DATE DUE FOR RETURN

This book may be recalled before the above date.

PERCEPTIONS OF JUSTICE

Perceptions of Justice

Issues in indigenous and community empowerment

Edited by

KAYLEEN M. HAZLEHURST
Centre for Community and Cross-Cultural Studies
Faculty of Arts
Queensland University of Technology
Brisbane, Australia

Avebury

Aldershot · Brookfield USA · Hong Kong · Singapore · Sydney

Published by
Avebury
Ashgate Publishing Limited
Gower House
Croft Road
Aldershot
Hants GU11 3HR
England

Ashgate Publishing Company
Old Post Road
Brookfield
Vermont 05036
USA

A CIP catalogue record for this book is available from the British Library.

Library of Congress Catalog Card Number: 94-73715

ISBN 1 85972 079 X

Reprinted 1996

Printed and bound by Athenæum Press Ltd.,
Gateshead, Tyne & Wear.

Contents

Figures and tables   vii

Acknowledgements   viii

Introduction: Post-colonial governance: The maturing
contract - *Kayleen M. Hazlehurst*   ix

I   Aboriginal justice reform in Canada: Alternatives to state
control - *Luke McNamara*   1

II   Systemic discrimination, Aboriginal people, and the
miscarriage of justice in Canada - *Shirley McMullen
and C.H.S. Jayewardene*   27

III   Moral panic and juvenile justice in Queensland: The emergent
context of the *Juvenile Justice Act* 1992 - *Richard Hil*   51

IV   Indigenous women and criminal justice: Some comments
on the Australian situation - *Chris Cunneen and Kate Kerley*   71

V   Race, gender, and the sentencing process in a New Zealand
District Court - *Heather Deane*   95

VI   'Striking a Balance': Lessons from problem-oriented policing
in British Columbia - *Gregory Saville and D. Kim Rossmo*   119

VII   Achieving the 'Good Community': A local police initiative
and its wider ramifications - *D.B. Moore and J.M. McDonald*   143

VIII   Native policing in Canada: A critical inquiry - *Tonio Sadik*   175

IX   Urban policing and Aboriginal social health: Research
and action - *Graham Brice*   197

X   Retrieving the 'Decent Society': Law and order politics in New
Zealand 1984-1993 - *Paul Havemann and Joan Havemann*   217

XI   Towards a cross-cultural theory of Aboriginal criminality
- *Russell Smandych, Robyn Lincoln and Paul Wilson*   245

Index   275

Figures and tables

Table 5.1 Race and gender of the sample; numbers and percentages 102

Table 5.2 Frequency of convictions for selected offences; men and
women; percentages: N = 269 104

Table 5.3 Age and gender of the sample; percentages: N = 298 105

Figure 5.1 Employment patterns of sample 106

Table 5.4 Employment and gender; numbers and percentages:
N = 298 106

Figure 5.2 Patterns of employment and gender 107

Table 5.5 Employment and race; numbers and percentages:
N = 298 107

Figure 5.3 Patterns of employment and race 108

Figure 5.4 Marital status of the sample; N = 298 109

Figure 5.5 Remand status of the sample; N = 298 111

Figure 5.6 Patterns of remand by gender 112

Figure 5.7 Patterns of remand by race 112

Table 5.6 Frequency distribution of sentences; numbers and
percentages; N = 298 113

Acknowledgements

Preparation of this volume was generously supported by the Faculty of Arts, Queensland University of Technology as part of the Community and Cross-Cultural Studies Program. As editor, I wish to thank successive Deans, Professors Paul Wilson, Peter Lavery and Roger Scott, and Professor Cameron Hazlehurst, Head, School of Humanities, who have each encouraged and facilitated the completion of this work.

I particularly wish to thank Glenda Wiltshire for her tireless assistance and cheerfulness in wordprocessing and preparing this manuscript for publication. I gratefully acknowledge the help of Sharon Petersen for her assistance in the earlier wordprocessing, Sally Whitehead for the compilation of the index, and Hilary Kent for her meticulous copy editing.

Introduction:
Post-colonial governance:
The maturing contract

Kayleen M. Hazlehurst[1]

The last decade has seen a growing recognition of the afflictions borne by the descendants of the dispossessed peoples of post-colonial societies.

Research in Canada, Australia, and New Zealand in particular has begun to elucidate the links between continuing material and spiritual impoverishment, social collapse and criminality. Major inquiries have matured our understanding of the ways in which both action and inaction by governments at all levels have often been damaging even as they have sought to ameliorate intolerable conditions.

Structural impediments to reform are being identified. There is a deepening awareness that a massive effort is necessary to harmonize the delivery of human services. Criminal justice systems are seen as susceptible to constructive change but limited in their potential if they are not integrated with active community responses to prevent crime.

Somehow government initiatives must become a welcome contribution to solutions, rather than a lamented cause of further distress. But, as many observers are beginning to appreciate, the beginning of wisdom lies less in government initiatives than in the regeneration of communities. Re-empowered peoples can do for themselves what no outsiders, however well-meaning, can do for them. The more we know about the bitter and socially dangerous nexus between long-term disadvantage and intergenerational crime, race and overimprisonment, or unemployment and rising juvenile offending, the greater the likelihood that a commonality of experience will emerge.

One discernible collective conviction is that we need to do more than simply remedy the institutional failings of the criminal justice system. We have to replace those reasons for despair with reasons for optimism in the hearts and minds of the people the justice system most readily affects. Thus, the re-involvement of communities in justice decisions and justice delivery is no small milestone. The authors in this book explore a variety of avenues and opportunities for reforms of this nature. They bring to bear perspectives from three countries, several social science disciplines, and a blend of practical experience and sustained scholarly inquiry.

Critiques of Canadian, Australian, and New Zealand systems are frequently directed towards the hindering or determining factor of the political will - the extent to which governments are prepared to make genuine commitments to and investments in community and social recovery. Closely tied to the question of political will is the issue of inventiveness. The lack of creative energy and the absence of imagination in policy and programme development, so obvious in the past, have begun to yield to systematic review and occasional inspiration.

One thing is certain, says Luke McNamara in his examination of systemic discrimination and overimprisonment of Aboriginal peoples, 'tinkering' with the system will not work. McNamara discusses the inherent limitations of the conventional Canadian justice reform model in reducing offending and incarceration of Canadian Native peoples, and provides a preliminary assessment of emerging 'autonomy-based' initiatives.

Effective justice reform in Canada, he claims, will not take place 'unless strategies are made operative within the context of an exercise by Aboriginal communities of autonomy, based on a constitutionally recognized right of self-government' (2). McNamara specifically supports the adoption of strategies which encourage the development of dispute resolution processes and social control mechanisms which enhance local autonomy and effective intervention. This approach, he stresses:

... looks beyond the mere fact of over-representation and seeks to confront the underlying reality of dispossession - and offers the possibility of genuine alternative strategies for dealing with matters of social harmony and the maintenance of order in Aboriginal communities (20).

Explanations of disproportionate indigenous incarceration take three major directions. One focuses upon the behaviour of Native people, a second on the treatment of Native people within the criminal justice system. Studies in the first category seek to ascertain whether, and to understand why, indigenous people commit proportionally more crimes.

Thus, age structure and population growth have been important factors to our understanding. National inquiries have scrutinized structural and operational aspects of the justice system which have long been of concern to social scientists.

Studies in the third category focus upon socioeconomic and demographic factors which contribute to, or indeed induce, this criminality. As in McNamara's conclusions, McMullen and Jayewardene detect a general belief among these researchers that whatever the demographic, social, and economic conditions, Native criminality has been due to the marginalization of Aboriginal societies following colonization. 'The argument here is that there has been a breakdown of Native societies because control of their own destinies has been removed from them' (28).

In the 'strikingly similar' findings of Canadian commissions of inquiry, evidence has been marshalled of racism within police ranks, excessive surveillance of Native people, over-charging and over-use of pre-trial detention against Native suspects, trivialization of the experiences of Native victims, and inadequate care of Native prisoners (38). At the heart of systemic discrimination, one witness to the Law Reform Commission contended, the real issue may in fact be 'cultural imperialism' (44).

The history and concept of policing were themselves founded upon a fundamental commitment to a specific moral and social order and style of peacekeeping. The role of police, as their primary enforcers, begs the question of whose law and order is being enforced and whether other styles might be more effective. Any changes within the criminal justice system must take into account, and reflect, such understandings. McMullen and Jayewardene take this further by saying:

> The criminal justice experience of the Aboriginal people of Canada raises the question of the propriety of policing as it is now conceived, especially for multicultural countries like Canada, which foster and encourage ethnic and cultural pluralism (44).

In his essay on 'Moral Panic and Juvenile Justice in Queensland', Richard Hil expresses deep concern about the limited life opportunities of working class youth - many of them indigenous or of immigrant background - on the dole or on skills-training programmes, and the way these influence 'attitudes and orientations to their immediate environment' (57). The looming prospect of unemployment and dependency alienates many young people resulting in trends towards 'school absenteeism, delinquency and petty offending' (57).   Politicians and administrators seem devoid of an understanding of this, he says.

Hil sees a clear connection between the negative economic and social forces which shape the life experiences of disadvantaged young people and their conflict with the criminal justice system.   Where there is increased policing of streets, parks, and shopping centres - public spaces habitually occupied by young people - the criminalization of working class youth is inevitable (58).   Hil attempts to trace the emergence of the Queensland Juvenile Justice Act (1992) within this broader social, economic, and political context.

During times of economic crisis, 'crackdowns' through more severe legislation and policing of 'problem populations' - the unemployed, the socially marginalized and disaffected - do little to reduce long-term offending or to protect potential victims, Hil contends (67).   Rather, solutions to the problems of offending among disadvantaged cohorts and communities:

> ... must be generated by a concern with the quality of life experienced by people within such areas. This means taking stock of issues such as unemployment, poverty, deprivation, racism and all those factors which lead to the oppression of these people (68).

Chris Cunneen and Kate Kerley write about the 'profound silence' which has surrounded the impact of the Australian criminal justice system upon Aboriginal and Torres Strait Islander women. Even when issues of race and colonialism have resounded through major inquiries, the issue of gender is seldom highlighted (71).   But 'interacting ideologies of class, race and gender' have continued to support processes of colonization and neo-colonialism. Aboriginal women in Australia have been affected by a long history of 'protectionist' and other legislation - first by sexual and labour exploitation as domestic servants and later through policing strategies more vigilant in areas of public order than in the defence of Aboriginal women against domestic violence. Consequently, Aboriginal women are significantly over-represented in female prisoner populations. Aboriginal women are also more likely to be imprisoned for assault and other offences against the person (81).

Cunneen and Kerley point to the dearth of empirical data on the specific experiences of Aboriginal women. In recent years there has been growing alarm at the high levels of alcoholism, child neglect, family violence, and sexual assault in Aboriginal communities. Australian and

Canadian researchers have asserted 'a strong relationship between the contemporary condition of indigenous men as a result of colonization and the use of male violence against indigenous women, and the then subsequent criminal activity by indigenous women' (81).

The dysfunctional emphasis upon masculine control in the colonial relationship has resulted in the misuse of traditional law in more remote areas. Poverty, frustration, and the inflammatory influence of alcohol have combined to provide justification for horrific levels of violence against Aboriginal women, and have resulted in the trivialization of the experiences of victims by police and courts.

Aboriginal women are now subjected to three sources of law: Western law, Aboriginal law, and 'bull-shit' traditional law! It is clear, say Cunneen and Kerley, that 'Aboriginal women are not able to rely on the structures of criminal justice for their protection' (88). The under-reporting of crime against them can be traced to a general distrust of that system, a poor police response, and inappropriate attitudes towards Aboriginal women which reach as far as the judiciary. It would seem evident, say these authors:

> ... that an understanding of the specific function of criminal justice agencies within the history of Australian colonialism is necessary to explain why such a deliberate punitive approach is taken in regard to Aboriginal women. (90)

Is the Australian experience replicated elsewhere? Heather Deane has conducted a study of race, gender, and the sentencing process in New Zealand. In her examination of data from one District Court, she found no evidence of racial discrimination between Maori and Pakeha. In this busy, high volume court the defendants were sentenced in an equitable and routine manner. Most of the sample were 'young, unemployed, and single and nearly one-quarter were first offenders' (114). About one-third of the defendants were given community-based sentences, and there was some indication that women might receive community service orders more frequently than men.

In contrast to research on issues of race, gender, and sentencing conducted in Britain and North America, Deane says her New Zealand study did not demonstrate extra-legal factors influencing sentencing. In Deane's analysis, those who committed more serious offences, or who had more than one previous conviction, received more severe penalties. 'Their sentences were different for these reasons, irrespective of their race, gender, employment situation or marital status', she said (114). Further studies will be needed to establish whether the record of the court examined by Deane is typical of New Zealand practice. But it is consistent with a growing international interest in the New Zealand criminal justice system for its innovative leadership in juvenile justice, and its apparent ability to operate relatively free of systemic bias or prejudice.

Ironically, and perhaps because they have been the most criticized, police in Canada, New Zealand, Australia, and Britain could well be considered pioneers in community regeneration. It was the rigorous self-examination and the reshaping of police thinking towards community policing principles during the 1980s which led to some of the most innovative projects in crime prevention and community development.

In Canada, the question of whether police patrols should respond primarily to calls for service or cultivate new responses has become a central debate. Incident-driven policing has been the traditional form of policing in urban areas for the past 40 years. With the illustration of two case studies, Gregory Saville and Kim Rossmo examine the development of 'problem-oriented' policing in British Columbia. The objective of this community-based policing has been to work with members of the community in order to attack the causes of social problems, rather than merely their symptoms. A four-stage approach to community problems is employed. This involves the scanning and analysis of specific problems, followed by the design of a situational response, and a later assessment of this response. Officers who have been taught and are able to utilize problem-oriented skills usually recognize their advantage.

The success of this approach is most obvious in 'highly turbulent' environments, say Saville and Rossmo (137). Problem-oriented policing clearly has relevance in other contexts - for indigenous communities for example. Not only should it have a more flexible and less damaging effect, but its potential for achieving better sociocultural fit and increased community participation in crime prevention is obvious. Saville and Rossmo conclude that police leaders should actively seek to strike a balance between community expectations for incident-driven policing and their needs for a problem-solving response.

Having personally spearheaded this process of change in Australia, David Moore and John McDonald are able to focus attention upon the fundamental philosophical and structural requirements for the achievement of 'the Good Community'. The most important question today, they say:

... is not: what sort of police officers do we need to maintain order in the community? Nor is it: what type of police organization best keeps the peace? *The question is: what sort of community do we want, and how do we best achieve that community?* (144).

The real significance of neighbourhood watch schemes, beat policing, store-fronts, community liaison units, and other community consultative processes, is the socially constructive way in which they approach problems of public safety and public order. In fostering citizen participation, they concentrate more directly upon the social causes of crime, and awaken the community's potential for self-healing.

Family group conferences, which so revolutionized the New Zealand juvenile justice system during the 1980s, have been increasingly appreciated and adopted throughout Australia since the early nineties. While longitudinal studies have yet to produce conclusive evidence of the value of conferences against recidivism, they have already proved preferable over other procedures.

Family group conferences respect the rights of victims to respond to, and to dissipate, their anger and resentment. They arrange and oversee material reparation and, in the opinion of researchers in both countries, are powerfully reformative and socially reintegrative of offenders:

The currency of conferences is ethical rather than legal, social rather than administrative. Fulfilling agreements is a matter of maintaining honour, regaining dignity, restoring trust (168).

In the experience of Moore and McDonald, the real success of social reform should not be measured in terms of its impact upon officialdom, but 'in terms of its impact upon the general citizenry' (170). Where this reform has been implemented 'the state arranges and coordinates a collective response to crime by the community of people most affected':

The process occurs at the very first point of contact with the justice system, seeking justice for victims and offenders in a community that will be strengthened by its collective response to the incident (170).

At the heart of this impetus to build community accountability into the treatment of young offenders is not the question of whether the state should provide softer or tougher punishment, but whether it is possible to guide young people away from lifestyles of crime towards more socially responsible behaviour. It is a democratic process, say Moore and

McDonald, which 'respects people's rights while reminding them of their duties' (170). In rendering social awareness in the offender, society might reduce the short and long-term harm of crime.

Of course, a collective response need not only be initiated by the state. In examining the history of Native policing in a Southern Ontario Native community, Tonio Sadik underscores the need to move away from the Western 'crime control' model towards alternatives more in keeping with ideals of local control and self-governance. While the political and practical consequence of this have been, and continue to be, complex there are some added benefits:

> ... by exploring potential alternatives available to them, Natives may find more constructive means of dealing with problems in their communities, while at the same time strengthening their claims of sovereignty (191).

Sadik, however, warns against the superficial imposition or oversimplification of so called 'traditional' alternatives to policing. To ensure that viable and appropriate alternatives are implemented, Sadik advises that communities 'begin to institute alternatives *along side* current structures of policing' (191).

In 1991 in Australia the published findings of the National Inquiry into Racist Violence and the Royal Commission into Aboriginal Deaths in Custody were condemning of the 'endemic' and 'insidious' racism which permeates the institutions and procedures of justice. The intrusion of the state's instruments of coercion is not limited to what is usually thought of as the criminal domain. For indigenous people, the police presence can be pervasive, and too often a signal of conflict. A two-phased study of state housing in Adelaide city characterized Aboriginal perceptions of police interaction with Aboriginal residents as extremely stressful. Reporting on these findings, Graham Brice explained that Aboriginal people believed themselves to 'be in receipt of negative "special attention" from police in Adelaide' (205).

Compared to non-Aboriginal households, police interaction was alleged to be excessively intrusive, frequently intimidating, and sometimes violent. This disturbing perception was particularly common among the most disadvantaged group - female Aboriginal sole-parents. It is well established, said Brice, that 'Aboriginal males are subjected to a very high level of police interaction and incarceration' (208). Interviews with these Aboriginal women, therefore, reflected their having witnessed the harassment and arrest of partners, children, brothers, and other male relatives.

At a meeting between the Aboriginal community and police and government representatives following the release of the Adelaide report, it was emphasized that bureaucracies need to challenge the attitudes and structures which have institutionalized racism. There was a need to change the police culture through cross-cultural training, the recruitment of Aboriginal officers, and the establishment of a special Aboriginal section at police headquarters. Improved relations in the future would be further linked to the increased employment of alternative approaches. Community justice mechanisms, such as dispute resolution services, would offer a means of decriminalizing and solving some of the underlying problems related to common forms of Aboriginal offending. Sport and recreational facilities would help to defuse street-level confrontation between youth and police. Moreover, the creative involvement of police with young people through police youth clubs, and their participation in educational programmes reaching Aboriginal students in schools and kindergartens, were warmly received by care-givers.

Paul and Joan Havemann provide an analysis of recent developments in New Zealand, which demonstrate the importance of placing problems of community breakdown into a broader political context. Over the past decade New Zealand has actively sought to reshape the state in an attempt to manage its mounting fiscal and ideological crises. The Report of the Royal Commission on Social Policy (1988) 'set out a radical participatory social democratic agenda for citizenship based on the principles of voice and choice' (221). The Roper Inquiry into Violence (1987) 'went to the heart of New Zealand's gendered culture of violence at a structural rather than victim-blaming level' (221). Institutionalized gender inequalities in employment were tackled by rigorous reviews, and through the Employment Equity Act (1990).

One of the most promising efforts of the Labour government of the 1980s was to promote citizenship through the New Zealand Bill of Rights Act (1990). Attempts to settle ethnic inequalities and antagonisms through the Treaty of Waitangi (Amendment) Act (1985), and to devolve power to tribal regions through the Rununga Iwi Act (1990) have promoted biculturalism. In fact, so significant were these reforms for the Maori people that this period was described by one commentator as 'the Maori Constitutional Revolution' (221).

Law and order and the achievement of the 'decent society' have remained central themes in the evolution of the New Zealand state. In

Havemann and Havemann's opinion, however, this is far from resolved. Efforts by New Zealand governments to control crime have been through 'greater technological efficiency in the formal apparatus', through promoting crime prevention and community policing strategies, and (if one were to take the most pessimistic view) by 'reintegrating the family into the archipelago of control' (218).

On the other hand, governments 'have consistently denied the contradictions inherent in their programmes', they contend:

> Repressive, traditional law and order policies and platforms have been juxtaposed with explicit acknowledgments of the links between crime and unemployment and anomie, yet the links between unemployment, anomie, and Labour and National's social and economic policies are consistently unacknowledged (218).

Havemann and Havemann express concern that the price of the 'decent society' may be a state which increasingly turns 'to coercion rather than legitimation to manage the crisis' (222). They discuss associations between the rise of the Right and increased spending on law and order identified by researchers in Britain and Canada, and compare these with New Zealand trends.

Among the rich allusions to the role of family, community, and marae there is still 'little or no real attempt to reinforce Maori legal structures' within these new manifestos. In the wider setting, it is hard to see what difference a handful of neighbourly residents and a few police can make against 'a crime wave which results from still-unaddressed structural causes' (238). Finally, Havemann and Havemann say: 'Unless different social movements are radically re-aligned and empowered, socially just outcomes for all which might mitigate crime and violence seem unlikely' (239).

Expressing an underlying impulse throughout the work of all the contributors to this volume, Russell Smandych, Robyn Lincoln and Paul Wilson articulate the need for the development of a general theory of aboriginal criminality and of contemporary processes of decolonization. Sharing similar historical, demographic, and geographical features, Canada and Australia are particularly suitable for cross-cultural analysis, they say. Yet, no systematic collaborative research has been undertaken in these two countries.

Recent inquiries and political events have placed indigenous issues upon national and international agendas. As pressure upon governments to address matters concerning aboriginal crime and justice has mounted, criminological research has received more considered attention. Over the past two decades research has tended to be insular, centring upon 'small localized studies of offending behaviour, sentencing disparities and police or public attitudes' (245). A cross-national synthesis of local studies and national data, on the other hand, might allow us to move from 'description to explanation' (245), facilitating the development of more useful causational and reformative theories.

In providing a summary of Canadian and Australian findings the authors conclude that at every step of the way indigenous people are cumulatively disadvantaged within criminal justice systems. Clusters of explanations focus upon the possibility of 'racist bias, visibility, cultural factors, legal and extra-legal considerations and over-policing' (251). These do not satisfy Smandych, Lincoln and Wilson. 'Such explanations are often provided at the micro-level to explain differences found in specific data, but they fail to provide general explanatory value' (251).

Other explanations suggest that, when measuring inmate rates, we qualify standard population ratios by a closer examination of age distributions. It is inevitable that we will see higher rates of imprisonment among more youthful indigenous populations. Another standard predictor of imprisonment is socioeconomic status. When these powerful factors are carefully examined, the role of ethnicity in over-representation will need to be re-assessed. More importantly, social class and underprivilege - which governments may be able to do something about - may join race in political salience.

Questions of differential age (younger population) and class distributions (lower socioeconomic status), differential commission of crime (minor and more frequent), differential offence patterns (high profile in public spaces), differential treatment (excessive policing or discrimination) and processing within the criminal justice system (accumulative disadvantage), therefore, provide the broad loci of explanation. We should also add the historical context (experiences of colonization and paternalism).

While informative, these analyses do not, in themselves, tell us a great deal about how to undo the damage. But there would be few criminologists who would not seek to link cause to cure, when they admonish current administrations or call for social and policy reform. Smandych, Lincoln, and Wilson, however, feel that this is not sufficient. The arguments of scholars and other professional commentators are 'rarely followed through very far', they say, 'either in terms of developing more adequate theoretically-informed research, or more appropriate (theoretically defensible) criminal justice policy' (256).

In recent years increasing numbers of comparative criminologists have urged the development of 'more generalizable cross-cultural theories of crime based on the systematic collection and analysis of cross-national crime data' (257). Smandych, Lincoln, and Wilson examine pioneering work by LaPrairie, Marenin, and Braithwaite in this direction, and observe several steps by which this might be achieved.

Clearly, the unequal attention of the criminal justice system is not reserved for indigenous people alone. But because they stand as one of the most underprivileged sectors of colonized countries they are particularly vulnerable. Specific ethnic or racial groups, social classes and increasingly, youth, are also vulnerable.

There is a haunting familiarity in the questions raised by criminologists in Canada, Australia, and New Zealand about indigenous overrepresentation in prisons, and those raised in studies of African American crime in the Bronx, or of youth offending in Manchester. International studies have typically focused upon patterns of criminality, or upon contributory socioeconomic and demographic factors - identifiable variables, collectable statistics.

Perhaps it is because our collective conscience is sharper, or because the social dangers are so great - but increasing numbers of social scientists today are displaying concern that their work appears to produce little practical or social benefit. Measurement of the extent of the damage is no substitute for evidence that their work is leading to social repair. Where are the social architects? Where are the busy workers? What part of our blueprint is missing? Where should we look for prospects of community regeneration?

Governments alone cannot be expected to transform social life. But they can recognize and support the abilities of individuals and groups to experiment and explore local capacities to do so. In this experimental field, programmes for the rehabilitation and social reintegration of offenders must form a greater proportion of government spending.

The idea of Native-run alcohol rehabilitation centres, so successfully functioning in Canada, has been repeatedly resisted in Australia - for no apparent reason, other than that they are seen to be a 'foreign' invention. As Australian Aboriginal people have been begging governments for such centres for several years, pride rather than reason seems to be dominating here. The conviction of bureaucrats to explore alternative justice programmes, repeatedly recommended by expert inquiries since the late-seventies, has faltered under the weight of lethargy. Community healing approaches, so potent in the rebuilding of severely broken-down collectives, are almost nonexistent. Australia certainly could not be accused of employing a broad repertoire of regenerative institutions.[2]

Conscious decisions need to be made to rechannel resources, presently consumed in the processing and incarceration of indigenous offenders, into preventative areas. At the very least, demands by police and corrections for funding increases should be granted, conditional upon some of those monies being spent upon preventative and rehabilitative programmes, in partnership with communities. Such a strategy would represent a maturing of the contract between government and the people to solve intractable social problems.

Ultimately, the measure of our success will not be signposted by superficial changes in party philosophy or official policy, nor in the creation of more enlightened manifestos - even though their inauguration may well give us historical cause to congratulate ourselves. It will be when such ideas are manifested through action in the lives of ordinary citizens and the underprivileged. The question of 'what sort of community do we want, and how can we best achieve it?', is surely the people's question. When we see the people creating the definitions and arranging the collective response, then we will see a shift in power.

At this point in our history we are unskilled. We simply do not know how to rebuild collapsed sectors of society, nor how to redirect destructive behaviours, attitudes, and lifestyles. We only know how to lay welfare nets, catch the unfortunate, and respond to crime.

Some may say that such ambitions are naive and utopian. Others take a more hardy view. If the processes of social decline can be scientifically analysed and understood, we should equally be able to identify, understand, and apply the processes of social reconstruction. We should at least do the research before dismissing the proposition. In a modest way the authors in this volume have sought to contribute towards such a science of social regeneration.

Notes

1. Kayleen M. Hazlehurst (Ph.D Toronto) is a Senior Lecturer, in Cross-Cultural Studies at the Queensland University of Technology. Since 1972 she has worked as a researcher and consultant in Australia, Canada, and New Zealand. Her most recent books are *Political Expression and Ethnicity: Statecraft and Mobilisation in the Maori World* (Praeger, 1993)

and *A Healing Place: Indigenous Visions for Personal Empowerment and Community Recovery* (Central Queensland University Press, 1994); (ed.) *Legal Pluralism and the Colonial Legacy* (Avebury 1995); (ed.) *Popular Justice and Community Regeneration* (Praeger 1995).

2.   See Kayleen M. Hazlehurst (1994) *A Healing Place: Indigenous Visions for Personal Empowerment and Community Recovery, op cit.*

I   Aboriginal justice reform in Canada: Alternatives to state control

Luke McNamara[1]

Introduction

The extent of documentation of the suffering of indigenous peoples at the hands of imposed criminal justice regimes is becoming increasingly overwhelming.[2] In Canada, a quarter of a century of growing concern about the criminal justice experience of Aboriginal peoples[3] has seen the evolution during the 1980s of 'justice' as a key element of the indigenous political agenda (Erasmus 1989). At the same time 'Aboriginal justice' has developed as an important component of the discipline of 'justice studies' (Harding, Couse and Schriml 1988) as well as an increasingly distinct field of academic research (Horn and Griffiths 1989; Harding and Forgay 1991). One important manifestation of this rising profile has been the establishment of a series of public inquiries into the problems of over-representation and systemic discrimination which indigenous peoples routinely face when they come into contact with the various agencies of criminal justice administration (McNamara 1992b).

This essay provides an outline of the Canadian justice reform process, including a critique of the inherent limitations of conventional approaches, and a preliminary assessment of the emergence of autonomy-based initiatives. No detailed discussion of the circumstances of Aboriginal contact with the agencies of the criminal justice system nor of the various reform strategies which have been attempted during the last two decades will be possible here.[4] However, some specific references to the extent of over-representation and to the failure of the conventional reform model will be necessary to support the argument that effective justice reform will not take place in Canada

unless strategies are made operative within the context of an exercise by
Aboriginal communities of autonomy, based on a constitutionally recognized
right of self-government.

Reforming the justice system: 'tinkering won't work'

> The first step is to recognize that tinkering won't work and what will
> work is empowerment. Until the justice system can accommodate the
> reality of our self-determination, it can hardly begin to deal with over-
> representation of natives in prisons, the lack of native jury members or
> judges, discrimination in policing or corrections (McCormick in Hamilton
> and Sinclair 1991: 258).

If one thing has emerged very clearly from the latest 'attempt' at
Aboriginal justice reform it is that many Aboriginal people see no value in
'modification' to the systems of criminal justice administration which
currently operate in Canada. For more than 20 years actual and proposed
reforms to police, courts and prisons have been advanced on the basis that
the system was in need of a bit of an overhaul rather than anything in the
way of fundamental changes to its basic structure and underlying principles.
    In important respects, the 1975 National Conference on Native Peoples
and the Criminal Justice System established the framework for the pattern of
Aboriginal justice reform that followed (Ministry of the Solicitor General
1975). Based on the objective of ensuring 'the equitable treatment of native
peoples within the Canadian criminal justice system' (ibid: 3), the conference
adopted 'guidelines for action' which included closer involvement of native
persons in the planning and delivery of justice services, greater control by
native communities over service delivery, cultural sensitivity training for
non-native staff in the criminal justice system, recruitment of native persons
for service functions at all stages of the criminal justice system, increased use
of native para-professionals, and a greater policy emphasis on prevention,
community-based diversions and alternatives to imprisonment, and the
protection of young persons (ibid).
    Since this landmark meeting more than 20 reports have made numerous
recommendations designed to address the problem of Aboriginal contact with
the criminal justice system. The vast majority of these contributions follow
the broad pattern established in 1975. The Alberta Task Force on the
Criminal Justice System and Its Impact on the Indian and Métis People of
Alberta (Cawsey 1991: Vol 3: 4-7) identified the following '"Top Ten"

Trends in Recommendations' between 1967 and 1990:

- Have cross-cultural training for non-Native staff;
- Employ more Native staff;
- Have more community-based programmes in corrections;
- Have more community-based alternatives in sentencing;
- Have more special assistance to Native offenders;
- Have more Native community involvement in planning, decision-making and service delivery;
- Have more Native advisory groups at all levels;
- Have more recognition of Native culture and law in Criminal Justice System service delivery;
- Emphasise crime prevention programmes;
- Self-determination must be considered in the planning and operation of the Criminal Justice System.

Recently several commentators have begun to examine more closely which notions of justice and social control inform conventional approaches to justice reform (Brown 1987). For example, Harding (1991) has questioned why the indigenization of policing came under serious consideration as a reform strategy during the 1970s. He concludes (ibid: 370):

> Though lip-service was given to [indigenization] as a step towards more Aboriginal self-government, it seems clear that the need for a more effective social control system was the paramount consideration ... Like cross-cultural training, Native constable programmes were primarily concerned with making policing more effective. They were not fundamentally concerned with reducing incarceration rates of Aboriginal people, though the supporters of the programme would likely prefer this to happen. If it didn't however, the programme would not be seen to have failed. Social control, not self-determination, was the main concern.

Havemann (1988: 81) has reached a similar conclusion, suggesting that indigenization 'has evolved as an ameliorative policy within the criminal justice system ... [which] compounds the net-widening effect of the hybridized social service and order-maintenance policing which indigenous people experience'.

The dominant element of the majority of Aboriginal justice reforms that have been implemented since the 1970s has been commitment to the assumption that ensuring justice for Aboriginal people need not involve questioning the legitimacy of the criminal justice system, nor the endorsement of autonomous Aboriginal justice values and dispute resolution processes. In this respect the analysis of the process of justice inquiries offered by Mannette (1992a: 71) is particularly apt:

Following Burton and Carlen (1979), the role of official discourse is to assign blame in terms of the temporary failure of an essentially reformable system. Emphasis on human fallibility is often made to reinforce the notion that, had actors adequately discharged their functions, the crisis which has led to state intervention would have been averted. Having been seen to publicly and authoritatively take charge in the assignment of blame, the state process of official discourse transforms an ideological phenomenon (that is, eroded public confidence in judicial process) into a material event (that is, the inquiry and its report). The material event is worked up according to principles of administrative rationality and legal coherence (for example, the use of lawyers, judges, quasi-judicial format etc.). Of key importance is the representative inclusion of minority constituents. Through the inquiry process, via their lawyer representatives, minority factions are included and given voice. Crucially, some of their recommendations are incorporated into the majority findings. Thus, minority factions are seen to collude in the inquiry process and 'consent' is manufactured.

Aboriginal consultants to the Law Reform Commission of Canada (1991: 28) suggested that 'involving more Aboriginal persons in the present system merely diverts resources, personnel and attention in the wrong direction, away from the creation of Aboriginal justice systems'. In many ways, these comments capture the essential inadequacies of the reform strategies which have predominated in Canada (and in Australia) for the last two decades. As Zimmerman (1991: 2-3) has observed:

In Canada today, native people are fed up with studies such as this, which describes a deplorable situation they already know too well, cite statistics and authorities, recommend changes, but ultimately amount to nothing. To examine the criminal justice system and to recommend changes is called 'tinkering'. Most native people are past believing that tinkering within the mainstream justice system is a worthwhile pursuit. They want, they need a system of which they have ownership

- one which they shape according to their values, traditions and beliefs. No amount of tinkering with the non-native justice system will fully and finally answer that need.

It may be rather too optimistic to state categorically that the last few years have seen the emergence of a new era in Aboriginal justice reform, but there have certainly been some promising advances. The most recent round of reform initiatives reflect, perhaps for the first time, an awareness of the value of indigenous autonomy as both a necessary foundation and a vital ingredient of future justice strategies. Whether the limitations of 'official discourse' identified by Mannette (1992a) affect the practical outcome of this particular reform push remains to be seen.

The latest round of commissions and inquiries

The Royal Commission into Aboriginal Deaths in Custody (Johnson 1991) has dominated the established Aboriginal justice reform agenda in Australia since the mid 1980s. In Canada, although there has been no parallel in terms of the specific focus on the issues of custodial deaths, a similar phenomenon can be identified: the resort to independent inquiries to address fundamental questions about the impact of the social control institutions of the dominant culture on Aboriginal peoples. A justice reform pattern initiated more than a decade earlier (Ministry of the Solicitor General 1975) became a highly prominent feature of the Canadian political agenda with the establishment of the Royal Commission on the Donald Marshall Jr., Prosecution in Nova Scotia in 1986 (Hickman 1989).[5]

In the Prairie region the phenomenon seems to have taken a particularly strong hold.[6] Between March 1991 and March 1992 reports of government appointed investigations into the impact of the criminal justice system on Aboriginal peoples were produced in Alberta (Cawsey 1991), Saskatchewan (Linn 1992a; Linn 1992b) and Manitoba (Hamilton and Sinclair 1991).

At least at one level the recent popularity of public inquiries dealing with the Canadian Aboriginal justice issue is explainable, and indeed, must necessarily be considered, as part of a serious bringing into question of the conventional and institutionalized framework of justice administration, including the inherent capacity of the system for 'improvement'. To varying degrees recent provincial and national inquiries have demonstrated this shift in the tenor of the recommendations which they contain. The Task Force on the Criminal Justice System and its Impact on the Indian and Métis People of Alberta commented that:

> ... within the last five to ten years there has been a marked increase in the
> devolution of control of many aspects of the criminal justice and social
> welfare systems from the government to aboriginal people (Cawsey 1991:
> Vol 1: 1-4).

Several inquiries have been very tentative in terms of recognizing the
relationship between justice reform and the indigenous autonomy agenda
(Linn 1992a, Linn 1992b; Cawsey 1991). Others however, have strongly
endorsed the centrality of this relationship (Law Reform Commission of
Canada 1991). Of particular significance are the recommendations contained
in the *Report of the Aboriginal Justice Inquiry of Manitoba* (Hamilton and
Sinclair 1991) which advocate for Aboriginal communities a level of
autonomy in the administration of justice unprecedented since the erosion of
traditional Aboriginal social and political institutions following Manitoba's
entry into the Canadian federation in 1870 (McNamara 1992b; Hamilton and
Sinclair 1991; Milloy 1990; Brogden 1991).

While these reports contain hundreds of recommendations for alleviating
the circumstances of Aboriginal contact with the criminal justice system,[7] the
key element of this push for autonomy-based justice reform is the
establishment of Aboriginal justice systems. The Aboriginal Justice Inquiry
of Manitoba recommended that:

> Aboriginal justice systems should be established in Aboriginal
> communities, beginning with the establishment of Aboriginal courts. We
> recommend that Aboriginal communities consider doing so on a regional
> basis ... We suggest that Aboriginal courts assume jurisdiction on a
> gradual basis, starting with summary conviction criminal cases, small
> claims and child welfare matters. Ultimately, there is no reason why
> Aboriginal courts and their justice systems cannot assume full jurisdiction
> over all matters at their own pace (Hamilton and Sinclair 1991: 642).

The Law Reform Commission of Canada (1991: 16) recommended that:

> Aboriginal communities identified by the legitimate representatives of
> Aboriginal peoples as being willing and capable should have the authority
> to establish Aboriginal justice systems. The federal and provincial
> governments should enter into negotiations to transfer that authority to
> those Aboriginal communities.

The Aboriginal Justice Inquiry of Manitoba noted that '[t]he call for separate, Aboriginal controlled justice systems was made repeatedly in our public hearings throughout Manitoba ...' (Hamilton and Sinclair 1991: 256). The essence of the proposal is that every component of the justice system operational within an Aboriginal community - from police, to prosecutor, to court, to probation, to jails - must be controlled by Aboriginal people (ibid).

The Commissioners considered a range of possible legal bases for the establishment of Aboriginal justice systems before settling on the 'treaty-based' option preferred by the Assembly of Manitoba Chiefs. The establishment of Aboriginal justice systems then, would be based on:

Federal-Indian negotiations leading to a recognition of the right of Aboriginal people to establish and maintain Aboriginal courts as an aspect of the 'existing treaty and aboriginal rights of the aboriginal peoples,' as recognized and affirmed by section 35 of the *Constitution Act*, 1982 (ibid: 311).

This approach places the justice system proposal firmly within the context of Aboriginal self-government. Indeed, the Commissioners recommended that both federal and provincial governments specifically recognize the right of Aboriginal self-government by constitutional amendment (ibid). The basic point of identification then, is with the immediate political aspirations of Aboriginal peoples of Canada, rather than with the policies of assimilation and paternalism that have historically informed criminal justice reform strategies.

Unlike the Aboriginal Justice Inquiry of Manitoba, the Law Reform Commission of Canada did not locate its recommendation for the creation of Aboriginal justice systems within the context of Aboriginal self-government. In fact, the Commission expressly distanced itself from the whole self-government debate:

We recognize that the call for completely separate justice systems is part of a political agenda primarily concerned with self-government. We need not enter that debate. Aboriginal-controlled justice systems have merits quite apart from political considerations (Law Reform Commission of Canada 1991: 14).

The Commission justified its departure from the general principle that 'criminal law and procedure should impose the same requirements on all members of society' (ibid: 14) on the basis of 'distinct historical position of

Aboriginal persons' which has given them a 'different constitutional status' (ibid: 14-15).

This point of departure between the Aboriginal Justice Inquiry of Manitoba and the Law Reform Commission of Canada raises a fundamental question about the status of Aboriginal justice systems. Should autonomy in the administration of justice be advanced within the wider paradigm of Aboriginal self-government? A brief examination of formal responses to the recommendations of the Aboriginal Justice Inquiry of Manitoba confirms just how crucial resolution of this basic question is likely to become.

Representatives of Aboriginal organizations in Manitoba and across the country registered their approval of the Aboriginal Justice Inquiry of Manitoba's conclusions about the impact of the justice system on Aboriginal people, and generally endorsed its plan for change. For example, the report was described by the Grand Chief of the Assembly of Manitoba Chiefs as 'a solid piece of work with recommendations that represent fundamental social change in this province and elsewhere' (Fontaine in Santin 1991). The overwhelmingly positive response appears to have been based on a belief that the justice concerns of Aboriginal people had finally been addressed in a serious and constructive manner by an independent inquiry, and that it signalled a departure from the era of internal reforms and 'tinkering' within the justice system that had failed significantly to improve the system's capacity to deal effectively with Aboriginal people.[8]

On 28 January 1992 the provincial government released its formal response to the *Report of the Aboriginal Justice Inquiry of Manitoba*. The Justice Minister announced a number of reforms which would, he promised, result in a 'better justice system in Manitoba for aboriginal people than anywhere in the country' (McCrae in Campbell and Weber 1992). However, the Manitoba Government refused to endorse the autonomy-based reform direction charted by the Aboriginal Justice Inquiry of Manitoba on the basis that '[s]uch key recommendations as an aboriginal justice system, separate criminal codes, civil codes, and charters of rights for First Nations are not achievable within the current constitutional framework' (McCrae in Roberts 1992).

After jointly considering the government's response to the *Report of the Aboriginal Justice Inquiry of Manitoba*, the Assembly of Manitoba Chiefs, the Manitoba Métis Federation, the Indigenous Women's Collective, and the Aboriginal Council of Winnipeg registered their 'profound disappointment with the limited vision and political will reflected in the Province's response' (Assembly of Manitoba Chiefs 1992). At the heart of the dissatisfaction registered by Aboriginal organizations was their view that '[t]he same government that has accepted the recognition of the inherent right to self-government simultaneously refuses to recognize one of the most vital components of inherent jurisdiction, i.e. the right of jurisdiction over justice' (ibid).[9]

Aboriginal self-government: a necessary context?

For more than a decade the issue of Aboriginal self-government has been a major topic on the formal Canadian political agenda (Wherrett and Brown 1992). Angus (1991: 35) has observed '[i]f the success of a lobbying effort is measured by the extent to which an issue gains acceptance on the national political agenda, the early 1980s may be looked upon as the heyday of Native rights activism in Canada in the 20th century'. While it would be premature and disappointing to accept without question that at the end of this century the limited gains of the period between 1982-1987 will represent the greatest achievement of the Aboriginal rights movement,[10] the significance of this era clearly deserves recognition. While ultimately unsuccessful in terms of the objective of achieving a constitutional amendment recognizing the right of Aboriginal self-government, the process played a significant role in creating the constitutional reform environment of the early 1990s in which Aboriginal organizations appeared so close to their objective of a constitutional framework for political autonomy.

Brock (1991) has argued that Canada's experience with the development of Aboriginal self-government between 1982 and 1987 is best described as 'paradoxical':

> In this period, the concept of aboriginal self-government matured and while the issue was not resolved in the constitutional forum, it developed significantly in other policy arenas. However, constitutional failure to entrench aboriginal self-government contributed to its success in other areas and possibly to its future development as a constitutional issue (ibid: 273).

One example of this development has been in the area of statutory recognition of regional self-government agreements, including the 1984 *Cree-Naskapi (of Québec) Act* and the 1986 *Sechelt Indian Band Self-Government Act*. Both statutes have been characterized as 'non-constitutional self-government arrangements' (Dawson 1991: 8) and have the general effect of granting to the identified Indian bands, powers broadly equivalent to those of municipal governments. Section 14 of the *Sechelt Indian Band Self-Government Act* outlines the range of matters over which the band is empowered to assume jurisdiction. These include zoning and land use planning, education, local taxation, health services, and social/welfare services. Criminal justice jurisdiction is limited to the power to impose fines or imprisonment for summary conviction offences under band laws.[11] Essentially, the Act transfers to the Sechelt band those powers previously exercised by the federal government under the *Indian Act*, and under section 25 transfers reserve lands to the band 'for the use and benefit of the band and its members' (Taylor and Paget 1989).

In general terms the *Cree-Naskapi Act* achieves a similar purpose: replacing the *Indian Act* for the incorporated Cree and Naskapi bands (Peters 1989). Under the terms of the Act, the Cree and Naskapi bands exercise local government powers in relation to matters such as land and resource use and zoning, local taxation, and pollution control and environmental protection.

Isaac (1991: 2) has concluded that the *Cree Naskapi Act* 'was, for all intents and purposes, as close to self-government or self-determination that any piece of legislation could achieve within the constitutional framework of the country'. Elsewhere Isaac (1989) suggests that the Act 'offers the Cree and Naskapi a unique and autonomous level of government within Canada and is able to satisfy the native aspirations for power and control' (cited in Isaac 1991: 2).

Without questioning the legitimacy or value of either of the self-government arrangements discussed here, Isaac's conclusions reveal the limitations of delegated statute-based forms of limited Aboriginal self-government in terms of accommodating the full range of autonomy aspirations, and, in particular, the justice demands of many Aboriginal communities.

Aboriginal justice systems of the type recently proposed in Canada are fundamentally inconceivable without the prior recognition of Aboriginal self-government on a scale far more substantial than that which has been delegated to Aboriginal communities in Sechelt, British Columbia, and in the James Bay region of Québec.[12]

Canada's most recent attempt at macro-constitutional reform appeared to hold the promise of just such a level of recognition. With the collapse in June 1990 of the Meech Lake Accord (which effectively ignored the self-government aspirations of Aboriginal peoples) it became clear that the basic political concerns of Canada's Aboriginal peoples could no longer be dismissed (Turpel and Monture 1990; Asch and Macklem 1991).

Thus it came as no great surprise when in September 1991 the Government of Canada produced a package of constitutional reform proposals which included a proposal for the recognition of the right of Aboriginal self-government (Government of Canada 1991):

> The Government of Canada proposes an amendment to the Constitution to entrench a general justiciable right to aboriginal self-government within the Canadian federation and subject to the Canadian Charter of Rights and Freedoms, with the nature of the right to self-government described so as to facilitate interpretation of that right by the courts. In order to allow an opportunity for the Government of Canada, the governments of the provinces and the territories, and aboriginal peoples to come to a common understanding of the content of this right, its enforceability would be delayed for a period of up to 10 years (ibid: 10).

The proposal envisioned that 'aboriginal governments would potentially exercise a combination of jurisdictions presently exercised by the federal, provincial and municipal governments ... [including] ... land and resource use, language and culture, education, policing and administration of justice, health, social development and community infrastructure (ibid: 8).

The initial response of Aboriginal organizations to the federal government's original proposals was not positive. In particular, concerns were expressed about the ten year 'waiting period' (Campbell 1991), the implications of entrenching a 'justiciable' right to self-government (Indigenous Bar Association 1991), and the failure to describe the rights as inherent. Following a preliminary assessment of the proposals Chartrand (1992: 63) observed:

> Aboriginal people have a moral and legal right under Canadian and international law to require Canada to recognize an inherent right to self-government of Aboriginal peoples as equal partners in the federation. The federal government's position is nothing short of a simple re-affirmation of colonial superiority, an attitude which has been time and time again discredited as pure racism.

Following the contribution in February 1992 of the Special Joint Committee of the Senate and the House of Commons (Beaudoin and Dobbie 1992) - which recommended 'the entrenchment in section 35 of the *Constitution Act*, 1982 of the inherent right of aboriginal peoples to self-government within Canada' (ibid: 29) - and the formal recognition in March 1992 that Canada's four major Aboriginal organizations - The Assembly of First Nations, the Native Council of Canada, the Métis National Council and the Inuit Tapirisat of Canada - were entitled to participate fully (Branswell 1992), the constitutional reform negotiation process began to take shape. For several months an apparently successful Multilateral Meeting on the Constitution (MMC) process continued until the Charlottetown Accord was formulated on 28 August 1992. The package included the following draft amendment to section 35 of the *Constitution Act, 1982*: 'The aboriginal peoples of Canada have the inherent right to self-government'. It also provided for a formal self-government negotiation and implementation process which would be available to Aboriginal communities in all regions of Canada. However, in a national referendum on 26 October 1992 a majority of voters in seven of twelve provinces and territories rejected this package of constitutional amendments.

In light of the failure of the 'Canada round' to produce an acceptable package of constitutional reforms, the immediate future of the struggle for recognition of indigenous autonomy rights in Canada is unclear, particularly given the significant 'fatigue factor' which must inevitably arise after more than a decade of attempted constitutional reform. In the long term greater discussion of the meaning and content of the 'inherent right of Aboriginal self-government' can only increase the prospects of the implementation of recent proposals for the creation of Aboriginal justice systems.

A framework for the creation of Aboriginal justice systems

The task of translating an endorsement of autonomy-based criminal justice reform at the broad policy level into viable programmes within Aboriginal communities will necessarily involve the formulation of an appropriate framework particularly as the number and scope of such initiatives increases. One of the primary dangers of pre-defining the 'limits' of potential exercises of Aboriginal autonomy in the field of justice administration is that the result may be a stifling of legitimate autonomy-based alternatives to the existing system. The debate over the status of the *Canadian Charter of Rights and Freedoms* during the latest constitutional reform round was indicative of this concern. But clearly certain 'boundary' or jurisdictional issues need to be addressed.

In the context of Aboriginal justice systems, jurisdiction refers to a range of issues including: the sphere in which autonomous institutions would operate; the matters that would be dealt with and the 'laws' that would apply; and the way in which institutions would interact with each other, and with the non-Aboriginal criminal justice system. As has been suggested earlier many of these issues can only be adequately addressed in relation to the broader context of Aboriginal self-government. Following the failure of the 'Canada round' of constitutional reform in October 1992 it is perhaps even more imperative to explore just how responsibility for the administration of justice and maintenance of social harmony/order in Aboriginal communities might operate within the broader scheme of Aboriginal autonomy in the Canadian context. Clearly, concerns about jurisdiction over 'criminal matters' and 'law and order' constituted one of the major 'sticking points' during the constitutional reform debate in relation to the question of Aboriginal self-government. As one commentator observed, '[t]he notion of scores of Indian bands across the country enacting their own criminal law stirs visions of anarchy in a lot of legal brains' (Dafoe 1991: D2).

During the course of the last decade proposals for the creation of 'Aboriginal courts' or related institutions have been made with increasing frequency in Canada. For the most part these proposals have failed to conceive of ways of administering justice in Aboriginal communities that are substantially different to the dominant 'Western' adjudication process, and indeed have tended to perpetuate approaches based on exercising jurisdiction within a specified geographic area.

Aboriginal justice systems with a territorial jurisdiction base are inadequate to meet the justice aspirations of a large number of Canada's Aboriginal peoples. Proposals based on this approach suffer from a failure to reflect an accurate conception of the nature of the justice 'problem' in many Aboriginal communities (McNamara 1992b; La Prairie 1990; and Brodeur, La Prairie and McDonnell 1991). Further, they have generally been seen as dependent on several other contentious issues such as the settlement of land claims, and the whole question of status under the *Indian Act* (Morse 1982). They assume that the situation of First Nation reserve communities and status Indians is the norm in Canada, and fail to recognize the legitimate autonomy rights of all of Canada's Aboriginal peoples.

The extent to which proposed models in Canada have been limited to territorial and semi-autonomous approaches reflects, at least in part, the tendency to rely on the United States system of tribal courts as a guide to possible developments in Canada. For example, Morse (1980) considered the viability of the tribal court system in the United States as a model adaptable to the situation of Aboriginal peoples in Canada, and suggested that 'it would appear appropriate for us in Canada to consider seriously the implementation of a similar institutional framework' (Morse 1980: 1). More recently Hemmingson (1988) has undertaken a detailed analysis of the jurisdiction of tribal courts in the United States, on the basis of which he has made a series of recommendations as to the jurisdictional structure of such courts in Canada. Neither analysis seriously questions the relevance of the United States model, given the particular needs and aspirations of Canada's Aboriginal people (Osnaburgh-Windigo Tribal Council 1990; and Rudin and Russell 1991). Specifically, they fail to recognize that the purpose for which tribal courts were originally established in the United States and the reasons for which they are being endorsed now in Canada are fundamentally different. Although there have been several efforts in recent years to reshape and expand tribal courts in line with renewed assertions of sovereignty (American Indian Lawyer Training Program Inc., 1982), the legacy of the original rationale for the establishment of such courts in the 1880s - to 'contain' Indians on allotments of land or reservations (Deloria and Lytle 1983) by application of the 'police idea' (Barsh and Henderson 1976) - remains in the limited and fragile jurisdiction exercised by tribal courts today (Kickingbird 1976; Clinton 1976).

In Canada proposals for the establishment of Aboriginal justice systems have emerged in an entirely different context and from a completely different perspective. They have evolved as part of the indigenous autonomy paradigm and in substantial part from the perspective of indigenous legal cultures, and not from within the narrow limits of the legal philosophy of the non-Aboriginal state. However, comprehensive models consistent with these differences have been slow to develop, partly because of a strong tendency when attempting to identify and recognize traditional or alternative justice processes to '... require permanent and specialized institutions wielding absolute judicial or executive powers ...' and to fail to '... imagine justice without police, bailiffs, and prisons ...' (Coyle 1986: 615).

At first glance the recommendations of the *Report of the Aboriginal Justice Inquiry of Manitoba* appear to belong to the category of significant but ultimately inadequate conceptualizations of how Aboriginal autonomy rights can be given effect in relation to matters currently dealt with by the non-Aboriginal criminal justice process. It proposes that:

All people, Aboriginal and non-Aboriginal, within the geographical boundaries of a reserve or Aboriginal community be subject to the jurisdiction of the Aboriginal system in place within that community (Hamilton and Sinclair 1991: 321).

As suggested above, apart from its apparent limitations, the immediate difficulty which is raised by this approach is that of defining an Aboriginal community and its physical boundaries. For Hamilton and Sinclair (1991: 318) a partial resolution of this problem is found by determining that 'it is not necessary, in our opinion, for Aboriginal communities to "own" or have a valid legal claim to the land they occupy in order to be identified as Aboriginal communities for purposes of establishing Aboriginal justice systems'. With limited exceptions the scheme of comprehensive Aboriginal justice systems proposed by the Commissioners would operate only within the boundaries of the community, where 'Aboriginal courts must have exclusive, original jurisdiction ...' (Hamilton and Sinclair 1991: 327).

In relation to specific communities, proposals for territorial Aboriginal justice systems are clearly appropriate. For example, Brodeur, La Prairie and McDonnell (1991) have recommended in *Justice for the Cree* that an autonomous system should operate within the established boundaries of Cree lands in the James Bay region of Québec, and that 'any person perpetrating an offence on Cree territory should answer to the Cree system of justice for his or her behaviour' (Brodeur, La Prairie and McDonnell 1991: 130). However, to create a generally applicable model of territorial Aboriginal justice systems is to ignore the fact that one of the primary motivations for the establishment of autonomous Aboriginal justice structures in Canada is the inadequacy of the non-Aboriginal system in dealing justly and effectively with Aboriginal offenders (including the substantial numbers living in urban centres and other predominantly non-Aboriginal communities), and the manner in which it has denied the inherent autonomy rights of Aboriginal peoples.

The recommendations for the establishment of Aboriginal justice systems contained in the *Report of the Aboriginal Justice Inquiry of Manitoba* represent a significant advance on conventional approaches to Aboriginal justice autonomy including the question of jurisdiction, and the capacity to apply traditional or other Aboriginal dispute resolution mechanisms. In relation to Aboriginal persons living outside of distinct Aboriginal communities, the report proposes that the autonomy-based approach could include 'alternative dispute resolution mechanisms and alternative measures attached to the existing court system, which take into account, or are based upon, the cultures of Aboriginal people' (Hamilton and Sinclair 1991: 327).

The Law Reform Commission of Canada (1991) has also made a significant contribution to the development of a more flexible understanding of Aboriginal justice systems. Most importantly, the Commission conceives of territoriality as one of only several possible bases for the exercise of jurisdiction by Aboriginal justice structures:

> Jurisdiction could be based on the offender, the offence or the location of
> the offence: any one of these criteria might be appropriate.   An
> Aboriginal justice system might automatically acquire jurisdiction where
> the offender is an Aboriginal person, or jurisdiction might be optional in
> that case ...   Jurisdiction might also be simply divided on the basis that
> any offence committed on a reserve or designated territory (or perhaps by
> an Aboriginal person on a reserve) will be dealt with by a local
> Aboriginal justice system.   Thus, although we have not devised precise
> jurisdictional rules - and it would be inappropriate for us to do so - it is
> clear to us that a workable formula can be achieved through the process
> of negotiation that is contemplated by our proposal (ibid: 22).

Ultimately, the jurisdiction of Aboriginal justice systems must be
compatible with, and indeed based on, the jurisdictional structure of
Aboriginal governments.   The whole shape of Aboriginal justice systems
must be allowed to develop in terms consistent with the broader movement
towards realization of the inherent right of Aboriginal self-government.
Frameworks such as those articulated by the Aboriginal Justice Inquiry of
Manitoba and the Law Reform Commission of Canada represent an attempt
to conceive of 'justice' in terms which may be fundamentally different from
the principles which underlay the existing Canadian system of criminal law
and criminal justice administration.

This approach has implications beyond the jurisdictional structure of
Aboriginal justice systems.   It is becoming increasingly apparent that
Aboriginal autonomy in the field of justice is not simply a matter of
establishing Aboriginal courts, no matter how comprehensive.   Meaningful
autonomy must include the right to 'define' justice, and to adopt and apply
laws and processes consistent with this definition.

Indeed, perhaps the most challenging aspect of the task of reconciling
Aboriginal autonomy and justice reform is that of formulating a framework
for the creation of Aboriginal justice systems that is not simply flexible in
jurisdictional terms, but also capable of achieving objectives which are
fundamentally different from those of the dominant system.   As was noted
in the *Report of the Aboriginal Justice Inquiry of Manitoba*:

> At the most basic level of understanding, justice is understood differently
> by Aboriginal people ...   The purpose of a justice system in an Aboriginal
> society is to restore the peace and equilibrium within the community, and

to reconcile the accused with his or her own conscience and with the individual or family who has been wronged. This a primary difference. It is a difference that significantly challenges the appropriateness of the present legal and justice system for Aboriginal people in the resolution of conflict, the reconciliation and the maintenance of community harmony and good order (Hamilton and Sinclair 1991: 22).

When applied to the task of creating a framework for the creation of Aboriginal justice systems, recognition of this difference must translate into support for the right of Aboriginal communities to shape key elements of their justice environment. For example, this must include the power to define 'crime' or social disorder in terms relevant to the community. In this respect the approach taken by the Aboriginal Justice Inquiry of Manitoba is central. The Commissioners recommended that:

Aboriginal communities be entitled to enact their own criminal, civil and family laws and to have those laws enforced by their own justice systems. If they wish they should also have the right to adopt any federal or provincial law and to apply or enforce that as well (Hamilton and Sinclair 1991: 323).

While recommending that 'Aboriginal traditions and customs be the basis upon which Aboriginal laws and Aboriginal justice systems are built' (ibid: 323), it is significant that the Commissioners do not conceive of customary law as 'fixed in some static sense' (ibid: 323). Rather 'Aboriginal customary law' is seen as having 'continued to evolve slowly to meet the changing needs, values and circumstances present within Aboriginal communities', and thus somewhat equivalent to common law (ibid: 323). Given the distinctive nature of Aboriginal concepts of justice (Dumont 1990), simply granting to Aboriginal communities a certain amount of control over justice institutions is inadequate. As Mary Ellen Turpel (1992: 98) has commented in relation to the recommendations of the Royal Commission on the Donald Marshall Jr., Prosecution,

... [W]hen the Commissioners recommend the establishment of a pilot-project, summary-conviction Native Criminal Court on a Mi'kmaq reserve, enforcing exclusively Canadian law (not Mi'kmaq or tribal law), they fail to realize that this just makes the sense of injustice seem closer to home. What is required is something more respectful of Mi'kmaq norms.[13]

A corollary of the law-making capacity proposed by the Aboriginal Justice Inquiry of Manitoba is the right to employ dispute resolution mechanisms and decision-making processes that are equally consistent with Aboriginal cultures. Indeed, it is crucial, if respect for Aboriginal autonomy is to be genuine, that non-Aboriginal notions of what justice looks like (Coyle 1986) not be permitted to infringe on legitimate forms of justice administration so completely so as to render meaningless the characterization of Aboriginal justice systems as autonomous. As an Anishinabe presenter asserted during hearings conducted by the Aboriginal Justice Inquiry of Manitoba:

> Our communities have resolved disputes for centuries with various mechanisms such as the Council Fire where heads of families would meet to adopt widows and children or extend friendships and alliances. Our people would seek advice from Elders, and from medicine men and women who could conduct ceremonies such as the shaking tent. From them we would learn the teachings and gain knowledge that would assist us in mending relationships, setting our lives straight along the path again. We can use these traditional dispute resolution mechanisms in designing structures and approaches that will work today (Kelly-Kinew 1991).

Justice initiatives based on respect for Aboriginal cultures must also reflect the broader context of Aboriginal autonomy. As Hazlehurst (1988: 311) has observed in relation to parallel developments in Australia:

> If alternative dispute resolution mechanisms are to be established in Aboriginal communities as a means of diverting relatively minor problems away from the formal justice system and into the hands of the community itself, the principle of self-determination and dispute ownership must be embedded in the structure of such initiatives.

Finally, it is worth noting that the development of alternative dispute resolution processes in the context of justice administration is supportable not only in terms of exercising Aboriginal autonomy and adopting aspects of Aboriginal cultures. As the authors of a study prepared for the Aboriginal Justice Inquiry of Manitoba concluded,

> The most recurring theme within the [alternative dispute resolution] literature is that non-adversarial based approaches to justice are more appropriate for resolving a wide variety of conflict situations than

litigation through the courts' (ARA Consultants 1990: 59).

As this example illustrates, the creation of Aboriginal justice systems need not be seen as a development which is in competition with the general reform direction of the wider criminal justice system. Indeed, several commentators have suggested that the non-Aboriginal justice system might be 'improved' by incorporating certain Aboriginal processes and norms (Ross 1992). Support for alternative dispute resolution mechanisms is likely to be one of the most important elements of the interface between the two systems. Further, a flexible approach to achieving 'justice' in Aboriginal communities is not likely to result in systems which seriously threaten the principles of justice upon which the dominant system purports to be based.

Conclusion

In the context of a discussion of alternatives to territorial sovereignty for Aboriginal peoples, Hall (1992: 41) has observed:

Perhaps the most useful role that non-natives can play in the effort to achieve native self-government is not to design regimes of self-government but rather to demonstrate methods by which non-native legal and governmental structures can coexist with native sovereignty.

This approach can be applied in the context of criminal justice reform, and specifically, in relation to the adoption of a strategy which supports the development of autonomous dispute resolution and social control mechanisms. The initial aim of this direction should not be the creation of a generally applicable uniform regime of Aboriginal justice systems, but rather, endorsement of a justice administration policy which is designed to *support* rather than *shape* a range of community-based initiatives.

This approach would be compatible with the ongoing self-government negotiation process (assuming that this process *will* be ongoing and has stalled only temporarily). Indeed, the rejection of the Charlottetown Accord in October 1992 demonstrates that there may be significant impediments to the alignment of justice reform with the broader autonomy aspirations of Canada's Aboriginal peoples. However, this arrangement represents a major and necessary advance on the conventional and demonstrably ineffective strategy of 'tinkering' with the existing justice administration system. Conventional state-sponsored and state-controlled reform strategies are based on the fallacious assumption that a regime which has oppressed Aboriginal people for more than 100 years can effectively dispense 'justice' if only it undergoes a relatively painless sensitization process. In sharp contrast, autonomy-based reform is consistent with a more sophisticated conception of the nature of the justice problem in Aboriginal communities - an approach which looks beyond the mere fact of over-representation and seeks to confront the underlying reality of dispossession - and offers the possibility of genuine alternative strategies for dealing with matters of social harmony and the maintenance of order in Aboriginal communities.[14]

References

American Indian Lawyer Training Program Inc. (1982) *Indian Self-Determination and the Role of Tribal Courts. A Survey of Tribal Courts*, Oakland: American Indian Lawyer Training Program Inc.

Angus, M. (1991) *'... And the Last Shall Be First'. Native Policy in an Era of Cutbacks*, Toronto: NC Press Limited.

A.R.A Consultants (1990) *Feasibility Study of Alternative Dispute Mechanisms for Aboriginal People in Manitoba*, research paper prepared for the Aboriginal Justice Inquiry of Manitoba.

Asch, M. and Macklem, P. (1991) 'Aboriginal Rights and Canadian Sovereignty: An Essay on R. v. Sparrow', *Alberta Law Review*, 30: 465.

Assembly of Manitoba Chiefs (1992) 'Aboriginal Organizations Propose Partnership With Province in AJI Implementation', News Release, 3 February.

Barsh, R. and Henderson, J.Y. (1976) 'Tribal Courts, the Model Code and the Police Idea in American Indian Policy', *Law and Contemporary Problems*, 40: 25.

Beaudoin, G.A. and Dobbie, D. (1992) *A Renewed Canada: The Report of the Special Joint Committee of the Senate and the House of Commons*, Ottawa: Supply and Services Canada.

Branswell, H. (1992) 'Natives win full role in drafting unity package', *Winnipeg Free Press*, 13 March: A4.

Brock, K.L. (1990) 'The Politics of Aboriginal Self-Government: A Canadian Paradox', *Canadian Public Administration*, 34: 272.

Brodeur, J.P., LaPrairie, C. and McDonnell, R. (1991) *Justice for the Cree: Final Report*, Nemaska: Grand Council of the Cree (of Québec) and the Cree Regional Authority.

Brogden, M. (1991) 'Introduction: Criminal Justice and Colonization', in S.W. Corrigan and L.J. Barkwell (eds) *The Struggle for Recognition: Canadian Justice and the Métis Nation*, Winnipeg: Pemmican Publications.

Brown, D. (1987) 'Politics of Reform', in G. Zdenkowski., C. Ronalds and M.

Richardson (eds) *The Criminal Injustice System: Volume 2*, Sydney: Pluto Press.

Campbell, D. (1991) 'Indians say 10-year wait an outrage', *Winnipeg Free Press*, September: 10.

Campbell, D. and Weber, T. (1992) 'Province rejects separate Native justice system', *Winnipeg Free Press*, 29 January: A1.

Canada, Government (1991) *Shaping Canada's Future Together: Proposals*, Ottawa: Supply and Services Canada.

Canada, Ministry of the Solicitor General (1975) *Native Peoples and Justice. Reports on the National Conference and the Federal-Provincial Conference on Native People and the Criminal Justice System, Edmonton, February 3-5, 1975*, Ottawa: Ministry of the Solicitor General.

Cawsey, R.A. (1991) Task Force on the Criminal Justice System and its Impact on the Indian and Métis People of Alberta, *Justice on Trial*, Edmonton: Province of Alberta.

Chartrand, L. (1992) 'Beads and Trinkets Take on New Form in Federal Constitutional Proposals for Aboriginal Peoples in Canada', *Constitutional Forum*, 3: 62.

Clinton, R. (1976) 'Criminal Jurisdiction Over Indian Lands: A Journey through a Jurisdictional Maze', *Arizona Law Review*, 18: 503.

Coyle, M. (1986) 'Traditional Indian Justice in Ontario: A role for the present?', *Osgoode Hall Law Journal*, 24: 605.

Cunneen, C. (1992) 'Policing and Aboriginal Communities: Is the concept of over-policing useful?' in C. Cunneen (ed.) *Aboriginal Perspectives on Criminal Justice*. Monograph Series No. 1, Sydney: Institute of Criminology, Sydney University.

Dafoe, J. (1991) 'Manitoba's inquiry into Aboriginal justice merits vastly more than wariness', *The [Toronto] Globe and Mail*, 7 September: D2.

Dawson, M. (1991) 'Bridging the Constitutional Gap: Aboriginal Sovereignty/Canadian Sovereignty', paper presented at the Canadian Bar Associations' *Bridging the Constitutional Gap Conference*, Winnipeg, April 5-6.

Deloria, V. and Lytle, C. (1983) *American Indians, American Justice*, Austin: University of Texas Press.

Erasmus, G. (1989) 'Epilogue: The Solutions We Favour For Change', in B. Richardson (ed.) *Drumbeat: Anger and Renewal in Indian Country*, Toronto: Sumerhill Press.

Hall, G.R. (1992) 'The Quest for Native Self-Government: The Challenge of Territorial Sovereignty', *University of Toronto Faculty of Law Review*, 50: 39.

Hamilton, A.C. and Sinclair, C.M. (1991) Public Inquiry into the Administration of Justice and Aboriginal People, *The Report of the Aboriginal Justice Inquiry of Manitoba. Volume 1: The Justice System and Aboriginal People*, Winnipeg: Province of Manitoba.

Harding, J. (1991) 'Policing and Aboriginal Justice', *Canadian Journal of Criminology*, 33: 363.

Harding, J., Couse, K. and Schriml, R. (1988) *A Defence of Justice Studies: A History and Analysis of the Human Justice Program*, Regina: Prairie Justice Research, University of Regina.

Harding, J. and Forgay, B. (1991) *Breaking Down the Walls: A Bibliography on the Pursuit of Aboriginal Justice*, Regina: Prairie Justice Research, University of Regina.

Havemann, P. (1988) 'The Indigenization of Social Control in Canada' in B.W. Morse and G.R. Woodman (eds) *Indigenous Law and the State*, Dordrecht: Foris Publications.

Hazlehurst, K.M. (1988) 'Resolving Conflict: Dispute Settlement Mechanisms for Aboriginal Communities and Neighbourhoods?', *Australian Journal of Social Issues*, 23: 309.

Hemmingson, R.H. (1988) 'Jurisdiction of Future Tribal Courts in Canada: Learning From the American Experience', *Canadian Native Law Reporter*, 3: 1.

Hickman, A. (1989) Royal Commission on the Donald Marshall, Jr., Prosecution, *Report*, Halifax: Province of Nova Scotia.

Horn, C. and Griffiths, C.T. (1989) *Native North Americans: Crime, Conflict and Criminal Justice. A Research Bibliography*, 4th ed., Burnaby: Northern Justice Society Resource Centre, Simon Fraser University.

Indigenous Bar Association (1991) Constitutional Committee, *Presentation to the Joint Committee on a Renewed Canada*, 18 December.

Isaac, T. (1989) *An Analysis of the Native Self-Government in Canada: The Cree-Naskapi (of Québec) Act*, M.A. thesis, Dalhousie University.

Isaac, T. (1991) 'The *Constitution Act, 1982* and the Constitutionalization of Aboriginal Self-Government in Canada: *Cree-Naskapi (of Québec) Act*', *Canadian Native Law Reporter*, 1: 1.

Johnson, E. (1991) Royal Commission into Aboriginal Deaths in Custody, *National Report*, Canberra: Australian Government Publishing Service.

Kaiser, H.A. (1990) 'The Aftermath of the Marshall Commission: A Preliminary Opinion', *Dalhousie Law Journal*, 13: 364.

Kelly-Kinew, P. (1988) 'Presentation No. 121', *Public Inquiry into the Administration of Justice and Aboriginal People - Transcript of a Community Hearing*, Winnipeg, 19 October: 1211.

Kickingbird, K. (1976) 'In Our Image ... After Our Likeness: The Drive for the Assimilation of Indian Court Systems', *American Criminal Law Review*, 13: 675.

LaPrairie, C. (1990) *If Tribal Courts Are the Solution, What is the Problem?*, consultation paper prepared for the Attorney General of Nova Scotia.

Law Reform Commission of Canada (1991) *Aboriginal Peoples and Criminal Justice: Equality, Respect and the Search for Justice*, Ottawa: Law Reform Commission of Canada.

Linn, P. (1992a) *Report of the Saskatchewan Indian Justice Review Committee*, Regina.

Linn, P. (1992b) *Report of the Saskatchewan Métis Justice Review Committee*,

Regina.

Mannette, J. (1992a) 'The Social Construction of Ethnic Containment: The Royal Commission into the Donald Marshall Jr. Prosecution', in J. Mannette (ed.) *Elusive Justice*, Halifax: Fernwood Publishing.

Mannette, J. (ed.) (1992b) *Elusive Justice: Beyond the Marshall Inquiry*, Halifax: Fernwood Publishing.

McNamara, L. (1992a) 'Aboriginal People and Criminal Justice Reform: The Value of Autonomy-Based Solutions', *Canadian Native Law Reporter*, 1: 1-13.

McNamara, L. (1992b) 'The Aboriginal Justice Inquiry of Manitoba: A Fresh Approach to the "Problem" of Over-representation in the Criminal Justice System', *Manitoba Law Journal*, 21: 47-79.

McNamara, L. (1993) *Aboriginal Peoples, the Administration of Justice and the Autonomy Agenda: An Assessment of the Status of Criminal Justice Reform in Canada With Reference to the Prairie Region*, Winnipeg: Legal Research Institute, University of Manitoba.

Milloy, J.S. (1990) *A Partnership of Races: Indian and White. Cross-Cultural Relations and Criminal Justice in Manitoba, 1670-1949*, research paper prepared for the Aboriginal Justice Inquiry of Manitoba.

Morse, B. (1980) *Indian Tribal Courts in the United States: A Model for Canada?*, Saskatoon: Native Law Centre, University of Saskatchewan.

Morse, B. (1982) 'A Unique Court: s.107 Indian Act Justices of the Peace', *Canadian Legal Aid Bulletin*, 5: 2/3, 131.

Osnaburgh-Windigo Tribal Council Justice Review Committee (1990) *Tay Bway Win: Truth, Justice and First Nations*, report prepared for the Ontario Attorney General and Solicitor General.

Peters, E.J. (1989) 'Federal and Provincial Responsibilities for the Cree, Naskapi and Inuit Under the James Bay and Northern Québec, and Northeastern Québec Agreements' in D.C. Hawkes (ed.) *Aboriginal Peoples and Government Responsibility. Exploring Federal and Provincial Roles*, Ottawa: Carleton University Press.

Roberts, D. (1992) 'Separate native justice rejected for Manitoba, *The [Toronto] Globe and Mail*, 29 January:A1.

Ross, R. (1992) *Dancing With A Ghost: Exploring Indian Reality*, Markham: Octopus Publishing Group.

Rudin, J. and Russell, D. (1991) *Native Alternative Dispute Systems: The Canadian Future in Light of the American Past*, Toronto: Ontario Native Council on Justice.

Santin, A. (1991) 'Findings, recommendations exactly what natives expected', *Winnipeg Free Press*, 30 August: 5.

Taylor, J.P. and Paget, G. (1989) 'Federal/Provincial Responsibility and the Sechelt' in D.C. Hawkes (ed.) *Aboriginal Peoples and Government Responsibility. Exploring Federal and Provincial Roles*, Ottawa: Carleton University Press.

Turpel, M.E. (1992) 'Further Travails of Canada's Human Rights Record: The

Marshall Case' in J. Mannette (ed.) *Elusive Justice*.

Turpel, M.E. and Monture, P.A. (1990) 'Ode to Elijah: Reflections of Two First Nations Women on the Rekindling of Spirit at the Wake for the Meech Lake Accord', *Queen's Law Journal*, 15: 345.

Wall, B. (1992) 'Analyzing the Marshall Commission: Why it was Established and How it Functioned', in J. Mannette (ed.) *Elusive Justice*, Halifax: Fernwood Publishing.

Wherrett, J. and Brown, D. (1992) *Self-Government for Aboriginal Peoples Living in Urban Areas. A Discussion Paper Prepared for the Native Council of Canada*, Kingston: Institute of Intergovernmental Relations, Queen's University.

Wildsmith, B.H. (1991) 'Getting at Racism: The Marshall Inquiry', *Saskatchewan Law Review*, 55: 97.

Zimmerman, S. (1991) *'The Revolving Door of Despair': Native Involvement in the Criminal Justice System*, Ottawa: research paper prepared for the Aboriginal Justice Inquiry of Manitoba and the Law Reform Commission of Canada.

Notes

1. Luke McNamara is a Lecturer in the Faculty of Law at the University of Wollongong. He has completed a Master of Laws thesis on Aboriginal justice reform in Canada, and has written several articles about criminal justice and indigenous peoples in Australia and Canada. He is a co-editor of *Australian-Canadian Studies* and is currently conducting research on the role of racial vilification legislation in both countries.

2. As Cunneen (1992: 91) has observed in the context of a discussion of policing, '[m]uch of the work of the 1970s and 1980s was directed at proving that the policing of Aboriginal people was racist.... There is no doubt that the evidence is in: Aboriginal people are policed in a way different from, and at a greater level than, non-Aboriginal people'.

3. While conscious of the difficulty of appropriate terminology in relation to indigenous peoples I have adopted the term 'Aboriginal' throughout this article on the basis that it is currently the term that is most commonly adopted to embrace all first peoples in Canada including First Nations (or Indians), Inuit and Métis. This usage is also consistent with section 35 of the *Constitution Act, 1982* which offers a definition of 'aboriginal peoples of Canada'.

4. Statistical information on rates of arrest and incarceration for Aboriginal peoples in Canada is contained in McNamara (1993), chapter 1. Chapter 2 reviews the various reform initiatives which have been implemented in the Prairie region of Canada.

5. For a summary of the events and circumstances which led to the creation of the Marshall Royal Commission, see Wall (1992). The conclusions and recommendations of the Royal Commission (Hickman 1989) have attracted

considerable attention including substantial criticism. See the excellent collection of articles in Mannette (1992b); also Kaiser (1990); and Wildsmith (1991).

6. That is not to suggest that Aboriginal justice is not an important issue in other parts of Canada. Indeed, reports produced recently in Ontario (Osnaburgh/Windigo Tribal Council Justice Review Committee 1990), Quebec (Brodeur, La Prairie and McDonnell 1991) and by the Law Reform Commission of Canada (1991) illustrate that the concerns of Aboriginal people about how they are treated by the existing justice system is receiving attention in all parts of the country and is truly a matter of national significance.

7. For a detailed discussion of the range of recommendations contained in several recent reports see McNamara (1993), particulary chapters 3 and 4.

8. For example, the National Chief of the Assembly of First Nations indicated that the recommendations of the Inquiry reflected an understanding that 'making small changes to the current system is simply not appropriate or adequate': Press Release, 29 August 1991.

9. The Manitoba Government was represented on the Manitoba Constitutional Task Force which recommended in October 1991 constitutional recognition of the inherent right of Aboriginal self-government (Fox-Decent 1991).

10. Yet, this possibility, however unpalatable, cannot now be rejected out of hand given the collapse (once again) of the constitutional reform process as signalled by the Canadian electorate's refusal to endorse the reform package contained in the Charlottetown Accord.

11. This power under section 14(1)(p) is stated to be subject to section 14(2) which states:

    A law made in respect of the class of matters set out in paragraph (1)(p) may specify a maximum fine or a maximim term of imprisonment or both, but the maximum fine may not exceed two thousand dollars and the maximum term of imprisonment may not exceed six months.

12. Several other recent initiatives can be placed within the category of non-constitutional Aboriginal government arrangements, although they do not involve a formal delegation of legislative authority. Of particular interest is the plan announced in March 1992 by the Lheit-Lit'en Nation of northeastern British Columbia to replace the existing *Indian Act* system of govermnment with an elders council which it is anticipated will take over the functions of government on 1 July 1993. In contrast to the limited powers accepted by the Sechelt, the new Lheit-Lit'en government plans to assume a range of powers broadly equivalent to those of a province without the support of provincial or federal enabling legislation. Significantly, the initiative includes a proposal for the establishment of a separate justice system including a 'native healing and restoration centre': D. Wilson, 'Natives to create new society. B.C. Band will become self-government laboratory', *The Globe and Mail* (13 March 1992) A1.

13.   The Government of Nova Scotia has recently acted on the recommendation to
       which Turpel (1992) refers. However, according to an outline prepared by the
       Nova Scotia Department of Attorney General, the pilot project to be
       established in cooperation with the Shubenacadie Band on the Indian Brook
       Reserve is most accurately described as an 'Adult Diversion Pilot Programme'
       rather than an Aboriginal or Mi'kmaq court. A formal agreement was signed
       on 1 October 1992 by Shubenacadie Band Chief Reg Maloney, the Attorney
       General of Nova Scotia, Joel Matheson, and the Minister Responsible for
       Aboriginal Afffairs, Guy LeBlanc.
14.   This essay is based upon a detailed analysis of autonomy-based justice reform
       in Canada, submitted as a Master of Laws thesis at the University of
       Manitoba (McNamara 1993).

II Systemic discrimination, Aboriginal people, and the miscarriage of justice in Canada

Shirley McMullen and C.H.S. Jayewardene[1]

'When the Mohawks of Akwesasne devised their own proposed judicial code, they made the ultimate punishment the turning over of natives to the "white" system. That explains a lot about how Natives view the justice system ... They don't trust the British-based adversarial approach - with its European values and focus on incarceration - to provide justice to Canada's 1.2 million Aboriginal people', so claimed Sherri Barron (1990). A relevant and perhaps a more appropriate question may be how the criminal justice system has viewed Native people. That there was something lacking in the way that system treated them appears to be an accepted fact. On 8 July 1990, the Canadian Minister of Justice addressed a letter to the Law Reform Commission under subsection 12(2) of the Law Reform Commission Act requesting 'the Commission to study, as a matter of special priority, the Criminal Code and related statutes and to examine the extent to which these laws ensure that Aboriginal persons ... have equal access to justice and are treated equitably and with respect' (Law Reform Commission 1991).[2]

Studies of Canada's Aboriginal population indicate that they are disproportionately involved with Canada's Criminal Justice System (Cawsey, Little Bear, Franklin, Bertolin, Galet, Cooper and Gallagher 1991; Clark and Clark and Associates 1989; Hamilton and Sinclair 1991a, 1991b; Hylton 1980; Jackson 1988; Jolly 1982; Jolly and Birkenmayer 1981; Liang 1967). Official statistics show first, that about 9.6% of the federal penitentiary population (National Parole Board 1989) are Native Canadians who collectively comprise 2-3% of the total population of Canada; second, that while the number of inmates in penal institutions tended to fall, the number of Native inmates, both male and female, tended to increase (National Parole

Board 1989); third, that these figures have been and are relentlessly increasing (Law Reform Commission 1991; National Parole Board 1989); and fourth, that the rate of admission to penal institutions is much higher for Native women than for Native men (Law Reform Commission 1991).

Attempts to explain the disproportionate involvement of Native people in the Canadian criminal justice system has taken two major forms. One form focuses on the behaviour of Native people: the other on the treatment of the Native people by the criminal justice system. Falling into the first category are studies which accept the figures as a revelation that Native people do in fact commit more crime than non-Native people. These studies search for the causes of their criminality (LaPrairie 1990a), focusing on their social, economic and demographic conditions. Some have considered the possibility of discovering that Native people are in reality under-represented in the system, if the age structure of their population is taken into consideration (Havemann, Foster, Couse and Matanovich 1985; LaPrairie 1990a). The inordinately large crime figures, they speculate, may be attributable to the size of the 14-25 years old age group. No attempt has, however, been made to test empirically this speculation. Havemann and his colleagues also point to socio-economic status as an added contributory factor.

The analysis of arrest data for the City of Winnipeg led Bienvenue and Latif (1972) to conclude that their socio-economic status and the area of residence could account for the over-representation of people of Indian ancestry in the arrest statistics. Pertinent in this connection is the fact that the data on ethnic origin is collected on a self-report basis and a recent decreasing reluctance or an increasing willingness of Native people to identify themselves as Native people could account for the increase in the numbers (British Columbia Native Indian and Métis Education Club 1975; National Parole Board 1989). Also contributing to the increasing numbers could be a differential rate of growth of the Aboriginal population (National Parole Board 1989). There exists, however, a general belief that whatever the demographic, social and economic conditions contributing to their criminality may be, their criminality is really due to the 'marginalisation of Aboriginal societies as a result of colonization' (Hyde and LaPrairie 1987). The argument here is that there has been a breakdown of Native societies because control of their own destinies has been removed from them. Those criminologists contributing to this point of view contend that 'deflecting responsibility to the criminal justice system rather than addressing fundamental problems of social and economic disparity as reflected in reserve life, almost assures the continuation of the problem' (LaPrairie 1990b).

Falling into the second category are studies that have tended to focus their attention on the decision making points within the criminal justice system, looking for peculiarities in the manner in which Native people are treated by the different segments of that system. An examination of the statistical data led Hamilton and Sinclair, who headed the Manitoba Aboriginal Justice Inquiry, to acknowledge the operation of a differential treatment factor. This, however, did not obviate the possibility that their 'current state of social and economic distress' resulting from the social, economic and cultural repression and oppression of previous generations did make them commit more crime than non-Native people. The two together apparently conspired to produce the disproportionality (Hamilton and Sinclair 1991a).

Native people are over-represented at the police level of the criminal justice system (Cawsey et al 1991). This over-representation could possibly be due to their over-involvement in crime. This is the official position. The official crime rate among Native people is much higher than that among non-Native people. However, as all crime is never recorded and only a proportion of that crime gets recorded, over-representation at the police level need not necessarily mean over-involvement in criminal activity. Differential enforcement could be responsible for it. The type of crime in which a group indulges may be the crime to which the police pay special attention, because these crimes are more visible, are considered to be specifically disruptive of society, or are committed by people the police consider specially criminal. Street crimes are usually more visible to the police than other types of crimes, and groups whose socio-economic conditions favour the commission of this type of crime could well be seen as being over-involved in crime. Again, street crimes are considered to be 'more disruptive of society than other crimes' and, as such, groups engaging in these crimes become the target of police activity. Such groups can also be seen as being over-involved in crime (Lewis 1989).

The police point out that their day-to-day experience leads to the empirical observation that particular groups of people are criminal. They fail, however, to appreciate that this experience may be the result of police extra-surveillance leading to an increased detection of engagement in crime (Quigley 1990). Instead, they attribute the 'observed criminality' to cultural differences preventing these groups from fashioning their behaviour according to Canadian rules and Canadian law. Police crime prevention and crime control activities call not only for this extra-surveillance but also for police intervention at a point before the actual commission of a crime. As far as Native people are concerned, most of their criminal activity is believed to revolve around the consumption of alcohol and they tend to become a crime statistic more because of a police penchant for proactive policing than because of the actual violation of the law (Jayewardene 1972, 1975).

Native people are also over-represented in admissions to correctional institutions. This, of course, is not surprising if they are over-represented at the police level. However, their over-representation at the level of correctional institutions was greatly enhanced (Cawsey et al 1991), indicating the operation of discriminatory factors at each succeeding point of decision-making in the criminal justice system. There is a reduction in numbers as suspected offenders pass through the criminal justice system (Sellin 1937). In the United States, an increasing concentration of blacks has been noted at each succeeding level of the criminal justice system. Barros and her colleagues (1970) who refer to this phenomenon as the 'blacking' of the defendant cohort has attributed it to white offenders being filtered out from the criminal justice system at a faster rate than black offenders. Havemann and his colleagues (1975), who have noted the 'blacking' phenomenon in connection with the Aboriginal people of Canada, identify 'discriminatory, discretionary practices and powers of officials in the criminal justice system, particularly those who may exercise influence over which offenders are apt to be imprisoned' as a possible source while Cawsey and his colleagues (1991), state 'the courts appear to contribute to the over-representation of Aboriginal people in prison in a direct and significant manner'.

Studies on sentencing have sought to discover the existence either of an unwarranted disparity in disposition - the incarceration of Native people for offences for which non-Native people are not incarcerated - or an unwarranted disparity in sentence length - the sentencing of Native people to longer terms of incarceration than non-Native people. These studies have controlled for legal variables such as the seriousness of the offence and criminal record. The findings reveal that, on the average, Native offenders are given much shorter sentences than the non-Native offenders, which has been interpreted as a judicial leniency toward Native offenders (LaPrairie 1990; Havemann et al 1985). Judges, testifying before the Task Force on the Criminal Justice System and its Impact on the Indian and Métis People of Alberta, also alluded to this greater leniency referring to it as a 'Native discount' (Cawsey et al 1991). A second finding in these studies is the restriction of the judicial leniency in sentencing to relative minor cases and the imposition of more severe sentences when serious offences are involved (Harrell 1977). The overall impression of judicial leniency, hence, results from a much greater involvement of Native offenders in relatively minor crimes (Hagan 1974). Third, is the seemingly contradictory finding that though Native offenders are given shorter sentences by the courts, they spend more time incarcerated. Incarceration while waiting for trial and incarceration for the non-payment of fines accounts for part of the discrepancy. Finally, the studies indicate that Native offenders are less likely to receive non-custodial sentences such as probation (Schmeiser 1974).

Evaluating the existing studies on sentencing disparity, LaPrairie (1990a) states the data 'provide no definitive answers to the question of racial bias or unwarranted disparity in the sentencing of Aboriginal people, but highlight some of the contradictions that exist', while Head and Clairmont (1989) caution 'such discrimination has been much more subtle, sporadic and driven either into earlier stages of the charge/conviction/sentencing process or into the "backroom" of the court'. Loath to attribute it to outright racism, the various Commissions of Inquiry have tended to point an accusing finger at an encrusted discrimination stemming from the seeming neutrality of the extant criminal justice system demanding a continuation of the traditional perspective of substantive criminal law that every one be treated equally. Interpreted as a requirement for identical treatment and applied as such, it has only recently been recognized that such application of the law to a people discriminated against for generations, abused and oppressed and reduced to a 'state of social and economic distress' cannot possibly result in equality (Andrews v Law Society of British Columbia 1989; Canadian National Railway Co v Canada (Canadian Human Rights Commission) 1987). 'The concept of equality in court proceedings', Chief Judge Lilles is cited as observing, 'is based on the premise that any law is equally applicable to, understood by and concurred in, by all those subject to it. It is, in fact, an assumption of cultural homogeneity; it operates to maintain the existing sociological order. In non-legal terms, this assumption is patently false' (Cawsey et al 1991).

Given the discretionary power of judges and the apparent judicial practice of individualizing sentences, differential sentencing outcomes seem inevitable. The extent to which factors other than those legitimately involved in this individualizing process play a part in the sentencing of Native offenders cannot be determined from a statistical analysis which does not examine all the variables, legal as well as extra-legal, considered by courts in reaching sentencing decisions (LaPrairie 1990a; Havemann et al 1985). A study by LaPrairie and Griffiths (1982) indicated that 'significant socio-cultural differences' rather than ethnicity was responsible for the over-representation of Native juveniles at all stages of the criminal justice system. Hagan (1974, 1975) used a model, developed by Hogarth (1971), to test the hypothesis that 'offender characteristics interact with judicial attitudes to produce disparities in sentencing'. This model presents sentencing as a dynamic, subjective process in which variables such as attitudes and beliefs, perception of social and legal constraints, relevant case facts and cognitive styles, resulted in each judge's individual interpretation of reality. His study led him to the conclusion that 'among those judges who have an active concern for law and order, there appeared to be no abuse of discretion or differential treatment of minorities. Offence seriousness and not race determined their sentencing decisions. Judges who were less concerned about law and order, however, appeared to use part of their discretion to provide lenient treatment to indigenous offenders'.

Unfortunately, systemic discrimination - structural arrangements of the system which operate to produce unintended ill effects for a group of people - act to nullify this leniency. One form of leniency is the fining of offenders instead of sentencing them to imprisonment. Native people, together with the poor, are usually unable to pay the fine and, spared incarceration for the crime, they nevertheless end up incarcerated for the non-payment of the fine. Hickman and his colleagues (1989) have defined systemic discrimination as 'what happens when a specific act, policy or structural factor - intended or unintended - results in adverse effects for members of certain specific groups'. There are a number of such acts, policies and structural factors which adversely affect Native people, the most blatant of which is the operation of the jury system.

As the Law Reform Commission (1991) points out, 'trial by jury ... is in part intended to allow an accused person to be judged by people who are likely to understand the accused's motivations and who perhaps share common attitudes and expectations'. It is believed that the desired result would be achieved through the random selection of the jury from the community in which the accused is tried. Operationally, the random selection is limited to the first stage of a multi-stage selection process - the preparation of the jurors' roll - and even here, restricted to a certain segment of the community. Educational and other such qualifications exclude some from participation while occupation exempt others from jury service. Then, in the creation of the jury panel, the efficiency of postal and telecommunication services to groups of people play a part. Placement on the jury panel depends on the celerity with which an individual responds to summons to serve. Finally, there is the selection of the actual jury in which the prosecution and defence could use 'peremptory challenges and stand asides' to exclude certain people (Hamilton and Sinclair 1991a). The process 'may result in a jury, none of whose members share the accused's race or ethnic association, even though that race or ethnic group is well-represented in the community as a whole. Even so, if no deliberate exclusion can be shown, the courts will recognize no cause for complaint' (Law Reform

Commission 1991).

Less obvious systemic discrimination exists in the operation of the certain Acts. The Provincial Offenses Act, designed to relieve courts of the unnecessary burden of adjudicating minor offenses, allows the police, in cases of minor highway traffic offenses and liquor offenses, to proceed by means of an offence notice which permits an out-of-court settlement by the police imposition of a predetermined fine. If, however, the police deem the circumstances of the case to require it, they are permitted to proceed by means of summons to court for trial and determination of penalty. When the second alternative is resorted to, there is a tacit message, unintended maybe, given to the court that this is a special case calling for special consideration. Courts tend to respond with prison penalties. In jurisdictions where there is a large Aboriginal population, it has been found that the tendency was for the police to proceed by way of summons to court. In Kenora, one such jurisdiction, the court option was utilized primarily in liquor offences, twice as frequently as was the practice in jurisdictions where the population was predominantly non-Aboriginal. The courts in these jurisdictions used prison penalties for these offences three times as frequently as courts in other jurisdictions (Jolly and Seymour 1983). Operating to influence court sentencing decisions for Native offenders in these cases are the conditions associated with the imposition of the non-custodial penalties. The sentencing options available to a judge in any and every liquor offence case are incarceration, discharge or probation with a requirement for treatment designed to deal with the offender's problem. When the offender is a Native person, the absence of treatment facilities for them limits these options (Clark et al 1989). Whatever the offence may be, the conditions required for non-custodial dispositions constitute a source of systemic discrimination. The information that is used by parole and probations officers for their pre-parole and pre-sentence reports makes the reports 'automatically loaded' against Native people. The higher than average unemployment rates on reserves provides little opportunity for job prospects (Havemann et al 1985) and the paucity of aftercare facilities makes it difficult for them to obtain parole (Hickman, Poitras and Evans 1989).

Making a considerable contribution to the problem, Hamilton and Sinclair (1991a) claim is culture conflict, a clash between the values treasured by the Native people and the values enshrined in the Canadian criminal justice system. Analysing Native concepts of justice, they point out how 'differing concepts of crime and justice, conceptual misunderstandings and communication difficulties' as well as 'different concepts of the purpose of a legal system', has assisted in the failure to dispel the notion that the

Canadian criminal justice system was an instrument for the oppression and the exploitation of Native people. The cultural orientations of Native people did not permit them to utilize effectively the protection that the criminal justice system offered. Essentially non-adversarial, 'the Aboriginal person may not provide the court or even his counsel with evidence unfavourable to the opposing witnesses' (Indigenous Bar Association 1991). Then, reared to look upon lying, 'which would include not acknowledging those acts of which you were properly accused ...', as the most serious of crimes, the Native person would not be able to benefit from such concepts as the presumption of innocence (Ross 1989). The cultural differences and the culture conflict, it should perhaps be pointed out, as Brass (1979) has already done, does not call for an Aboriginal legitimization of behaviour deemed criminal in Canadian society. The same behaviour is condemned in both cultures. The difference lies in the culturally-dictated societal reaction to the behaviour. 'The laws, customs, and traditions that have been defined by [the Aboriginal] culture ... respect cultural imperatives that restrict interference and encourage restraint. Their primary purpose is to discourage disruption and to restore harmony when it occurs' (Hamilton and Sinclair 1991a).

The Law Reform Commission interpreted the request of the Minister of Justice as a call for them 'to propose reforms that will offset the sorry results of a history of disadvantage and suffering within the system - reforms that can be proceeded with as a matter of special priority' (Law Reform Commission 1991). In the performance of this task, they discovered that Aboriginal people viewed the criminal justice system as 'an alien one, imposed by a dominant white society', characterized by the 'abuse of power and the distorted exercise of discretion', incomprehensible to them and insensitive to their customs, traditions and beliefs. They desired an Aboriginal system of justice - a system that was 'Aboriginal-designed, Aboriginal-run and Aboriginal-populated from top to bottom'. Although the details of the desired system were unknown, it was, most importantly, a system which challenged 'both common and civil law concepts', placed less reliance on statute law and depended on customary practices, which would vary from community to community, as 'the binding force promoting harmony within the community' (Law Reform Commission 1991). The various commissions inquiring into the relationship between Aboriginal people and the Canadian criminal justice system had also made similar discoveries. The challenge posed to all of them was whether the Canadian criminal justice system should be made to accommodate such a system, especially when the Aboriginal desire was seen as 'a natural outgrowth of their aspirations to self-government and sovereignty' (Law Reform

Commission 1991). The Law Reform Commission had, from its very inception, established and adopted a 'uniform, consistent and comprehensive approach to law reform'. It was their belief that 'all those coming to or residing in Canada should accept Canadian rules, and the outer limit of allowable behaviour should be set by the criminal law'. Sympathetic to the Aboriginal position, the Law Reform Commission recommended the creation of an Aboriginal Justice System 'through a process of negotiation and agreement'. The provisions of sections 25 and 35 of the Canadian Charter of Rights and Freedoms, they claimed, permitted distinct treatment to be afforded the Aboriginal people. What was more, 'legal pluralism, in the form of Quebec's control over civil law, and divided jurisdiction ...' already characterized the Canadian system.

Because of the impossibility of accomplishing overnight the fundamental changes needed for the establishment of an Aboriginal Justice System, the Law Reform Commission as well as the other Commissions of Inquiry proposed the adoption of a two-pronged approach in which short term ameliorative reforms would be immediately effected while steps would be taken to ensure that the long-term goal of an Aboriginal Justice System would be ultimately reached. On the claim that 'a pervasive lack of knowledge about Aboriginal people on the part of the justice system personnel' contributed to the inequitable treatment meted out to them, the short term proposals called for a rectification in the form of an increased involvement of Native people at all levels of the criminal justice system on the other side of the divide, of increased and improved cross-cultural training given non-Native people working in the system, and of incorporation into the system of Native innovations by enlarging existing Native-controlled programmes which involve Elders' Councils in 'diversion, bail supervision, preparation of pre-sentence reports and speaking to sentence' (Indigenous Bar Association 1991). These recommendations, if implemented, would give Native people a more representative system. There would be more Native judges, more Native lawyers, more Native clerks of court, more Native correctional officers and more Native managers of the correctional system, but as Ovide Mercredi, presently President of the Assembly of First Nations, has pointed out, 'it would still be your law that would apply, it would still be your police forces which would enforce the law, it would still be your courts that would interpret them, and it would still be your correctional system that houses the people that go through the court system' (Law Reform Commission 1991). The system would be akin to the U.S. Tribal Court System which has been described as 'a pale mirror of the U.S. Court system' (Osnaburgh/Windigo Tribal Council Justice Review Committee 1990) and the establishment of which in Canada has been denounced as not accomplishing a great deal (Rudin and Russell 1991). The solution is to 'find alternatives to the existing system' (Law Reform Commission 1991). What the desired alternative was remained unknown. Also unknown was the reason for their living dislike of the existing criminal justice system especially when Native participation in and contribution to the system was being increased. Perhaps it was their experience that the reforms outlined, first conceptualized and promoted in the early 1970's, were being implemented in a political and ideological setting which called for an assimilationist policy for Native people (James 1979; Harding 1991), despite a Government commitment to multiculturalism.

It is not unreasonable to look in judicial decision-making for the roots of over-representation at the prison level. Restricted as it might be by mandatory penalties, the sentences imposed on offenders is ultimately decided upon by the judge. The impact of judicial decision-making, however, is contingent on police activity. The police decide who are the offenders taken to court and what are the charges laid against them. The police exercise of discretion in law enforcement has a considerable impact on the type of person who is labelled criminal (Jayewardene and McWatt 1983) as well as on the nature of the prison population. However, as LaPrairie (1990a) point out, 'it is difficult to explicitly point to differential police charging and arrests as the basis for disproportionate incarceration rates'. Hamilton and Sinclair (1991a) argue that the differential crime rate of the Native people is partly due to the way in which they and their behaviour are categorized and stigmatized by the police. The police keep them under greater surveillance, tend to stop and check them at a greater frequency (Hamilton and Sinclair 1991a; Quigley 1990; Greenaway 1980) and charge them for minor offences, where merely the formal requirements for a charge exists (Law Reform Commission 1991), simply because they believe that such people may tend to commit more serious crimes. Perceived to be a danger to public order, Native people 'are given much less latitude in their behaviour before the police take action' (Hamilton and Sinclair 1991a). Differential charging has been found to account for the inordinate number of Native people charged with being drunk and disorderly (Finkler 1976; Harding 1971) and this differential charging, especially in the North, has been attributed to the police perception of what drinking does to a Native rather than to his drunken and disorderly behaviour (Jayewardene 1979-1980). 'Many Aboriginal people are arrested and held in custody, where a non-Aboriginal person in the same circumstances either might not be arrested or might not be held', claim Hamilton and Sinclair (1991a).

In recent times, there have been outcries of police racism stemming from the manner in which Native people and members of visible ethnic minorities were being treated by the police. A number of public inquiries have consequently been conducted into the conduct of the police in different parts of the country. The factors that precipitated these inquiries and formed their main focus have varied, but all of them have extended the investigation into the operation of all segments of the criminal justice system and their relationship with minority groups, in many, with Native people exclusively. The differential treatment accorded Native people and ethnic minorities by the Nova Scotia Justice System was investigated as a part of a Royal Commission (Hickman et al 1989a, 1989b; Apostle and Stenning 1988; Archibald 1989; Clark et al 1989; Edwards 1989; Government of Nova Scotia 1988; Head and Clairmont 1989) inquiring into the 1971 conviction of a 17-year-old Micmac Indian Donald Marshall Jr. of Sydney, Nova Scotia, accused of stabbing to death an acquaintance (Harris 1986). Flawed police investigation and perjured testimony were found to the reasons for this miscarriage of justice. The confrontation between Blood Tribe members, the people of the Town of Cardston and the R.C.M.P., and the concern over the manner in which the police handled sudden deaths of Blood Tribe members led to Alberta's Commission of Inquiry into Policing in Relation to the Blood Tribe (Rolf 1991a, 1991b). The police investigations of the abduction and murder on 13 November 1971 of a 19-year-old Cree girl, Helen Betty Osborne of Norway House, Manitoba, attending school in The Pas, Manitoba, in which charges were laid against the suspects only in 1986 (Priest 1989); and the shooting death of Native leader John Joseph Harper in 1988 by Robert Cross, a Winnipeg police officer (Kaila and Brosnahan 1989), resulted in the Public Inquiry into the Administration of Justice in relation to the Native peoples of Manitoba (Hamilton and Sinclair 1991a, 1991b).

The much publicized arrest of the prominent Winnipeg Lawyer Harvey I. Pollock Q.C., who had represented the Harper family at investigations into Harper's death and had been very critical of the manner in which the police had conducted the original investigation, and the subsequent staying of the charges of sexual assault laid against him, led to the inquiry into the behaviour of the Winnipeg police (Hughes 1991). The recognition of a general problem in the relationship between the Native community in Alberta and the criminal justice system resulted in the Alberta Aboriginal Justice Inquiry (Cawsey et al 1991; Government of Alberta 1991a, 1991b). Confrontation between Toronto's black community and the police following the shooting deaths of Mississauga teenager Michael Wade Lawson, and of

Lester Donaldson, a black man who had been crippled four months earlier by a police bullet, resulted in Ontario's Race Relations and Police Task Force (Lewis 1989). The 1987 shooting of black teenager Anthony Griffin by a Montreal Urban Police officer and the ensuing hostile relations between the police and the black community resulted in a Commission of Inquiry established by the Quebec Human Rights Commission, to inquire into the allegations of 'discriminatory treatment and racist behaviour' toward visible and ethnic minorities by the police (Bellemare 1988).

Witnesses appearing before these and other similar inquiries have related how Native people have been insulted and humiliated by the police, how they have been denied adequate police protection and how they have been framed for crimes that they did not commit. The witnesses also complained about their inability to obtain any redress for police misdeeds. Complaints of police misdeeds are investigated by the very police against whom the complaint was lodged. When complaints were lodged against police officers, attempts were always made to exonerate them. After they had lodged a complaint, witnesses found themselves subjected to police harassment. Not only did they feel that there was no point in reporting abuses, they were fearful of doing so (Cawsey et al 1990). In an increasing number of instances, Native people and members of visible minority groups have shown a growing reluctance to accept the police version of the incident and have been insistent in their demand for a public inquiry. Jack Aubury (1991) has pointed to the existence of a 'fairly consistent pattern of reaction' to these cases. An initial reaction to any complaint has always been denial. When denial failed to silence the voices of those complaining, attempts at a cover-up have been made. When the cover-up is found unacceptable, one or more public inquiries have been conducted, each revealing the shortcomings of the system and police misdeeds. When an adverse conclusion is reached, and disciplinary action is taken against any police officer, a violent reaction is evoked from the police brotherhood. The police brotherhood demonstrates, declaring their support for the disciplined officer in some instances (Story 1990), denouncing the Police Chief claiming that he had stabbed them in the back in other instances (King 1992), and calling for his resignation and/or the resignation of the Attorney General in still other instances (Hoffman 1989).

In strikingly similar conclusions, all these Commissions of inquiry acknowledged the existence of evidence of over-policing, of over-surveillance, of over-charging, and of the over-use of pre-trial detention. All of them also found evidence of under-policing, of cunctation in responding to Native calls to the police, and of police apathy in the investigation of crimes committed against Native people. The complaints made against the police indicate the existence of four types of police behaviour that could be considered not only unnecessarily obnoxious and definitely discriminatory but even racist (Jayewardene and Talbot 1990). There is first, verbal abuse. The police, witnesses claimed, make derogatory references to Native people and have even addressed them in derogatory terms (Cawsey et al 1990). Police officers frequently use expletive adjectives which Hamilton and Sinclair (1991b) concluded revealed definitely a racist attitude. Heard at the police station, especially after a tragic encounter between the police and members of Native groups, were also racist jokes (Gillmor 1988), which were considered to be nothing more than innocuous ethnic jokes even by the Chief of Police (Hamilton and Sinclair 1991b). Native people were always looked upon as drunkards, as uncivilized and unprincipled (Jackson 1988), to whom the word truth had absolutely no meaning, and, as if to remind them that, when they were dealing with Native people, they were dealing with an entirely different species, some police officers had their billy clubs etched with the words 'For Indians, hold here'.

Then, there is physical abuse. There is the shooting and beating of Native people by the police in 'other than extreme circumstances' (Lewis 1989). When a shooting occurs, it is always justified with the police claiming sometimes that it was only an accident (Kaila and Brosnahan 1989) and at other times that it was the result of a police officer, who perceived his life to be in danger, acting in self-defence (Wiecek 1990). These cases, however, are rare, but the publicity that is given them, with the same story repeated over and over again in the press, during the long period it takes to bring the investigation of the incident to a satisfactory conclusion, makes shooting appear a common occurrence (Jayewardene 1993).

Not so rare are cases where the physical abuse does not result in death. As a part of the daily routine of police work or in special crime prevention programmes, the police single out Native people, stop and interrogate them, and often, especially if they show any signs of resentment, assault them, arrest them and lay a number of frivolous charges against them. Native suspects being transported, witnesses appearing before the Commissions claimed, sometimes 'accidentally fall out of moving police cars'. In addition to these obvious forms of physical abuse are less obvious forms. A classic example exists in the case of Kitty Nowdluk-Reynolds, a victim of a rape, who was arrested by the R.C.M.P. in her home in Surrey, British Columbia, because she failed to answer a summons to appear in court. She was to be taken to her home town of Iqaluit, North West Territories, where the rape occurred, to testify at the trial of her assailant Inusiq Shoo. Because her

R.C.M.P. escort overslept and they missed their flight, the trip took eight days, during which period she was forced to go without a shower, spend time in five separate jails, working three days in the prison laundry in one. She was finally transported, handcuffed, in the same van as her rapist to a court house where her evidence was not required because the accused pleaded guilty. After the case, she was given a plane ticket to Vancouver where she arrived late at night to be taken by the R.C.M.P., who, refusing to drive her home, dropped her on a highway to catch a bus (Bindman 1992). Stranding Native persons in town appears to be a not uncommon practice of the police. During an investigation, Native persons in a remote settlement or reserve, arrested and taken to town for questioning are not taken back after the questioning. They are released on their own recognizance and asked to find their way back (Alberta Federation of Métis Settlements 1990). In places such as High Level, Peace River and Valleyview Native, persons walking home 'are picked up by the R.C.M.P., thrown into gaol and at times charged with several offences'. Non-Native persons walking home are not subjected to the same treatment: sometimes they are offered a ride home (Métis Nations of Alberta 1990).

Third, there is the trivialization of victimization, resulting in the underpolicing of the Native people. Police fail to extend to Native people, the same degree of protection that they extend to non-Native people. Responsible for this poor response is the police belief that Native problems are always alcohol-related. When a Native person in custody shows signs of physical distress, the condition is considered related to inebriation and no action is taken unless death appears imminent. When a Native person is reported missing, he is thought missing because of an alcohol-related problem (Rolf 1991a). When the police are called by Native people, the response time has been found to be 'inexplicably long' (Clark 1989). The slow response rate has been linked to the stereotyped views held by the police of Native people as heavy drinkers and their belief first, that the summons is to deal with an alcohol-related domestic problem (Rolf 1991a), which would turn out to be a 'temporary situation that will disappear in the morning', and second, that any violence that might occur would not be serious enough to be of any real danger to the individuals (Clark 1989). Of course, there is the complicating problem of limited police staff and large patrol areas.

More serious is the manner in which the police investigate non-natural deaths of members of Aboriginal groups. When the 48-year-old Native Leo Lachance was leaving a gun and pawn shop in Prince Albert, Saskatchewan, he was shot in the upper chest. Although he was shot in broad daylight and in front of witnesses, it took the police two days to arrest Carney Nerland, the owner of the shop, who was responsible for the shooting (Jenish and Sampson 1991). When Coreen Thomas, a young Native woman from a reserve outside Vanderhoff, British Columbia, was struck down and killed by a car driven by a 22-year-old white man, Richard Redekop, under the influence of alcohol and at a speed of over 70 miles an hour, the R.C.M.P. officer investigating the case demurred at the suggestion that charges should be laid against the driver, on the grounds that the key issue in deciding whether criminal charges should be laid was whether there was contributory negligence on the part of the dead girl in running in front of the car (Cocking 1977). The inquiry of Hamilton and Sinclair (1991b) into the case of Helen Betty Osborne led them to the conclusion that the fact that she was a Native did influence the R.C.M.P. inquiry into her death.

Fourth is the unwarranted suspicion of involvement in criminal activity, resulting in active harassment. Police in cities tend to patrol bars where Native people congregate rather than private clubs frequented by businessmen (Quigley 1990). In Operation SHOCAP (Serious Habitual Offenders Comprehensive Action Programme) in Edmonton, approximately 50% of the young offenders identified as those with the greatest likelihood of re-offending and subjected to intensive policing were Native (Cawsey et al 1991). Native people seen on the streets are stopped and asked for identification for no other reason than that they are Native people. 'The police would never approach a (white) stockbroker and ask for I.D.' was the response given to a speculative query as to what would have been the situation if J.J. Harper, the Indian Chief who was shot, had been a white stockbroker (Gillmor 1988). Not only is there an unwarranted suspicion of involvement in criminal activity, there is also the unwarranted assumption of guilt in cases where Native people are suspects. The case of Donald Marshall Jr. of Halifax, Nova Scotia, is an example. Convicted and sentenced to life imprisonment, Marshall spent eleven years in prison before the last of several R.C.M.P. reviews of the case found the existence of evidence that confirmed his innocence. This evidence had apparently been available at the time of Marshall's very first appeal but had then not been shown to either the lawyer for the crown or the lawyer for the defence. It was kept in the Attorney General's department in a 'separate set of files marked with green labels and containing secret R.C.M.P. reports on politically-sensitive matters' (Harris 1988). The Royal Commission appointed to inquire into this case concluded 'this miscarriage of justice could have and should have been prevented or at least corrected quickly, if those involved in the system had carried out their duties in a professional and competent manner' (Hickman et al 1989). Regarding the initial investigation, the Commission observed that the investigating officer, MacIntyre, had identified Marshall as the prime suspect by the next morning not only without any evidence to support his conclusions but also in the face of evidence to the contrary. They concluded that 'the fact that Marshall was a Native was one of the reasons MacIntyre identified him as the prime suspect' (Hickman et al 1989).

In another case, a R.C.M.P. sergeant whose investigation led to the conviction of another Native man, Wilson Nepoose, for the strangulation murder of Marie Rose Desjarlais in 1986, was charged with perjury for his testimony at an Alberta Court of Appeal. In this case, pressure from the Federal Government to reopen the case made the R.C.M.P. admit that the investigation which led to the conviction was flawed (Curren 1992). There was evidence known to the police investigators which was not passed on to either the crown or the defence. Referring to other shortcomings in the investigation, Jack Ramsay, a former R.C.M.P. officer who investigated the case privately, observed 'R.C.M.P. errors in the case were difficult to excuse as honest mistakes or even as incompetence' (Barrett 1992). Non-disclosure of evidence available to the crown has also occurred in cases where non-Native persons have been accused of a crime committed against Native persons. In these cases, the result was a stay of proceedings. Bishop Hubert O'Connor, who was charged with the rape of two Native women and the indecent assault of two others, while he was the principal of St. Joseph's School, a residential school for Natives, near Williams Lake, British Columbia, had proceedings in the case against him stayed because the prosecuting crown counsels had failed to supply documents, drawings and transcripts to the defence (Sudlow 1992).

The inquiries into police misdeeds, Sunahara (1992) claims, focused on individual officers from a legal perspective and identified the cause of the objectionable behaviour as a personal deficiency in the individual officer. As each inquiry was conducted in isolation, and headed by lawyers whose normal orientation is the finding of personal responsibility, the similarity in the behaviour of officers separated by a breadth of geography and time went unnoticed, and the possibility that it might be 'an institutional response that many police officers in a similar position would have made' went unrecognized. Underlying the behaviour of the individual officer, he claims, is the 'social and subcultural characteristics of policing as an institution'. The verbal abuse to which the Native people were subjected, he contends, is only an expression of the 'cynicism and callousness which some officers develop as they progress through their careers' (Delattre 1991) and which, though looked upon as flippancy and humour by the police, often gets interpreted as aggression and abrasiveness by the public. The differential treatment meted out to them and some other groups results apparently from the police desire to maintain amicable relations with organizations which form the institutional context in which the police must function, causing 'the police to subordinate their duty as peace officers to the practical exigencies of day to day life' and treat different groups differently (Sunahara 1992). The manipulation of evidence to obtain a conviction of a Native person and the 'inept and dilatory investigation' of crimes committed against Native people, has been attributed to the hierarchical, paramilitary structures of police services which relegate subordinate officers to play a secondary role in an investigation and effectively prevent them from speaking out when an investigation is being conducted improperly. The difficulty encountered by Native people in obtaining redress for police misdeeds is considered to stem from the central value of police culture - the loyalty of police officers to fellow officers - which leads them to overlook the transgression and errors of other officers subordinating 'their professional responsibilities to the desire to maintain solidarity with other officers'. Finally, their insensitivity in dealing with Native people, thought attributable to their ignorance of Native customs, is, in reality, an unwillingness to tailor policing methods to the needs of the community policed because the professional policing paradigm compels them to be guided by an ethos, internal to the police, reflecting 'the pressures and incentives of police bureaucracies' and not by community needs (Brown 1988).

The Native people envisage the problem differently. Whatever may be the contribution to the problem made by the personal idiosyncrasies of criminal justice personnel, by systemic discrimination and/or by the social and cultural characteristics of the policing institution, playing a much greater part and making a much greater contribution appears to be the very concept of policing. In the enactment of their role, the police perform a multitude of tasks, all of which derive from the conception of their role as that of maintaining law and order and this, to ensure people the quiet enjoyment of their lives. Police forces, differ greatly in what they do. There are a multitude of reasons given for these differences but all of them stem from the manner in which they structure order (Ericson 1982), from what they perceive the order-disturbing behaviour to be, and on whom they perceive to be disturbing that order. An analysis of the policing function in Canada (Talbot, Jayewardene and Juliani 1984) has led to the conclusion that, at times, when the order-disturbing behaviour was seen as a foreign invasion of, or infiltration into, a sparsely populated territory, the police translated the maintenance of law and order to mean the protection of the integrity of the country. At these times, policing strategy was keeping onside the population by acting as a service providing agency rather than a behaviour controlling one. At other times, when the problem was attacks from marauding bands of Indians and bandits, the maintenance of law and order was translated to mean the security of the territory for settlement. At these times, policing strategy comprised surveillance not of those in the area but of those coming into the area. Finally, at still other times, when communities were growing and developing, the maintenance of law and order was translated to mean the creation and maintenance of those conditions which would be conducive to prosperous development. Policing strategy assumed the form of enforcement of rules and regulations 'to bind the community together' (Stenning 1982), rules and regulations which would assist in the establishment of a specific moral order. Alluding to the etymology of the term, Hamilton and Sinclair (1991a) contend that the police 'can be understood as a social structure, which a community puts in place and mandates to enforce the political decisions of society'. This mandate, thought essential for the preservation of the ethos of society, ignores the greater policing objective of ensuring people the quiet enjoyment of their lives. In his remarks to the Law Reform Commission, Ovide Mercredi contended 'The real issue is what some people have called cultural imperialism, where one group of people who are distinct make a decision for all other people' (Law Reform Commission 1990). The criminal justice experience of the Aboriginal people of Canada raises the question of the propriety of policing as it is now conceived, especially for multicultural countries like Canada, which foster and encourage ethnic and cultural pluralism.

References

Alberta Federation of Métis Settlements (1990) *The Métis Settlements and The Criminal Justice System: Recommendations for Change*, A Submission to the Task Force on the Criminal Justice System and its Impact on Indian and Métis People of Alberta, July.

Andrews v Law Society of British Columbia (1989) 1 S.C.R. 143.

Apostle, Richard and Stenning, Phillip (1988) *Royal Commission on the Donald Marshall Jr Prosecution*, Vol. 2: *Public Policing in Nova Scotia*, Halifax: The Government of Nova Scotia.

Archibald, Bruce P. (1988) *Royal Commission on the Donald Marshall Jr Prosecution*, vol. 6: *Prosecuting Officers and the Administration of Justice in Nova Scotia*, Halifax: The Government of Nova Scotia.

Aubury, Jack (1991) 'Canada's Legacy of Unfair Legislation', *The Ottawa Citizen*, 3 August: B4.

Barrett, Tom (1992) 'Court Frees Native Convicted of Murder', *The Ottawa Citizen*, 10 March: A4.

Barron, Sherri (1990) 'Crime and Punishment, Their Native Land', Part IV, *The Ottawa Citizen*, 14 November: A6.

Barros, Colleen., Slavin, Andrea., McArthur, Virginia and Adams, Stuart (1971) *Movement and Characteristics of Women's Detention Center Admissions 1969*, Washington D.C: Department of Corrections, Research Report No. 39.

Bellemare, Jacques (1988) *Comité d'enquête sur les relations entre les corps policiers et les minorités visibles et ethniques, Rapport final*, Québec: Commission des droits de la personne du Québec.

Bienvenue, Rita M. and Latif, A.H. (1972) *The Incidence of Arrests among Canadians of Indian Ancestry*, paper, Canadian Sociology and Anthropology Meetings, May.

Bindman, Stephen (1992) 'Gross Injustice', *The Ottawa Citizen*, 8 December: A3.

Brass, Oliver J. (1979) *Crees and Crime: A Cross-Cultural Study*, Regina: The University of Regina.

British Columbia Native Indian and Métis Education Club (1975) Briefing Paper, in *Briefing Papers Pursed According to Workshop Topic: National Conference on Native People and the Criminal Justice System*, Ottawa: Canadian Intergovernmental Conference Secretariat.

Brown, Michael K. (1988) *Working the Street*, New York Russel Sage Foundation.

Canadian National Railway Co v Canada (Canadian Human Rights Commission) (1987) 1 S.C.R. 1114.

Cawsey, R.A., Little Bear, Leroy., Franklin, Janet., Bertolin, Cynthia., and Galet, Arnold., Cooper, Cleave and Gallagher, Michael (1991) *Justice on Trial, Report of the Task Force on the Criminal Justice System and its Impact on the Indian and Métis People of Alberta*, Vol. 1, Edmonton: The Government of Alberta.

Clark, Scott, Clark, G.S. and Associates (1989) *Royal Commission on the Donald Marshall Jr Prosecution*, Vol. 3: *The Mikq'mac and the Criminal Justice in Nova Scotia*, Halifax: The Government of Nova Scotia.

Clie, Cocking (1977) 'Bitterness Beyond the Graves', *Weekend Magazine*, 22 January: 4-10.

Curren, Reg (1992) 'Nepoose Probe Flawed: R.C.M.P. Official Admits', *Winnipeg Free Press*, 18 March: A4.

Delattre, Edwin J. (1991) *Against Brutality and Corruption: Integrity Wisdom and Professionalism*, Tallahassee, Florida Criminal Justice Executive Institute, Florida: Department of Law Enforcement.

Edwards, John L.J. (1989) *Royal Commission on the Donald Marshall Jr Prosecution*, Vol. 5: *Walking the Tight Rope of Justice: An Examination of the Office of the Attorney General*, Halifax: The Government of Nova Scotia.

Ericson, Richard V. (1988) *Reproducing Order: A Study of Police Patrol Work*,

Toronto: University of Toronto Press.

Finkler, Harold W. (1976) *Inuit and the Administration of Criminal Justice in the Northwest Territories, The Case of Frobisher Bay*, Ottawa: Ministry of Supply and Services.

Gillmor, Don (1988) 'The Shooting of J.J. Harper', *Saturday Night*, 4 December, 52.

Government of Alberta (1991) *Justice on Trial, Report of the Task Force on the Criminal Justice System and its Impact on the Indian and Métis People of Alberta*, Vol. 2: *Summary Report*, Edmonton: The Government of Alberta.

Government of Nova Scotia (1992) *Royal Commission on the Donald Marshall Jr Prosecution*, Vol. 7, *Consultative Conference November 24-26, 1988 Edited Transcript of Proceedings*, Halifax: The Government of Nova Scotia.

Greenaway, W.K. (1980) 'Crime and Class: Unequal before the Law', in John Harp and John R. Hofley, *Structured Inequality in Canada*, Scarborough: Prentice Hall.

Hagan, John (1974) 'Criminal Justice and Native People: A Study of Incarceration in a Canadian Province', *Canadian Review of Sociology and Anthropology*, Special Issue: 220-236.

Hagan, John (1975) 'Law, Order and Sentencing: A Study of Attitude in Action', *Sociometry*, 38: 2, 374-384.

Hamilton, A.C. and Sinclair, C.M. (1991a) *Report of the Aboriginal Justice Inquiry of Manitoba*, Vol. 1: *The Justice System and Aboriginal People*, Winnipeg: The Queen's Printer.

Hamilton, A.C. and Sinclair, C.M. (1991b) *Report of the Aboriginal Justice Inquiry of Manitoba*, Vol. 3: *The Deaths of Helen Betty Osborne and John Joseph Harper*, Winnipeg: The Queen's Printer.

Harding, James (1971) 'Canada's Indians: A Powerless Minority', in J. Harp and J.J. Hofley: *Poverty in Canada*, Scarborough: Prentice Hall, 232-252.

Harding, James (1991) 'Policing and Aboriginal Justice', *Canadian Journal of Criminology*, 33: 363-383.

Harrell, Andrew W. (1997) *The Effects of Alcohol Use and Ethnicity on Sentencing Decisions*, Ottawa: Department of Health and Welfare, Research Bureau, Non-Medical Use of Drugs Directorate.

Harris, Michael (1988) 'Warts and All', *Saturday Night*, November, 20-25.

Harris, Michael (1990) *Justice Denied, The Law versus Donald Marshall*, Toronto: MacMillan of Canada.

Havemann, Paul., Forster, Lori., Couse, Keith and Matanovich, Rae (1985) *Law and Order for Canada's Indigenous People*, Regina: Prairie Justice Research School of Human Justice, University of Regina.

Head, Wilson and Clairmont, Don (1988) *Royal Commission on the Donald Marshall Jr Prosecution*, Vol. 4: *Discrimination against Blacks in the Criminal Justice System*, Halifax: The Government of Nova Scotia.

Hickman, T. Alexander., Poitras, Lawrence A. and Evans, Gregory T. (1989) *Royal*

Commission of the Donald Marshall Jr Prosecution, Vol. 1: *Findings and Recommendations*, Halifax: The Government of Nova Scotia.

Hoffman, Richard (1989) 'Police Demand Minister Resign', *The Ottawa Citizen*, 16 January: A3.

Hogarth, John (1971) *Sentencing as a Human Process*, Toronto: University of Toronto Press.

Hughes, E.N. (1991) *Report of the Honourable E.N. Hughes Q.C. With Respect to the Process and Procedures in the Investigation, Charge, Arrest, Prosecution, Stay and Subsequent Actions of the October 3, 1990: Harvey I. Pollock Q.C. Case*, Winnipeg: The Government of Manitoba.

Hyde, Mary and LaPrairie, Carol (1987) *Amerindian Police Crime Prevention*, Ottawa: Solicitor General of Canada.

Hylton, John (1980) *Admissions to Saskatchewan Provincial Correctional Centres, Projections to 1993*, Regina: Saskatchewan Prairie Consortium, University of Regina.

Hylton, John (1981) 'Locking Up Indians in Saskatchewan: Some Recent Findings', *Canadian Ethnic Studies*, 13: 144-151.

Indigenous Bar Association (1991) *The Criminal Code and Aboriginal People*, Paper prepared for the Law Reform Commission of Canada.

Jackson, Michael (1988) *Locking Up Natives in Canada: A Report of the Special Committee of the Canadian Bar Association on Imprisonment*, Ottawa: Canadian Bar Association.

James, J.L.T. (1979) 'Toward a Cultural Understanding of the Native Offender', *Canadian Journal of Criminology*, 21: 453-462.

Jayewardene, C.H.S. (1972) *Crime and Society in Churchill*, Ottawa: Department of Indian Affairs and Northern Development.

Jayewardene, C.H.S. (1975) 'Violence among the Eskimos', *Canadian Journal of Criminology and Corrections*, 17: 4, 307-314.

Jayewardene, C.H.S. (1979-80) 'Policing the Indian', *Crime and/et Justice*, 7: 42-47.

Jayewardene, C.H.S. and McWatt, F. (1983) 'Définition Policière de la Délinquance', *Journal du Collège Canadien de Police*, 7: 2, 83-88.

Jayewardene, C.H.S. and Talbot, C.K. (1990) *Police Recruitment of Ethnic Minorities*, Ottawa: Ministry of Supply and Services, 1990.

Jayewardene, C.H.S. (1993) Police Killing of Citizens in Canada 1977-1992 (in preparation).

Jenish, D'Arcy and Sampson, Connie (1991) 'Give me a Medal', *Maclean's Magazine*, 29 July, 42.

Jolly, Stan (1982) 'Natives in Conflict with the Law', *Correctional Options*, 2: 82-98.

Jolly, Stan and Birkenmayer, A.C. (1981) *The Native Inmate in Ontario*, Toronto: Ontario Ministry of Correctional Services.

Jolly, Stan and Seymour, Joseph Peter (1983) *Anicinabe Debtor's Prison*, Toronto:

Ontario Native Council on Justice.

Kaila, Paul and Broshnahan, Maureen (1989) 'A Death in Winnipeg', *Maclean's Magazine*, 11 September, 16.

King, Mike (1992) 'Chief Stabbed us in the Back: Police Brotherhood', *The Montreal Gazette*, 1 February: A3.

LaPrairie, Carol (1990a) 'The Role of Sentencing in the Over-representation of Aboriginal People in Correctional Institutions', *Canadian Journal of Criminology*, 3: 3, 429-440.

LaPrairie, Carol (1990b) *If Tribal Courts are the Solution, What is the Problem?*, unpublished paper prepared for the Department of the Attorney General of Nova Scotia, cited in Law Reform Commission 1991.

LaPrairie, Carol and Griffiths, Curt Taylor (1992) 'Native Indian Delinquency and the Juvenile Court: A Review of Recent Findings', *Canadian Legal Aid Bulletin, Native People and Justice in Canada*, 5: 1, 39-46.

Law Reform Commission of Canada (1991) *Report on Aboriginal Peoples and Criminal Justice; Equality, Respect and the Search for Justice*, Ottawa: Law Reform Commission of Canada.

Lewis, Claire (1989) *The Report of the Race Relations and Policing Task Force*, Toronto: Government of Ontario.

Liang, Arthur (1967) *Indians and the Law*, Ottawa: Queen's Printer.

Métis Nations of Alberta (Métis Association of Alberta) (1990) *Submission to the Task Force on the Criminal Justice System and it Impact on the Indian and Métis People of Alberta*, April 20, cited in Cawsey et al 1991.

National Parole Board (1989) *Final Report, Canada, Task Force on Aboriginal People in Federal Corrections*, Ottawa: Ministry of Supply and Services.

Osnaburgh/Windigo Tribal Council Justice Review Committee: *Tay Bway Win: Truth Justice and First Nations* (1990), unpublished Report Prepared for the Ontario Attorney General and Solicitor General, cited in Law Reform Commission 1991.

Priest, Lisa (1989) *Conspiracy of Silence*, Toronto: M and S Paperback.

Quigley, Tom (1990) *Introducing Cross-cultural Awareness*, Paper, Western Workshop, Alberta, May.

Rolf, C.H. (1991a) *Policing in Relation to the Blood Tribe: Report of a Public Inquiry*, Vol. 1: *Findings and Recommendations*, Edmonton: The Government of Alberta.

Rolf, C.H. (1991b) *Policing in Relation to the Blood Tribe: Report of a Public Inquiry*, Vol. 2: *Executive Summary*, Edmonton: The Government of Alberta.

Ross, Rupert (1989) 'Leaving Our White Eyes Behind: The Sentencing of Native Accused', 3 *C.N.L.R.*, 1, cited in Law Reform Commission 1991.

Rudin, Jonathan and Russel, Dan (1991) *Native Alternative Dispute Resolution Systems: The Canadian Future in the Light of the American Past*, Toronto: Ontario Native Council on Justice.

Schmeiser, D.A. (1974) *The Native Offender and the Law*, Ottawa: Information

Canada.

Sellin, Thorsten (1937) *Research Memorandum on Crime in the Depression*, New York: Social Science Research Council.

Shernock, Stan K. (1990) 'The Effects of Patrol Officers Defensiveness Toward the Outside World on their Ethical Orientation', *Criminal Justice Ethics*, 9: 2, 24-42.

Statistics Canada, Canadian Centre for Justice Statistics (1991) *Adult Correctional Services in Canada*, Ottawa: Statistics Canada.

Stenning, Philip C. (1982) *Legal Status of the Police*, Ottawa: Ministry of Supply and Services.

Story, Alan (1990) 'Peel Police Ordered to Shed Protest Buttons in Fatal Shooting', *Toronto Star*, 12 July: A2.

Sudlow, Ron (1991) 'Bishop's Sex Trial Ends as Judge Stays Charges', *The Ottawa Citizen*, 8 December: A4.

Sunahara, David F. (1992) 'Public Inquiries into Policing', *Canadian Police College Journal*, 16: 2, 135-156.

Talbot, C.K., Jayewardene C.H.S. and Juliani, T.J. (1984) 'Policing in Canada: A Developmental Perspective', *Canadian Police College Journal*, 8: 218-288.

Wiecek, Paul (1990) 'Man shot after Pointing Toy Gun at Police', *Winnipeg Free Press*, 17 November: 1-4.

Notes

1.   Shirley McMullen, B.A. (Ottawa) is a graduate student at the University of Ottawa, Canada, completing her thesis on 'Police Racism'. She is employed presently as a Researcher in the Department of Justice, Government of Canada. C.H.S. Jayewardene, M.B., B.S. (Cey.) A.M., Ph.D. (Penn) is Professor of Criminology at the University of Ottawa, Canada. His main interest is the study of violence with special emphasis on its cultural aspects and on societal attempts at its control. He is the author of a number of books and articles on a wide variety of topics ranging from criminality among the Eskimos to fertility and mortality among the Ceylonese.

2.   Section 35 of the *Constitution Act* of 1982 refers to the 'Indian, Inuit and Métis' people as comprising the Aboriginal peoples of Canada.

III Moral panic and juvenile justice in Queensland: The emergent context of the Juvenile Justice Act 1992

Richard Hil[1]

> Crime is what the working class commit (John Braithwaite in Western 1983: 100).

> ...the shape of the juvenile justice system in a 'law and order' era is determined ultimately neither by an informed understanding of the needs and difficulties of the juveniles who pass through it, nor a commitment to justice, but by the pursuit of political legitimacy (Pitts 1990: 8).

> The Juvenile Justice Bill 1992 is based on a wide-ranging examination of programmes both in Australia and overseas... The result of this research and consultation is a complete reform package, which ranges from major crime prevention measures to court structures and penalties within a coordinated framework of well informed principles (Anne Warner, Minister for Family Services and Aboriginal and Islander Affairs, Queensland state parliament, August 1992).

Over recent years the 'juvenile crime problem' has come to represent one of the major social policy issues confronting state and territory governments across Australia. Talk of 'crisis', 'disorder', 'lawlessness' and a 'breakdown in law and order' (especially in relation to Aboriginal juveniles) is matched by calls for 'something to be done' and for action to be taken on policy and legislative fronts.

By and large such outpourings have come from politicians on both the left and right of the political spectrum, as well as from media pundits, 'experts' and members of a 'concerned public'. The 'law and order crisis' is seen as having arisen largely because the existing justice system has failed to deliver in terms of crime levels and/or is 'too soft' on offenders. Either way, it is argued that change in the response of governments to juvenile crime must occur.

It is against this general background of panic and concern that we consider the emergence of legislative change to Queensland's system of juvenile justice. However, before attempting to examine the broad context within which the legislation arose it is necessary to outline some of the main principles and provisions of the 1992 *Juvenile Justice Act*. Although the Act attempts to give greater emphasis to 'due process' in relation to the workings of the Children's Court (and many of the changes are to be welcomed), we focus briefly on some key principles guiding sentencing practice.

Punishment revisited: legislative reform and the justice model

The 1992 *Juvenile Justice Act* constituted a major reform of Queensland's approach to sentencing practice in relation to juveniles. Formulated in terms of a 'shake-up' to the *Children Services Act* 1965, the new legislation claimed to offer a new, expanded range of sentencing options including community service orders, immediate release orders, good behaviour orders, fines, probation orders, and graduated detention orders. In addition, the Act introduced two pre-sentence measures: formal cautioning (including cautioning by Aboriginal elders) and attendance notices. The latter was aimed at curtailing the possibility of arrest and detention of juveniles in watch houses.

According to the Act a principal objective of the Children's Court should be to:

 ... recognize the importance of families of children and communities, in
 particular Aboriginal and Torres Strait Islander communities, in the
 provision of services designed to:

 i) rehabilitate children who commit offences; and
 ii) reintegrate children who commit offences into the community
  (Queensland State Government 1992, Part 1:12).

Despite this emphasis on the importance of 'rehabilitation' and 'reintegration' in relation to young offenders the roles of parents and guardians are restricted largely to notification procedures and restitution. Indeed, the principle of parental restitution reflects a key element in the legislation. For example, if it appears to the court that 'wilful failure on the part of parent of the child to exercise proper care of, or supervision over, the child was likely to have substantially contributed to the commission of the offence' then the court may 'call on the parent to show cause ... why the parent should not pay the compensation' (Queensland State Government 1992, Sec. 197: 1, a,b). This provision, although overlooked in recent critiques of the Act (O'Connor 1993) illustrates the attempt by the state to broaden the scope of 'responsibility' from the offender to his or her family. Accordingly, it is the family and not the individual offender which may be regarded as directly culpable for crime and delinquency. Moreover, the principles of responsibility and restitution fit in neatly with recent populist assumptions about the general 'breakdown' in parental authority and the need for the restoration of greater discipline and control in the home.

Emphasis on the notion of offender responsibility is evident particularly in relation to the principles of sentencing in Section Four of the Act. Part One, Section Four of the Act states:

... a child who commits an offence should be:

i)   held accountable and encouraged to accept responsibility for the offending behaviour; and
ii) punished in a way that will give the child the opportunity to develop in a responsible, beneficial and socially acceptable way ... (Queensland State Government 1992, Part 1, Sec 4: 13).

Although the legislation calls for the court to give attention to 'relevant considerations' such as age, maturity and cultural background (Queensland State Government 1992, Part 1, Sec 4 [g]) the issues of 'relevance' is framed by the emphasis on individual responsibility. This necessarily defines the limits of judicial discourse and avoids reference to matters which are regarded as outside the immediate orbit of individual action and responsibility.

Enter the critics

In Queensland the burgeoning critique of the *Juvenile Justice Act* 1992 has taken as its starting point the legalistic ramifications of the so-called 'justice model' lodged in the heart of the new legislation. The Act is therefore seen as either restating an antiquated and narrow neo-classical view of crime and criminal behaviour through its focus on the 'offence rather than the offender' (O'Connor 1993), or as remiss in terms of providing adequate legal safeguards for juveniles (Wright and McMillan 1992). Despite claims to the contrary, criticism has also been generated by the very real possibility that the sentencing options outlined in the legislation, such as community service orders, are unlikely to receive the necessary funds for implementation from state government (O'Connor 1993: 11).

Moreover, in reinforcing a 'bifurcate' approach to juvenile justice in which the system responds strongly to 'hard-core' serious and repeat offenders and less punitively to other offenders, the Act reflects a central contradiction in the state's policy towards juvenile crime. On the one hand, the Act seeks to take a 'tough' retributive approach to the sentencing of particular (serious) offenders, without making any reference to wider social or economic factors impacting on their behaviour, while on the other hand supporting the rapid development of a primary crime prevention strategy (managed and administered by the Department of Family Services and Aboriginal and Islander Affairs) directed towards addressing the 'needs' of disadvantaged youth in 'targeted areas' (Hil and Seaton 1993). This separating out of offending populations of young people enables the state to keep up the appearance of being simultaneously tough and soft on crime. As John Pitts observes (1988: 29), such an approach is based largely on political pragmatism and is motivated by a desire to respond to 'public concern' and, more pressingly, to lessen state expenditure on criminal justice by placing increased numbers of offenders in community control programmes.

While such observations and critiques are vital in exposing the many shortcomings and contradictions associated with the Act, they have largely neglected the bigger question of why the legislation arose in the first place. Clearly, as in other cases of legislative reform in the area of criminal justice, such changes do not occur in a social, economic and political vacuum. It is argued here that the *Juvenile Justice Act* emerged in a context characterized by a number of interlocking forces which have served effectively to regard youth as a 'social problem' and juvenile crime as *the* problem of a recessionary society. In such circumstances new legislation dealing with juvenile crime was introduced on the populist premise that something 'tough' had to been done. In order to lay the foundations for this argument it is necessary to map out some of the broader shifts and changes in the Australian socio-economic structure over recent years.

The political economy of juvenile justice reform

There appears to be broad agreement that, in the words of Prime Minister

Paul Keating, the 'recession we had to have' has left deep scars on the nation in terms of high and long-term structural unemployment. Some of the most severe consequences of such developments have been experienced by working-class youth. Estimates of average levels of local youth unemployment vary widely from a low of 15% to 80%, or in the case of some rural and remote communities, 100%. Youth unemployment in Queensland is estimated to be around 25 - 35%. Nationwide, the decline in full-time employment began in the late 1960s and early 1970s, coinciding with a world-wide economic crisis exacerbated by a massive increase in oil prices. The rapid decline of Australia's manufacturing base brought about, in part, by deregulation policies and an entrenched fiscal crisis, led to the emergence of a growing service industry ('the hamburger economy') composed increasingly of low-paid, part-time labour. This had enormous implications for young people and particularly for young women.

Between 1969 and 1979 the proportion of unemployed teenagers in Australia (aged 15 - 19 years) increased from 3% to 17%. The 1983 post-war record unemployment level of well over 700,000, or about 10% of the total work force, increased the numbers of young people joining the dole queues. Since 1983 high unemployment has remained a key feature of the Australian economy with rates varying across states from 10% to 12%. The current rate in Queensland is a little in excess of 10%. Figures for youth unemployment are probably on the conservative side given the tendency of many youths not to register for unemployment benefit or to join one of a vast number of 'job creation' schemes. Also, many thousands of youths aged 16 - 19 years have had their unemployment benefits cut through changes in rules for claimants (as in South Australia). In addition, it has been estimated that approximately 430,000 young people between the ages of 15 and 19 are omitted from the officially promoted educational and training programmes (Beasly 1992: 76).

One indication of the impact of unemployment on working class communities in Australia has been an increase in the number of families on or below the poverty line. Indeed, as the Australian Catholic Bishop's Conference (1992) points out in a recent report entitled *Common Wealth for the Common Good*, between 80,000 and 100,000 children live in dire poverty or homelessness, 750,000-800,000 children live in poor families, 25% of school children live in poverty. Particular groups of people such as Aboriginal and sole parent families are disproportionately represented in the poverty data. In short, many thousands of young people and their families are likely to experience gross socio-economic disadvantage in contemporary Australia. Poverty and deprivation are the contributory harbingers of other problems such as child abuse, neglect and domestic violence. Moreover, the growing sense of alienation, despair and marginalization experienced by many young people, particularly in remote and rural areas, is evidenced by one major index: teenage suicide. In relation to the high level of adolescent suicides in the South Australian community of Broken Hill, Henry Lohse states:

> It is my opinion that another factor inherent in local suicide trends is one of socio-politics. Many suicide victims have few personal resources with which to deal with stressors, and they see few reasons in their lives to bother (Lohse 1992: 37).

Reflecting on the consequences of a recessionary economy on Australia's youth another commentator notes that: 'The plight of many young people in Australia in the last quarter of the twentieth century takes on Dickensian overtones' (Allegetti 1991: 123). The changing situation of young people within the Australian socio-economic structure and the moral panic generated over youth crime has led a number of state and territory governments, including Queensland, to increase control and surveillance of this section of the population. In other words, references in public discourse to young people as a 'problem' or a threat to the community, particularly as far as offending is concerned, has given the state a pretext to intervene more readily in working class communities and to employ state institutions to achieve the aim of social order.

Another important consideration in this process is the cost of juvenile crime to the state. It has been estimated (Potas, Vinning, Wilson 1990: xiii) that in 1986-7 the direct cost of some major categories of juvenile crime such as car theft, household burglary, vandalism, arson and shop stealing was in the region of $602 million. This figure is certainly an underestimate and takes no account of indirect costs incurred through hospitalization, sick leave, insurance payments, criminal compensation and so on. These figures reflect little of the misery and pain experienced by victims, most of whom come from disadvantaged and vulnerable backgrounds themselves. In light of such massive costs state governments have invested enormously in crime management. For example, estimates of Queensland state expenditure for 1992-3 (Government of Queensland 1992: 80) indicate that total fund allocated for law, order and public safety was $1,682,869,000 - nearly a half million dollars more than expenditure on social welfare and housing and only slightly less than the amount devoted to health.

Crimes of subsistence and mounting moral panic

For many working class youths the prospect of life on the dole, or on a skills or training programme, tends to shape attitudes and orientations to their immediate environment. Despite evidence of increasing retention rates among young people in schools - a trend encouraged by the looming prospect of unemployment and dependency - the alienation experienced by many working class youth tends to result in outcomes such as school absenteeism, delinquency and petty offending. Indeed, as Mike Presdee points out, politicians, administrators and planners seem devoid of an understanding of the consequences of unemployment upon the lives of young people in contemporary Australia:

> There has been a fundamental misunderstanding ... about how young working class people live: their expectations, hopes, fears, their happiness, their desperation ... (Presdee 1991: 180).

In a climate governed by the ideology of economic rationalism in which achievement is measured in terms of personal wealth and acquisition ('greed is good'), and the ability to compete in the marketplace, young working class people exercise their options for survival in a variety of often self-defeating ways:

> It is when young 15 year-olds, especially young women, finally leave school that the battle for an income, for survival begins in earnest. It appears that no matter how hard they try, in the end the way in which an income is achieved matters less and less (ibid: 187).

In a number of interviews conducted with young people in the Adelaide area Presdee found that 'subsistence crime' figured prominently as a strategy for achieving desired resources and, above all, income. Most had engaged in activities that crossed legal boundaries, such as non-attendance at school, vandalism, drug use, under-age carnal knowledge, drinking, smoking, breaking and entering, shoplifting, prostitution, driving offences, non-declaration of taxable income, etc. While such pursuits brought short-lived kudos for some young people, not to mention modest material gain, the end result was more likely to be an encounter with a disgruntled parent or guardian or, more ominously, a run-in with the local police.

As Presdee observes, the actions of working class young people are defined and constrained by the social and material realities of everyday life:

The pressures on relationships that resulted from being both unemployed and without subsistence confronted and consumed their everyday life, posing the singe most important problem of their social existence. At a time when they are at their most vulnerable they are rendered both useless and wageless and are unable to form relationships from any position of status or autonomy (ibid: 188).

Clearly, the negative economic and social forces allied against young people have a direct bearing on the ways in which they experience the world and their place in it. According to a detailed study of crime in New South Wales '... the presence of socio-economic disadvantage in a community significantly increases the risk of criminal offending in that community' (Devery 1991: 57). However, this is only half of the story. A significant factor in the increasing criminalization of working class youth, and particularly of those in Aboriginal communities, is the increased presence of police in public spaces such as streets, parks and shopping centres occupied by young people. Recent evidence in New South Wales and elsewhere indicates that public order legislation has been administered by the state in such a way as to ensure the extension of control and surveillance of the working class and particularly of Aboriginal communities (HREOC 1991; Kitchener 1992; Cunneen 1992). Not suprisingly, this has led to an increase in levels of street offences in a number of communities.

In Queensland recent evidence (Criminal Justice Commission 1992: 46) indicates that the most significant increases in offending among juveniles has been in the areas of shoplifting, property damage and car theft. By and large serious offending remains the province of adults and most juvenile offending is unplanned, opportunistic, episodic and transitory. Most children grow out of crime. Indeed, while the official figures indicate that juvenile crime has increased in Queensland over the past 20 years, the level of juvenile involvement in cleared crime has declined (Criminal Justice Commission 1992: 46).

Although official data should, at best, be viewed with caution, the general picture to emerge in Queensland is that rather than being the contemporary folk devils of our time, young people tend to offend, if at all, in petty and transitory ways. Indeed, approximately two-thirds of juvenile offenders do not offend (or get apprehended) again. However, despite such evidence, the prevailing image of young people manufactured by the media since the mid-1980s is one associated with violence, threat and disorder. The alleged emergence of 'street gangs' in major cities has generated moral panic over 'rapidly rising' juvenile crime. Graphic accounts of violent assaults against the elderly, shopkeepers, and innocent bystanders have often become the subject of glaring headlines and heated editorials calling for 'tough' new measures. In Western Australia during 1991-2 such imagery led to large public demonstrations in which 'community leaders', politicians and others called for 'harsher', 'tougher' penalties for juvenile offenders (*The Australian*, 7 November 1992).

In the light of such campaigns the Western Australian government passed the (now largely unused and discredited) *Crime (Serious And Repeat) Offenders Act*, 1992. The Act proposed mandatory 20-year sentences for repeat offenders and detention at 'Her Majesty's pleasure' for the most serious offenders. The Queensland government followed quickly in the wake of these measures. 'Tough new measures' were announced with indecent haste by Queensland Premier Wayne Goss who remarked that proposals to increase the power of courts to imprison young people under the age of 17 would give young offenders 'a taste of imprisonment to deter further youth crime'. Proposals to expand sentencing options for Queensland's Children's Courts were refereed to by the press as a 'New Crackdown on Young Thugs' (*Townsville Bulletin*, 1 February 1992) and, less dramatically, 'Goss Moves on Juvenile Crime' (*The Australian* 27 January 1992). The proposed measures were seen as an attempt to 'curb rising youth crime' or to 'shake-up the juvenile justice system'. The assumption underpinning such reports was that the juvenile problem had become a major threat to social order and something (tough) had to be done and seen to be done. As a senior police spokesperson remarked to a Townsville Bulletin reporter: 'Society was not being protected from thugs ... If these kids are running around the streets now what does this say to other youths of the same age?' According to this spokesperson, the juvenile justice system was 'a farce'.

In Townsville, Cairns, Brisbane and many other communities across Queensland, local newspaper reports referred with growing regularity to 'juvenile crime waves', 'thugs', 'street gangs' and young people 'out of control'. This in turn served to increase calls for 'crackdowns' and 'tough measures' either in the form of increased police powers or longer sentences. In a climate characterized by references to 'rising juvenile crime' and where the word 'youth' became increasingly synonymous with threat, fear and disorder (White 1990), Queensland - in concert with a number of other states across Australia - responded rapidly with the introduction of 'new' measures to deal with young offenders. At the same time, a populist and intellectual assault upon the apparent vagaries of the welfare model opened the door for the incorporation of the justice model in various forms of juvenile justice legislation. It was time to get 'back to justice'.

As Hudson (1987) and (Cohen 1985) point out, though originating from a general liberal critique of 'welfarism', the justice model proved convenient for the legal establishment in effectively avoiding any direct reference to the structural origins of youth offending, thereby enabling the juvenile justice system to operate within an abstract framework of 'due process'. The emphasis was to be on 'deeds' not 'needs'. For the legislative arm of the state, the justice model appeared to provide an intellectual justification for implementing 'hard-hitting', 'tough' measures against juvenile offenders, and especially for those deemed to be serious offenders. The government was also able to curry favour among the electorate by centring this model in the *Juvenile Justice Act* 1992 and in so doing it was able to demonstrate a commitment to 'getting tough on crime'. The more sober-sounding rhetoric from government ministers, however, was about 'law reform'. As the Minister for Family Services and Aboriginal and Islander Affairs, Anne Warner, pointed out during parliamentary deliberations on the *Juvenile Justice Bill* in August 1992: 'The reforms will place Queensland in the forefront of juvenile justice reform'.

The history of legislative changes to criminal justice suggests that such reforms tend to lead to a legion of unintended consequences. Perhaps the most probable outcome as far as the *Juvenile Justice Act* is concerned will be a significant increase in the number of young people being sentenced to custody. Indeed, we need only to look to the introduction of the 1982 *Criminal Justice Act* in England and Wales to appreciate some of the possible consequences of punitive sentencing practice. As John Pitts (1988: 149) points out, the introduction of this legislation, based squarely on the justice model, led to a rapid increase in the number of young people being sent to detention centres during the early 1980s. Between 1982 and 1984 there was a 200% increase in youth custody as well as a substantial increase in the average length of custodial sentences.

Such considerations appear to have escaped the notice of law reformers in Queensland. Given the hurried way in which the legislation was eventually pushed through parliament - much to the consternation and annoyance of many community organizations - it is difficult to avoid the conclusion that this was done at a politically apposite moment. The Act was passed on 19 August 1992, one month before to the state election.

Justice, punishment and political legitimacy

The shift in emphasis to a form of justice which seeks to punish, and punish harder, is as much about the pursuit of political legitimacy as it is about confronting the 'problem' of youth crime (Cohen 1985, Pitts 1990). In adopting a two-pronged approach to juvenile justice the Queensland state government is able simultaneously to address calls for tougher sentencing while at the same time alluding to the link between disadvantage and crime, as articulated in its crime prevention strategy. The approach to sentencing advocated in the *Juvenile Justice Act* is based firmly on the populist notion that if young people 'choose' to offend then they will reap the appropriate punishment of a tough-minded state. Queensland's approach to crime prevention, on the other hand, is informed by a perspective that recognizes the need to focus on issues of social and economic hardship. The rhetoric in this case refers to 'disadvantaged groups' and the need to develop strategies of 'community integration'. Unlike the *Juvenile Justice Act* there is no reference to the need to engage in the practice of retributive punishment. On the contrary, crime prevention policy is informed by a perspective which encourages young people to engage more actively in aspects of community life by having a direct say in the creation and management of community programmes and activities (Tansky 1992). While this approach is certainly not without it difficulties and may indeed end up as an exercise in extending and strengthening the net of social control of particular Queensland communities (that is, those defined as 'high crime' areas), it nonetheless indicates a radical difference in philosophy and practice to that of the *Juvenile Justice Act* (Hil and Seaton 1993).

This 'carrot and stick' approach to crime management is of course largely a caricature of the way in which the juvenile justice system actually functions. Indeed, most justice systems in Australia tend to be made up of a range of principles and practices incorporating aspects of welfare and justice models. Likewise, in Queensland sentencing practice in Children's Courts tends to involve a mixture of elements of these models and the precise form of judicial outcome depends as much on local tradition and the vagaries of individual magistrates, as on formal policy changes. Within the context of the new legislation, principles of welfare, for example, will be articulated through the content of social inquiry reports, when called for. No doubt such reports will be suitably tailored to reflect the primacy given to justice rather than welfare, and welfare workers will be required to steer an uneasy path between the court's desire to punish and the need to identify 'mitigating' factors. Such issues notwithstanding, the extent to which the welfare and justice models merge or collide in Queensland's system of juvenile justice is of less relevance than the general way in which the state develops its approach to the management of crime among working class youth. As John

Clarke has observed of the English system of juvenile justice:

> I am not convinced that the current juvenile justice is a war between these
> two [justice and welfare] abstract principles. Rather it needs to be seen
> as a system which criminalities working class youth, and manages the
> delinquent using a patchwork of processes and disposals which draw upon
> justice, retribution, rehabilitation and welfare (Clarke 1985: 419).

In Australia such a patchwork system of justice is reflected in a diverse
range of strategies to deal with working class youth crime. These may
include increased police powers (as recently advocated by the Criminal
Justice Commission), continued support for correctional institutions, higher
penalties for particular offences and the widening definition of particular
groups as 'high risk' or 'at risk' offenders. Hudson argues that the particular
mix of principles and practice advocated in crime control policies is governed
not simply by the introduction of 'new' reforms but rather by the prevailing
ideologies and policies of the time. In the context of a society experiencing
the ravages of economic recession, in which juvenile crime is perceived as
a threat to social order, the state seeks to promote populist, hard-hitting and
draconian solutions aimed at ensuring the continuance of existing social
arrangements. Such solutions are characterized by an increased emphasis on
punishment and retribution. Alternative, less brutalizing approaches
advocated by liberal reformers are inevitably caricatured as expressions of
do-goodery or as 'going soft on crime'. As Hudson states:

> It is not merely that the state does select the crimes of the disadvantaged
> as those to be taken seriously, it is that it must: in times of crisis, the
> street crimes of the poor are bound to be pinpointed as those which are
> a threat to the social order, for if the deteriorating conditions of the urban
> working class can be shown to be the product of their own wickedness
> rather than government neglect, then the government can justify itself in
> doing nothing to alleviate problems of decline and decay. It is not
> necessary to enter into debates about whether the under-privileged really
> do or do not commit more crimes than the privileged; it is not necessary
> to enter debates about whether unemployment, poverty and so forth really
> do have a direct causal connection with criminality, it is merely necessary
> to recognise the inevitability of this highlighting of the crimes of the
> disaffected during conditions of economic downturn (Hudson 1987: 165-
> 166).

It is precisely in the context of prolonged economic downturn in Australia since the mid-1980s that public discourse on the 'crime problem' has focused almost exclusively on crimes committed in working class, Aboriginal, and other disadvantaged communities. Young people and especially young Aboriginal people have experienced increased levels of regulation and surveillance and although there has been considerable variation between states in relation to law reform, such changes tend to be characterized by the implementation of punishment centred, 'law and order' policies. Government talk of 'crackdowns' and 'tough' approaches is directed continually towards the crimes of the powerless rather than crimes of the powerful. The government is thus able to claim enhanced legitimacy on the grounds that it is addressing public concern (Cunneen 1991).

This is not to suggest a simple conspiracy on the part of the state to increase control of working class communities. However it does point to a sequence of events and circumstances in which those in power set the parameters of discourse about crime and its perceived threat to social order, and seek 'solutions' by legislating for changes to policing and judicial practice in order to contain the emergence of 'problem populations' (Box 1987, Braithwaite 1979).

In such a climate public discourse on 'justice' or, more specifically, 'criminal justice', is increasingly characterized by reference to individualized action carried out by 'offenders' invariably from the more disadvantaged sectors of society. Thus the proponents of the justice model refer to free-floating notions of 'choice' and 'responsibility' as if these are utterly disconnected from the influence of poverty, unemployment and deprivation. John Pitts points out that a definition of justice, which turns on issues of individual rights and responsibilities, is almost certain to avoid reference to questions of power and inequality since these are considered as either tangential or irrelevant to the desired goal of due process:

The 'justice' model would have the victim of crime, the falsely accused citizen, and the correctly accused offender as individual moral actors engaged in discreet legal episodes in which social contracts between them (their rights and obligations) are violated. For those who see reform in terms of the manipulation of rights the programme which emerges from the unemployed ghetto will remain inconceivable and unworkable. It is inconceivable because it moves the issue of reform and change from a discourse on rights conducted between the theoreticians and practitioners of the criminal justice system to a struggle to impose some form of democratic control over the system of surveillance, policing and punishment by the actual and potential subjects of the system (Pitts 1988: 161).

From punishment and prevention to social development?

Despite the current dominance of the justice model in the Queensland legislation it is quite likely that once the 'unintended consequences' of increased rates of incarceration are identified the system will seek an alternative approach, as occurred in England during the late 1980s (Hudson 1987). In the wake of impending descriptions of a system in 'crisis' or at odds with humanitarian concerns, policy makers and liberal reformers may once more turn their attention to possible avenues of reform and change. While it is of course difficult to predict the precise nature of changes to be suggested by politicians and policy makers it is likely that much energy will be expended in the search for more 'technical' solutions to sentencing practice (for example, more training for magistrates, increased involvement of welfare workers and other human service personnel, more options to incarceration, etc.) or that the system will punish more selectively, and harder or softer.

The perennial question of 'what is to be done?' about youth crime derives its significance from broader ideological and political areas. In contemporary Australia, as in other industrialized states experiencing recession, juvenile crime has taken on the stature of a major 'social problem' requiring urgent 'solutions'. The use of the stick of punishment to deal with more serious offenders has certainly served the political purpose of responding to public concern. However, while all the available evidence demonstrates clearly that serious offending is primarily an adult activity, public discourse has been conducted in such a way as to suggest that all or most working class youth crime is serious. Clearly there are a small group of offenders for whom incarceration is necessary, but the vast majority of juvenile crime is of a irritating, nuisance variety. Having said this, however, all crime produces victims and a 'minor' offence can produce significant trauma and hardship. The question here is how should communities respond to juvenile offending?

There appears to be some agreement among theoreticians and criminal justice practitioners that it is preferable, where possible, to prevent young people becoming entangled in the justice system since this is likely to generate a process of labelling and the possibility of more rather than less offending and therefore even greater harm to working class communities.

For those young offenders who end up in custody the social and personal costs can be particularly high (Pitts 1990).

Practitioners dealing with young people already caught up in the system should, according to Stan Cohen (1985), attempt to adopt a position of 'moral pragmatism' by which the worker can help offenders to avoid the more damaging aspects of the system and (particularly) to search for alternatives to custody, although recognizing that the latter may lead to 'net widening'. The longer term project is to engage in political struggles which seek to draw back the net of social control and to help liberate the poor and disaffected from the realities of social and economic disadvantage. Some commentators (Harris and Webb 1987) maintain that the search for a 'solution' to juvenile crime from within the criminal justice system is fraught with difficulties and is ultimately bound to fail, as the rationale of the system is the control of working class and disadvantaged youth. Moreover, the system merely reflects existing inequalities of wealth and power in the wider community. Indeed, rather than diminishing such inequalities the system serves to exacerbate and enhance them. This is particularly so for young Aboriginal offenders who are massively over-represented in the juvenile justice system throughout Australia (Gale, Bailey-Harris, Wundersitz 1990; Cunneen 1992).

While adherents to the justice model turn a blind eye to the influence of structural inequality on offending, the social reality is that the young working class are criminalized for crimes against property and that the forces of law and order are disproportionately marshalled against this section of the community. Moreover, as the Youth Justice Coalition noted: 'The most deprived are subject to most crime and its control; are under-protected and over-controlled by authorities' (1990: 27).

Recent critiques of law reform in Queensland and elsewhere have recognized the need to move beyond mere 'technical' adjustments to the criminal justice system. Indeed, it has been argued that if the state is to intervene in working class communities it should be to address problems of high unemployment, poverty, homelessness and so on. According to Coventry, Muncie and Walters social policy in relation to young people should not be primarily concerned with crime and delinquency but rather with the quality of life for those living in low socio-economic areas:

We would argue that the issue of youth integration, empowerment and social development should take precedence over the narrow focus of crime prevention. Preventative strategies should be incorporated within and flow from broader attempts to improve the quality of life for young

Australians. A medium term objective would be to move beyond the direct provision of services to establish localised youth policies, involving multi-agency community partnerships (Coventry, Muncie and Walters 1992: 12).

In an attempt to engage various organizations in the pursuit of improving the quality of life for young people it is proposed that the state facilitates the co-ordination and co-operation of government departments such as Education, Family Services and Aboriginal Affairs, Health, Housing and Community Service as well as non-government bodies, voluntary organizations and young people themselves:

> The aim would be to construct an agency whose central objective is to facilitate a coordinated programme of youth advocacy. In the medium term, this would seek to prioritise opportunities for young peoples' empowerment in employment, housing and so on, and moving in the long term to seek institutional change and legislative reform which is capable of facilitating the broader social development of young people (ibid).

Such an approach would at least move the debate on juvenile justice from a narrow concern with crime prevention, to a recognition of the connection between disadvantage and offending and the need to facilitate a 'solution' in terms of 'social development' rather than punitive reaction. Such a social policy acknowledges that offending behaviour has its origins in the experience of material hardship and fractured relations brought about through structural disadvantage. Moreover, contrary to the current tendency of legislators and practitioners to label young people as 'at risk', 'serious' or simply 'young offenders' or 'delinquents', *a social development approach* seeks to engage all young people in community life and in so doing avoiding the punitive social reaction which such labels tend to attract. Except for the most dangerous of offenders their appears to be every reason to keep young people in the community. Indeed, as Andrew Rutherford (1986: 107) observes of Miller's achievements in decarcerating young offenders in Massachusetts, the evidence suggests that community programmes are as effective and possibly even more effective in terms preventing re-offending than prolonged periods in custody.

Although Queensland's approach to dealing with young people has often been innovative and progressive (at least in the liberal sense), as demonstrated in the widespread use of cautioning and in the development of the Youth and Community Combined Action programme, the main thrust of its sentencing practice is firmly wedded to the principles of punishment and retribution. These contradictory approaches to justice policy are in themselves symptomatic of the government's apparent willingness to place expediency and the quest for political legitimacy above a concern for the broader issues of equity, fairness, and social justice. As argued earlier, there is every likelihood that the Queensland experience will emulate that of England and Wales in untying the straightjacket of the justice model once its excesses - in the form of increased rates of incarceration - are recognized. In the meantime, Children's Courts will continue to practice a form of justice which obviates any reference to the structural origins of juvenile offending, thereby leaving the way open, as Stan Cohen puts it (1985), to punish and punish harder. Or, as Barbara Hudson comments:

To say that the circumstances of the individual committing an offence are irrelevant to sentencing is to take the criminal justice system out of the area of ordinary human interactions, and instead to elevate abstract descriptions of events and abstract decisions about which events are more significant and serious than others, into area of universalistic categories not subject to normal negotiating processes (Hudson 1987: 165).

Conclusion

This essay has attempted to trace the emergence of the *Juvenile Justice Act* in a broader social, economic and political context. It has been argued implicitly that in order to comprehend the origins of any 'new' criminal justice legislation, particularly legislation which professes 'far-reaching reform', it is necessary to locate its emergence in a particular historical moment. Most critiques of the *Juvenile Justice Act* have tended to focus on specific legal shortcomings in the legislation. Clearly these are crucial in ensuring that the rights of children and their families are protected. However, a more comprehensive critique of the Act and the ways in which the state responds to young people in Queensland requires a broader perspective on such matters. It has been demonstrated that the emergence of the *Juvenile Justice Act* came about through a number of interlocking forces and that, far from being simply an attempt to 'crackdown' on the 'problem' of juvenile crime, the Act is aimed at the control of 'problem populations' and the maintenance of social order. Moreover, as Ian Taylor (1981) has observed, it is in times of economic crisis that cohorts of working class people, particularly the unemployed, marginalized and disaffected, are defined and targeted as 'problem populations'. Against such a backcloth the introduction of punishment-centred legislation is designed to exercise more severe and 'tough-minded' approaches to crime management.

It has been argued that solutions - if indeed one can talk of 'solutions' - to the problem of offending in working class and disadvantaged communities must be generated by a concern with the quality of life experienced by people within such areas. This means taking stock of issues such as unemployment, poverty, deprivation, racism, and all those factors which lead to the oppression of these people. The pursuit of punishment as a central plank in penal policy may indeed placate those advocating stronger, tougher measures but it does little or nothing in the longer term to protect potential victims or to deal with factors leading to offending. Perhaps a policy of social development may offer a more productive and humane way forward in this respect. Moreover, as John Pitts has observed of policies in other countries:

... depoliticization, the deflection of public and political concern onto more appropriate phenomena and its concomitant political indifference, can sometimes clear the 'ideological space' in which quiet but effective reform can occur (Pitts 1990: 33-34).

References

Allegritti, I. (1992) *Social Problems: An Australian Perspective*, Wentworth Falls: Social Science Press.

Australian Catholic Bishops' Conference (1992) *Common Wealth for the Common Good*, North Blackburn: Australian Episcopal Conference of the Roman Catholic Church.

Beasly, B. (1992) 'Transitions to Nowhere: The Effects of Government Policies on Young Working Class People's Access to Employment/Training', in R. White and B. Wilson (eds) *For Your Own Good: Young People and State Intervention in Australia*, La Trobe University: Journal of Australian Studies (Special Issue).

Box, S. (1987) *Recession, Crime and Punishment*, London: McMillan.

Braithwaite, J. (1979) *Inequality, Crime and Public Policy*, London: Routledge and Kegan Paul.

Clarke, J. (1985) 'Whose Justice? The Politics of Juvenile Control', *International Journal of the Sociology of Law* 13: 2.

Coventry, G., Muncie, J., Walters, R. (1992) *Rethinking Social Policy for Young People and Crime Prevention*, Melbourne: La Trobe University, National Centre for Socio-Legal Studies, discussion paper series.

Cohen, S. (1985) *Visions of Social Control: Crime, Punishment and Classification*,

Cambridge: Polity Press.

Criminal Justice Commission (1992) *Youth, Crime and Justice in Queensland*, Brisbane: CJC.

Cunneen, C. (1991) 'Law, Order and Inequality' in J. O'Lacey and P. Sharp (eds), *Inequality in Australia*, Melbourne: Heinemann.

Cunneen, C. (1992) (ed.) *Aboriginal Perspectives on Criminal Justice*, Sydney: Institute of Criminology.

Devery, C. (1991) *Disadvantage and Crime in New South Wales*, Sydney: NSW Bureau of Crime Statistics and Research.

Gale, F., Bailey-Harris, R. and Wundersitz, J. (1990) *Aboriginal Youth and the Criminal Justice System*, Sydney: Cambridge University Press.

Harris, R. and Webb, D. (1987) *Welfare, Power and Juvenile Justice*, London: Tavistock.

Hil, R. and Seaton, S. (1993) 'Policy or Orthodoxy? Queensland's Response to Juvenile Crime', *Criminology Australia*, 4: 4, April/May.

Human Rights and Equal Opportunity Commission (HREOC) (1991) *Racist Violence: Report of National Inquiry into Racist Violence in Australia*, Canberra: Australian Government Publishing Service.

Hudson, B. (1987) *Justice Through Punishment: A Critique of the 'Justice' Model of Corrections*, London: McMillan.

Kitchener, K. (1992) 'Street Offences and the Summary Offences Act 1988: Social Control in the 1990s', in C. Cunneen (ed.) *Aboriginal Perspectives on Criminal Justice*, Sydney: Institute of Criminology.

Lohse, H. (1992) 'Suicide in Isolation: Actual and Attempted Suicides in Broken Hill', *Youth Studies*, 11: 1, Autumn.

O'Connor, I. (1993) 'Spare the Rod? New Laws, Old Visions', *Alternative Law Journal*, 18: 1, February.

Pitts, J. (1988) *The Politics of Juvenile Crime*, London: Sage.

Pitts, J. (1990) *Working with Young Offenders*, London: McMillan.

Potas, I., Vinning, A. and Wilson, P. (1990) *Young People and Crime*, Canberra: Australian Institute of Criminology.

Presdee, M. (1990) 'Deregulation, Youth Policies and the Creation of Crime', in Taylor, I. (ed.) *The Social Effects of Free Market Policies*, London: Harvester Wheatsheaf.

Queensland (1992) *Estimates of Receipts and Expenditure, State Budget 1992-3*, Budget Paper 2, Brisbane: Government of Queensland Publications.

Queensland State Government (1992) *Juvenile Justice Act 1992*, Brisbane: QSG.

Rutherford, A. (1986) *Growing Out of Crime*, Harmondsworth: Penguin.

Tansky, M. (1992) *Queensland Juvenile Crime Prevention Program*, Paper presented to the National Conference on Juvenile Crime, Canberra: Australian Institute of Criminology, September 22-24.

Taylor, I. (1981) *Law and Order: Arguments for Socialism*, London: McMillan.

Western, J. (1983) *Social Inequality in Australian Society*, Melbourne: McMillan.

White, R. (1990) *No Space of Their Own: Young People and Social Control in Australia*, Melbourne: Cambridge University Press

Wright, J. and McMillan, A. (1992) 'Juvenile Justice Bill 1992', *Transitions*, 2: 2, November.

Youth Justice Coalition (1990) *Kids in Justice*, Sydney: Youth Justice Coalition.

Youth Advocacy Centre (1993) *Juvenile Justice: Rhetoric or Reality?* Brisbane: Youth Advocacy Centre.

Notes

1.   Richard Hil B.A. (Hons) (Essex), M.Sc. (Bristol), C.Q.S.W. (Southampton), Cert.Ed. (Thames Polytechnic) is a Lecturer in Social Work and Community Welfare at James Cook University of North Queensland. His main interests are in the areas of juvenile justice and community corrections with a particular interest in theories of social control and lay tribunals. He is currently carrying out research on the Townsville Youth Assistance Panel.

IV Indigenous women and criminal justice: Some comments on the Australian situation

Chris Cunneen and Kate Kerley[1]

Introduction

> Much has been written about the impact of the criminal justice system on Aboriginal and Torres Strait Islander men. Few people want to consider its impact on indigenous women (Judy Atkinson 1990a: 6).

There has been a profound silence surrounding the issue of Aboriginal and Torres Strait Islander women in the Australian criminal justice system[2]. In fact there have been multiple silences on issues of gender, race and the processes of colonialism. By and large, Aboriginal women have remained invisible even where there has occurred considerable analysis of the impact of criminal justice on indigenous people in Australia. Indeed, the recent Royal Commission Into Aboriginal Deaths In Custody[3], having included eleven deaths of women in custody in its final report, did not make one recommendation out of its 339 with specific regard to women. Until recently there has also been inadequate attention to the problematic way in which the criminal justice system has failed to offer protection to Aboriginal women - particularly when they are subject to familial and other forms of violence (Atkinson 1990a).

The purpose of this essay is to explicate and review what we know about the way the criminal justice system impacts on Aboriginal women. We do so within the context of an analysis which acknowledges the intersectionality of race, gender and class. We argue further that the specific historical and contemporary forms of colonialism and neo-colonialism in Australia provide the explanatory context in which race, class and gender are experienced.

The interacting ideologies of class, race and gender support the continuing process of colonization. Such a process has a long history in the Australian context. Aboriginal women have been particularly affected by policies which saw the introduction of the so-called 'Protection' legislation, by sexual and labour exploitation as domestic servants (Huggins and Blake 1992) and by present policing strategies which over-emphasize public order maintenance and under-emphasize the protection of Aboriginal women from violence (Payne 1992).

To simply assert that Aboriginal people are subject to such oppression because of their cultural 'difference' is inadequate. The research reviewed in this essay reveals that no other non-Anglo ethnic minority is subject to the same level of criminal justice intervention in Australia as are Aboriginal people. To assert simple notions of cultural difference detracts from the inherently political status of Aboriginal and Torres Strait Islander people as indigenous people. Such an inherent political status flows from recognizable rights relating to self-determination and the possibilities opened by Aboriginal sovereignty. There is then a structural and ongoing tension between Aboriginal people and the Australian state.

It has also been argued that Aboriginal women have suffered because of their visibility in a society which enforces the invisibility of women (Scutt 1990: 4-5). The invisibility of women in anglo-Australian culture has been said potentially to 'pollute' any culture with which it comes in contact. This position has been projected onto Aboriginal women and manifests itself by distorting what elements of 'traditional' Aboriginal culture shall be recognized by the judiciary. Thus Bolger (1991) has shown how judicial officers have rationalized violence against indigenous women on spurious assumptions of cultural appropriateness. It has also manifested itself by the omission of women from serious consideration by the Royal Commission into Aboriginal Deaths in Custody. Similarly the lack of research about Aboriginal women in custody reinforces the 'invisibility' of women in society generally. It has been argued by Aboriginal women that urgent research is necessary in this regard (Selfe and Thomas 1992: 10).

We now turn to consider how the intersectionality of race, gender and class is evident in the empirical data relating to Aboriginal women and the criminal justice system.

Juvenile justice

Unfortunately most data which considers Aboriginal young people and juvenile justice does not distinguish the data between male and female youth. We do know however that Aboriginal young people generally are massively over-represented in the juvenile justice system particularly at the most punitive levels of intervention (incarceration). In Western Australia for example the rate of incarceration of Aboriginal youth is 539 per 100,000 compared to 9 per 100,000 for non-Aboriginal youth (Cunneen 1990: 16). One study which analyzed detection rates for female delinquency found that local government areas with the highest proportion of Aboriginal people in the population had, on average, four times the detection rate for female delinquency (Carrington 1990: 2).

The work of Gale, Bailey-Harris and Wundersitz (1990) is the most comprehensive study of the relationship between Aboriginal young people and the juvenile justice system. Aboriginal youth are described by the authors as being 'massively disadvantaged at every point in the South Australian system where discretionary decisions are made' (Gale, Bailey-Harris and Wundersitz 1990: 12). The authors stress there was clear evidence of class bias in the way decisions were made. Unemployed youth, and youth living in single parent families or with foster parents or relatives were far more likely to be arrested than receive the benefits of diversionary mechanisms. Residential criteria was also important. Youth from poorer socio-economic areas were more likely to be arrested than youth who presented officers with addresses from wealthier socio-economic areas (Gale, Bailey-Harris and Wundersitz 1990: 13). The study points to the important interplay between factors of class and race. Aboriginal young people display class characteristics which are likely to lead to more punitive decisions by criminal justice agencies. The class position of Aboriginal people is itself directly related to dispossession and colonization.

Aboriginal youth are gravely affected by such discriminatory practices. Many Aboriginal youth find it difficult to find work immediately they leave school. Further many Aboriginal youth come from single parent families, or are fostered or reside with relatives. The authors note another characteristic of the Aboriginal community is a high residential mobility rate. This is especially significant as Aboriginal youth move frequently from one relative to the next within their particular kin network (Gale, Bailey-Harris and Wundersitz 1990: 14) Therefore, this discrimination against so-called 'problem families' often dictates whether or not a youth will be arrested rather than ignored or cautioned, regardless of the offending behaviour involved. The extent and nature of state intervention into the lives of Aboriginal youth is decided upon on the basis of social, cultural and economic reasoning which places Aboriginal young people in a disadvantaged position. The authors also found this bias extended to the decision-making processes of diversionary panels designed to review police decisions.

The gendered form of colonization is particularly apparent with the way justice and welfare authorities have intervened against Aboriginal girls. The history of the removal of Aboriginal children is relatively well-documented and had begun under various state protection legislation of the late 19th and early 20th centuries (Edwards and Read 1988). For example a major function of the New South Wales Aborigines Protection Board was to gain control over Aboriginal children. The Royal Commission into Aboriginal Deaths in Custody identified the aims as:

i)   The reduction of Aboriginal birth-rate by removal of adolescents, particularly girls;

ii) Prevention of Aboriginal children's identification with the Aboriginal community by isolating them from their families and communities through adolescence; preventing or hindering their return to their families or the Aboriginal community at the end of their term of 'apprenticeship' (Wootten 1989: 18-19).

It is important to understand how this process of intervention was gendered. Goodall (1990) has argued that between 1900 and 1940 Aboriginal girls bore the heaviest impact of removal policies. The policy was targeted at pubertal girls and in its early years some 80% of the children removed were female, the majority of whom were aged 12 years and older (Goodall 1990: 4). Much of the non-Aboriginal anxiety at the time of the Board's inception was to do with the sexuality of Aboriginal females, be they girls or women. There were charges of Aboriginal girls being 'in moral danger' because of their sexuality (Goodall 1990: 9).

However, the use of juvenile 'status' offences has disappeared in most jurisdictions (Naffine 1989). Aboriginal girls are now more likely to be charged with a criminal offence. Thus it is important to consider the gendered aspects of policing Aboriginal youth - particularly in public places. Much of the debate around Aboriginal youth and criminalization has neglected the relationship between Aboriginal young women and the criminal justice system. The challenges of black youth to authoritarianism, particularly in the policing of public places, have been assumed to involve male youth. Yet there is evidence that Aboriginal girls in public places are also represented as posing a threat to good order (Cunneen 1989; Carrington 1990). It has also been argued that particular definitions of black femininity come into play.

> [P]opularised male discourses, mythologies and fantasies about the black female body underscore the hysterical fears expressed by extra-judicial agencies that the publicly visible presence of Aboriginal girls is somehow 'harmful to the local community' (an oft quoted phrase in Court Reports) ... Aboriginal girls because of white male discourses about black female bodies are subject to additional forms of regulation and surveillance for their use of public space (Carrington 1990: 8).

There is the interplay of gender and race in constructing Aboriginal girls as a threat. Goodall has argued that redefinition of Aboriginal youth as 'delinquent' developed in the postwar period with a shift from the genetically-based racist arguments concerning Aboriginal inferiority to arguments based on the psychologizing of environment and childhood. Characterizations of Aboriginal young women as sexually predatory and a menace acted as a 'powerful, although hidden, agenda in legal proceedings against Aboriginal girls' (Goodall 1990: 9). Equally with the shift from genetic based-theories to psychological-based theories of 'deviance', there continued to be a deep-rooted and pervasive pathologizing of Aboriginal cultures and familial structures.

The physical treatment of Aboriginal girls by police has also been shown to be motivated by both racist and sexist ideology. In interviews conducted with Aboriginal detainees in juvenile detention centres, girls stated that they were frequently abused by police officers with language that was both racist and sexist (Cunneen 1990: 41). The girls were told they were 'black sluts', 'black molls' and 'black bitches'. In Western Australia, one girl stated that an officer had 'talked real dirty' to her and had threatened her with rape (Cunneen 1990: 41). There were complaints about threats of rape and sexual assault (Cunneen 1990: 24). Similar evidence, including allegations of strip searches was presented to the New South Wales Youth Justice Coalition (Youth Justice Project 1990: 254). There were also allegations of police brutality including assaults (Cunneen 1990: 19).

The reports from the Royal Commission into Aboriginal Deaths in Custody also offer some insights into the specific processes of intervention into the lives of Aboriginal girls and young women. Six of the eleven women who died in custody had been removed from their families as children. In the case of Christine Jones (O'Dea 1990a) and Nita Blankett (O'Dea 1990b) removal had occurred at the age of five years. All six women had been institutionalized and been made the subject of welfare and juvenile complaints such as being neglected, uncontrollable, exposed to moral danger and truanting from school. There has been a profound history to state intervention into Aboriginal family life through the removal and institutionalization of children (Read, 1984). The effect of these policies, and in particular the effect of institutionalization and extensive separation from the family, has been referred to as constituting cultural genocide (Wootten 1989).

Aboriginal writers have noted that the visibility of Aboriginal girls on public streets makes them an obvious target for police intent on enforcing 'law and order' (Payne 1990: 11). When this is combined with police discrimination at pre-arrest stage, Aboriginal girls suffer biased treatment as a result of race, gender and class oppression. The broader context in which these social relations have been played out is the colonization process which has identified Aboriginal girls as specific objects for state intervention.

Arrest and police custody

It is imperative to understand that the use of police custody has a particular importance in an Australian context. Individuals can be held for significant periods of time in police cells or watchhouses after arrest for minor offences relating to public disorder. Such offences are usually found in summary offences legislation and relate to matters such as offensive behaviour. The enforcement of such legislation gives police wide discretionary powers of arrest. In addition in some jurisdictions in Australia, public drunkenness is a criminal offence which can result in an overnight stay in police custody until the matter is determined before a magistrate or Justice of the Peace. In other jurisdictions in Australia where public drunkenness has been decriminalized, the police still retain power to place an intoxicated person in police custody for their own protection. Individuals can also be held in police custody for significant periods of time if they are detained for fine default. Arguably then, the regime administered by the police has more immediate impact on Aboriginal women than the formal prison system itself.

Unfortunately there is little empirical evidence on the number of arrests of Aboriginal women by police. However there is some data available on the use of police custody. The figures in relation to the number of Aboriginal women in police custody can only be described in extraordinary terms. Aboriginal women comprise around 1.5% of all women in Australia. However they constitute almost half of the total number of women taken into police custody (Johnston 1991, Vol. 1: 194). One would have thought that this issue demanded an immediate investigation. Yet the National Report of the Royal Commission into Aboriginal Deaths in Custody simply notes that 'one of the disturbing findings of the National Police Custody Survey was the very high proportion of Aboriginal women placed in police custody' (ibid: 193). The Royal Commission offers no further specifically gendered analysis of the issue in the five volumes of the final report. Yet in some states and territories in Australia the majority of women held in police custody are Aboriginal. Indeed in Queensland, Western Australia and Northern Territory some 57%, 72% and 88% respectively of women in police custody are Aboriginal (ibid: 194). The sheer weight of such data should have demanded a response which considered the relationship between Aboriginality, gender, police practices and the use of custody. Indeed the Royal Commission noted, when discussing the general level of Aboriginal over-representation in police custody, that 'this disproportion in incarceration levels is a national disgrace, and one which shames Australia in the eyes of the international community' (ibid: 221). Yet despite the empirical evidence on the specific over-representation of Black women, they barely rate a mention.

The information we do have on Aboriginal women in police custody derives primarily from a National Police Custody Survey conducted in 1988 (McDonald 1990). It is possible to glean a little more information from the results of that survey which showed that Aboriginal women comprised 78% of all cases where women were detained in police custody for public drunkenness (ibid: 24). The report also notes that proportionately more females than males were detained in police custody for public drunkenness and good order offences compared to other offences (ibid: 24). Some further information from the police custody survey was available for Western Australia. In more than three of every four cases where Aboriginal women were placed in police custody the reason was public drunkenness or offences related to public disorder.

Indeed throughout Western Australia some 97% of the women placed in police custody for drunkenness were in fact Aboriginal women (O'Dea 1991, Vol. 1: 153).

It would appear that women in general are detained in police custody proportionately more for offences of public disorder than are men, and that Aboriginal women in particular are susceptible to being detained for these offences. Such a view is further supported by general figures (undifferentiated by sex) which showed that some two thirds of Aboriginal people placed in police custody were there for public drunkenness or other public disorder offences.

The empirical evidence strongly suggests that proportionately more Aboriginal women are detained in police custody for minor offences of public disorder than other groups. These figures are disturbing and raise many questions in relation to Aboriginality, gender and the policing of public places. It can be seen from reading the figures that the gender and race of Aboriginal women mean they are more likely to be treated punitively for public offences. As a result of being placed in police custody Aboriginal women are particularly vulnerable to police mistreatment. The National Inquiry into Racist Violence has outlined the allegations of various forms of police violence against Aboriginal women in custody (Human Rights and Equal Opportunity Commission 1991: 88-89). There is also the additional question of the impact of incarceration on community life. There is very little information available concerning the extent of incarceration at a community level, however a self-report study by Hunter and Spargo (1993) in the Kimberley region of north west Western Australia found that one in three Aboriginal women in the region had been locked-up in a police cell on one or more occasions.

The investigations into deaths of Aboriginal women in custody by the Royal Commission into Aboriginal Deaths in Custody also offer some insights into the specific processes involved in the use of police arrest and custody. Nine of the eleven women were in police custody (as opposed to adult or juvenile corrections) at the time of death[4]. Most were in police custody for the offence of public drunkenness. Others were there for fine default or offensive language. The place of death and the reason for custody would indicate that it is the penal regime administered by the police which should be a major concern for preventing the deaths of Aboriginal women. None of the women were in police custody for a serious offence. Indeed the reasons for incarceration can only be described as minor. In the majority of cases the 'crime' was victimless. Indeed there was potential for all of the women to have been offered alternatives to custody had these been available and had the custodial authorities been of the view to use alternatives. In other jurisdictions, and indeed for other women in the same jurisdictions, it might have been treated as a health rather than criminal problem.

The experience of the women who died in police custody shows that public space is regulated in a way that criminalizes its use by Aboriginal women. What we know from these deaths is that if Aboriginal women are visible in public they are likely to be 'scooped up and removed from the public view' (O'Dea 1990c: 28). They will then be left in a police lock-up with little supervision or no supervision, and with probably no enquiry as to their health.

One cannot fully appreciate the role of police without considering their instrumental role in enforcing a colonial order - particularly in the context of policing public space and public order. We saw that in the cases of Aboriginal women who died in custody, nearly all were apprehended for public order offences. Notions of offences in public places raise the issue of the construction of social space. It has been argued that social space as a construct defines particular activities and that the spatiality of social life can be considered to be constructed within parameters of race, gender and class relations (Cunneen 1988: 197). Complaints about the social visibility of Aboriginal people have a historical continuity. The popular 'remedy' for the Aboriginal 'problem' has been to make invisible the presence of Aboriginal people by the imposition of policing which seeks their removal from public space (Cunneen and Robb 1987: 192). The social relations of class, race and gender can be seen at a point of interaction. The policing of Aboriginal people reflects to some extent the policing of working class communities and their cultural use of public places. There is the gendered aspect to policing which has included the monitoring of women in public places to conform to the dominant definition of 'suitable behaviour' in the public sphere. There is also the specific policing of Aboriginality. Until recently, reserve areas were declared public areas. As a consequence, a degree of policing was possible in Aboriginal settlements which would have been unacceptable elsewhere (Cunneen 1988: 202). The social and spatial positioning of Aboriginal women is thus indicative of dominant power relations. Cowlishaw illustrates how Aboriginal people are positioned with regard to the use of public space by providing us with an example. Public seating was removed from a main street in a north-western New South Wales town because, as a Council member said 'Too many [Aborigines] sat on them, lounged all over them. It didn't look nice for the tourists'

(Cowlishaw 1986: 13).

Aboriginal women and imprisonment

The issue of Aboriginal women in Australian prisons has been raised on several occasions in recent years, but again the paucity of information is staggering (Howe 1988; Brown, Kramer and Quin 1988). The failure to conduct comprehensive research and to develop reform-driven policy is all the more reprehensible when we consider that Elizabeth Eggleston (1976) first noted the extreme levels of over-representation of Aboriginal women in gaol in the 1970s.[5]

Again in 1985 the New South Wales Task Force on Women in Prison in its chapter on Aboriginal women noted that 'no research information or clear policy is available specifically on Aboriginal women and the criminal justice system' (Howe 1988: 6). Unfortunately not a lot has changed, although since the Royal Commission into Aboriginal Deaths in Custody, we do have a little more empirical evidence on the extent and nature of over-representation.

Some of the information from Western Australia is the most detailed available on Aboriginal women in prison. At the 1986 Census Aboriginal people made up slightly less than 3% of the state's population. However Aboriginal women comprised 43% of all female prisoners at the time of the prison census on 30 June 1989, compared to Aboriginal men who comprised 35% of all male prisoners at the same time (O'Dea 1991, Vol. 1: 191). In addition the information available on the number of prison receptions over the twelve-month period of 1989 demonstrates an even greater over-representation of Aboriginal women who made up some 67% of women received into the prison system during the period. The comparable figure for Aboriginal men was 44% (ibid: 191).

The figures on prison receptions give a greater indication of who is going through the prison system over an extended period of time. Unfortunately most analyses rely simply on national prison census figures. While these figures do show Aboriginal women to be over-represented in the prison census, they tend to reduce the significance of the over-representation. The reason Aboriginal women are even more over-represented in the flow (or reception) data for prisons is because they are more likely to be serving short term sentences (ibid: 189). This point is itself related to the nature of the offences for which Aboriginal women are incarcerated and will be discussed further below. The Western Australian data show that there are significant differences in the reasons for imprisonment between Aboriginal women and non-indigenous women (ibid: 163).

Some 20% of the offences for which Aboriginal women were gaoled related to public disorder including disorderly conduct, drunkenness and other good order offences. However less than 3.5% of sentenced non-indigenous women were in prison for similar offences. It is significant then that one in every five Aboriginal women in prison in Western Australia during 1989 was there for a minor public disorder offence. This ratio compares to one in twenty-nine non-indigenous women in prison for the same offences.

Aboriginal women were also more likely to be in prison for assault than non-indigenous women (12.2% compared to 1.1%). Conversely 32% of non-indigenous women were in gaol for fraud and drug offences, compared to 2.5% of Aboriginal women. The over-representation of indigenous women in prison for offences against the person has been considered in the Canadian literature. LaPrairie (1989) has linked high levels of domestic violence to the disproportionate imprisonment of indigenous women for crimes of assault. She argues that there may be a strong relationship between the contemporary condition of indigenous men as a result of colonization and the use of male violence against indigenous women, and the then subsequent criminal activity by indigenous women. She suggests three ways that indigenous women's conflict with the law could be related to family violence; firstly indigenous women might retaliate against violence by the use of violence themselves; secondly indigenous women, in order to escape from violent or abusive situations, may resort to alcohol or drug abuse; and thirdly the victimization of indigenous women may itself cause abuse or neglect of others.

There has been considerable concern about the levels of family violence and sexual assault in Aboriginal communities in Australia (Atkinson 1990a; Bolger 1991; Payne 1992). It has also been suggested that the victimization of Aboriginal women in the area of domestic violence may have some bearing on the number of Aboriginal women in prison. Thomas (1991: 87) noted that 'almost all the Aboriginal women in Mulawa Gaol[6] had, at some stage in their lives, been sexually and/or physically abused'. Atkinson has stated that for Queensland 'almost 90% of Aboriginal women in prison experienced forms of sexual abuse as children, adolescents and as adults by both white and black males' (1990: 6). For Aboriginal women physical force may be the only resistance to domestic violence available given a range of pressures which militate against the involvement of the police (ibid; Dodson 1991, Vol. 1: 381). Atkinson (1990a) has also argued that Aboriginal women have been convicted and imprisoned for killing a person who has been violent to them. Langton (1991: 311) has suggested that the forms of violence that Aboriginal women use are more akin to customary obligations. The bald statistics on imprisonment rates do not indicate whether the convictions for offences against the person are related to issues of domestic violence or sexual assault. Indeed a proper consideration of the gender relations surrounding the imprisonment of Aboriginal women is a research/policy question which has been dramatically ignored (Selfe and Thomas 1992).

It could be argued that the different reasons for imprisonment between Aboriginal and non-indigenous women simply represent different offending patterns on the part of the two groups. But of course such a view begs as many questions as it might answer. Firstly a fundamental question which needs to be addressed is why are Aboriginal women being imprisoned on trivial charges related to drunkenness and public disorder? The extent to which Aboriginal women are brought before the courts and sentenced to imprisonment for minor offences is clearly problematic. A further question which flows from this is the extent to which the use of imprisonment by the courts is simply legitimating the processes of selective policing for particular offences. In other words, why are the women appearing in court for these offences in the first place?

In addition the question needs to be posed as to why imprisonment is being used as the sentencing option for Aboriginal women convicted of these minor offences. Why aren't Aboriginal women receiving the benefits of non-custodial options rather than the use of imprisonment? Commissioner Johnston has noted that the level of over-representation of Aboriginal people in non-custodial corrections is considerably lower than in custody, although these figures are not differentiated by sex. In other words Aboriginal people do not appear to be receiving the same benefits of non-custodial sentencing options. Johnston suggests that this may occur because of a 'belief held by judges, magistrates and parole authorities that Aboriginal offenders are either less able or less willing to comply with the requirements of non-custodial orders' (Johnston 1991, Vol.1: 217). Other evidence suggests that it may also occur, at least in the case of Aboriginal women, because of a patriarchal racism. Commissioner Dodson noted that one justice in Western Australia stated that he sentenced Aboriginal and Torres Strait Islander women to terms of imprisonment for 'welfare' reasons. 'Sometimes I sentence them to imprisonment to help them ...

To protect their welfare I put them inside for seven days. They get cleaned up and fed then' (Dodson 1991, Vol.1: 136). We wonder whether the same rationale would be used for the incarceration of non-indigenous women?

We would argue that particular conceptions of gender and Aboriginality have the effect of creating more punitive interventions in relation to Aboriginal women. A reading of the reports into deaths of Aboriginal women in custody by the Royal Commission into Aboriginal Deaths in Custody supports such a claim. Many of the women had been in prison on previous occasions. Yet what is remarkable in reading through these cases is that the women were being constantly criminalized because of poverty and alcohol addiction. In addition there was a pronounced punitiveness to the intervention.

For example Barbara Yarrie at the age of sixteen years was placed in Brisbane's maximum security adult women's prison for failing to pay a fine for under-age drinking. There were other occasions of imprisonment for fine default and in 1981 she was imprisoned for two months with hard labour for stealing $49 (Wyvill 1990a: 14-20). Fay Yarrie was the younger sister of Barbara Yarrie. At the age of seventeen she was sentenced to two months imprisonment in Brisbane Women's Prison for vagrancy. Only six months later she was again given two months gaol for vagrancy. At the age of eighteen she was given two and half years gaol for two separate property offences - one involving money for a taxi fare, the other a blanket for warmth. Her application for parole was refused. From this period until her death, Fay was in and out of police and prison custody (Wyvill 1990b: 3). Barbara Tier's first criminal conviction was at the age of twenty when she was fined $200 for a motor vehicle offence and allowed no time to pay. She was unemployed and subsequently spent a month in gaol for fine default. The Royal Commission analysed fourteen court appearances for minor offences by Barbara Tiers between 1971 and 1976. Of the six occasions she was sentenced to imprisonment, four were related to vagrancy. The periods of imprisonment she received for her poverty ranged from two to six months (Wyvill 1990c: 12). On another four occasions she was fined and allowed no time for payment. As a result she was imprisoned.

The empirical evidence shows that imprisonment for fine default also impacts differentially on Aboriginal women compared to non-indigenous women. For example there were large numbers of Aboriginal women in Western Australia who were put in prison for fine default. In 1989 almost three quarters (74%) of all women placed in prison for failing to pay a fine were Aboriginal. In addition fine default was the major immediate reason for the imprisonment of the majority of Aboriginal women. Some 61% of Aboriginal women received into prison in 1989 were there for fine default. In other words, over a one-year period, the majority of female fine defaulters were Aboriginal women and the majority of Aboriginal women were received into prison for fine default (O'Dea 1991, Vol.1: 207-208).

The discussion of poverty and fine default also raises the issue of the economic position of Aboriginal women. Aboriginal women have to contend with being less employed and poorer than non-indigenous women. According to the 1986 census 36% of Aboriginal women were in the paid workforce as compared with 48% of non-Aboriginal women. The level of unemployment was four times higher for Aboriginal people than others. For Aboriginal women in the fifteen to nineteen years age group the unemployment level was greater than 50% outside of urban centres (Australian Bureau of Statistics 1991: 21). In addition the median income of Aboriginal people was two-thirds that of non-Aboriginal people. Three quarters of Aboriginal women had median incomes of less than $9000 compared with 55% of Aboriginal men. Aboriginal families also have higher proportions of one-parent households and more dependent children than non-Aboriginal families (ibid: 13, 27). Given this economic position it is not surprising that fine default is a critical factor in the incarceration of Aboriginal women.

We have relied primarily on the situation in Western Australia in our discussion of the reasons for Aboriginal women's imprisonment. Such a reliance is mainly due to the relatively comprehensive data available from Western Australia. Similar information which would allow a discussion of fine default or prison receptions of Aboriginal women is not available from other states. While there are legislative differences between various Australian states and territories affecting the use of fine default or the criminalization of public drunkenness, we suspect the situation to be broadly similar at the national level.

Indeed recent national statistics indicate an extraordinary increase in the number of Aboriginal women in prison between 1987 and 1991 (Cunneen 1992: 13-14). A review of incarceration figures showed that the number of Aboriginal women in prison in all Australian jurisdictions rose from 78 in the 1987 prison census to 127 in the 1991 census. Such a change represented a 63% increase in the imprisonment of Aboriginal women during the four year period. New South Wales was the major contributor to the national increase in Aboriginal women in prison. Between 1987 and 1991 the number of Aboriginal women in New South Wales prisons rose by no less than 168%. It is worth noting that while the number of Aboriginal women in prison rose by 63% nationally, the corresponding increase for Aboriginal men was 24%. Thus in recent years there has been a general increase in the imprisonment of indigenous people in Australia. However that increase has disproportionately impacted on indigenous women.

In 1988 the Interim Report of the Royal Commission into Aboriginal Deaths in Custody by Justice Muirhead raised serious concerns about the level of Aboriginal imprisonment and argued that imprisonment should be used only as a last resort. Indeed Recommendation 1 of the Interim Report states that 'Governments ... [should] enforce the principle that imprisonment should be utilized only as a sanction of last resort'. The National Report of the Royal Commission, released in May 1991, deals in Recommendations 92 to 121 with imprisonment as a last resort and the methods involved in reducing the levels of Aboriginal imprisonment. One of the basic tenets of the Royal Commission has been that to reduce or stop Aboriginal deaths in custody there needs to be a reduction in the number of Aboriginal people in custody. State and territory governments appear to show little interest in the issue of Aboriginal women in prison, and in particular why the numbers of Aboriginal women in custody should be increasing at such a rate.

The continued and increased incarceration of Aboriginal people can be partly seen within the historical continuities of unprecedented intervention by criminal justice agencies (Eggleston 1976; Cunneen and Robb 1987) and also within the current political context of more pronounced recourse to 'law and order' measures (Cunneen 1992). However it is imperative that the current increases in the incarceration of indigenous women should also be contextualized within the gendered strategies of the colonial state in Australia. Such strategies have included the targeting of Aboriginal girls for removal to welfare institutions and the circumvention of child bearing capacities of Aboriginal women (Goodall 1990; Dodson 1991). Dodson has noted that 'there is concrete evidence to suggest that throughout the 'protection', 'assimilation', 'integration' eras of the twentieth century, Aboriginal women have been consciously nominated targets of government in its pursuit to destabilize and dismantle Aboriginal society' (Dodson 1991: 376). During the 'protection' era women lost their right to raise children through forced removals, segregation and welfarization. Today through criminalization and incarceration Aboriginal women are removed from their children. This separation and dislocation of the family structure serves to further restrict the 'culture bearing' capabilities of Aboriginal women (ibid: 376-377).

Aboriginal women and violence

In recent years Aboriginal women have drawn attention to the problems of family violence and sexual assault in various Aboriginal communities (Atkinson 1990a; Langton 1991, Payne 1990). Within the context of the Royal Commission into Aboriginal Deaths in Custody, Marcia Langton has noted that:

> While no Aboriginal women have died in custody in the Northern Territory during the 1989-1990 period, more women have died in alcohol-related murders than there have been [male] deaths in custody (Langton 1992: 11).

In a similar comparison Judy Atkinson (1990a: 6) has stated that 'in Queensland more women have died in one community than all the deaths in custody in that State'.

There has been little systematic research concerning the extent to which Aboriginal women experience male violence. However we do know that Aboriginal women are 10 times more likely to be homicide victims than non-indigenous women (Strang 1992: 25). Similarly there have been several reports and studies concerning the extent of family violence within Aboriginal communities (Atkinson 1990a; Bolger 1991). Atkinson has estimated that 88% of rape and assault cases in Aboriginal communities go unreported (Atkinson 1990b). Barber, Punt and Albers (1988: 96) have stated in relation to Palm Island that 'assault and rape are the two most underreported crimes on the Island and that it can take something as extreme as pack rape before a woman will complain'. Some Aboriginal women have analyzed the extent of family violence within the context of colonialism and argued that such violence has arisen out of dispossession, invasion and the fracturing of Aboriginal social control mechanisms (Atkinson 1990a: 6).

Inevitably a critical issue which arises is the extent to which the criminal justice system can provide protection for Aboriginal women in violent situations. As we discussed earlier, there have been silences around Aboriginal women in the criminal justice system. It is equally true to say that, with few exceptions (Bolger 1991), there has been little critical analysis of how the criminal justice agencies respond to the interests of Aboriginal women. There are many reasons why instances of family violence or sexual assault might not be reported to the authorities.

In New South Wales it has been shown that Aboriginal women are not being told about the processes of the legal system or how to access that system (Selfe and Thomas 1991: 8). Thus one reason for not reporting can be lack of access to information and lack of legal assistance. Aboriginal women may be reluctant to discuss violence against them because of the dominant racist discourse which encourages a reading of Aboriginal men's actions in the context of 'savage' (Pettman 1992: 70; Langton 1989: 3). To complain then may been seen as reinforcing racist stereotypes concerning Aboriginal men and Aboriginal family life. Aboriginal women may therefore be forced to compromise their own needs because recourse to institutions such as the police may be regarded as community betrayal (Dodson 1991: 387).

We would argue that a major issue involved in the non-reporting of family violence or sexual assault, is that police may not take such complaints seriously. Atkinson (1990a: 6) has noted that 'Aboriginal women are ashamed to report rapes and be subjected to the sneering interrogation of young white male policemen with their racially prejudiced and sexist questions'. The National Inquiry into Racist Violence received evidence from a Queensland serving police officer that during the course of a rape investigation involving an Aboriginal woman, he was told by a senior officer conducting the inquiry that 'you can't rape a coon' (Human Rights and Equal Opportunity Commission 1991: 108). There were also allegations that Western Australian police had arrested a woman who had attended a police station to make a complaint concerning violent threats from her husband (ibid).

A recent report by the Federal Race Discrimination Commissioner has also highlighted the problem of police attitudes and practices in relation to domestic violence in Aboriginal communities (Human Rights and Equal Opportunity Commission 1993: 28-30). The report noted that police officers on Mornington Island 'recognised that there was a problem with domestic violence, but rationalised its occurrence in essentially racist terms' (ibid: 28). In addition the appropriate legislation was not being utilized. Police officers acknowledged that no protection orders under the *Domestic Violence (Family Protection) Act* 1989, Queensland, had been utilized (ibid). The report was also concerned with the high level of sexual assault on the Island and the inadequate responses by police and other non-Aboriginal personnel (ibid: 43).

A further factor that needs to be considered is how judicial officers might respond to cases of family violence and sexual assault when they do appear in court. There has been considerable recent controversy concerning the attitudes of the (predominantly) male judiciary to women. There have also been some analysis of judicial attitudes to Aboriginal women in particular. Bolger (1991) and Payne (1992) have discussed the way in which appeals to Aboriginal customary law has been used in a way which legitimates physical and sexual violence against Aboriginal women. Bolger writes:

> Reading many court transcripts relating to cases of rape, murder and assaults on women is like reading the minutes of a male club. Judges, lawyers and witnesses act to confirm each other's prejudices - that men may be provoked into violence by women's actions, that women are inferior and that rape is not a serious offence in Aboriginal society and so on (Bolger 1991: 85).

Bolger has argued that while the police response to violence against women leaves much to be desired, there has at least been some recognition of problems in that area and training programmes have been put into place. On the other hand, the reaction of the judiciary has been inadequate. Bolger has referred to a number of Northern Territory cases which had occurred during the 1980s where it was accepted by the judge that violence and rape were in some ways acceptable within the Aboriginal community. In a similar vein, Payne has noted that Aboriginal women have been subject to three types of law, 'white man's law, traditional law and bullshit traditional law; the latter being used to explain a distortion of traditional law used as a justification for assault and rape of women' (Payne 1992: 37). According to Payne 'quasi-anthropologists and all manner of experts' have been used to justify rape and sexual assault as in some way traditional.

A number of factors are evident. Violence against Aboriginal women is a problem. For a number of reasons these crimes are not being reported. Not the least among those reasons is the inadequate response by the criminal justice agencies to the criminal victimization of Aboriginal women. The evidence shows that Aboriginal women are not able to rely on the structures of criminal justice for their protection.

Conclusion

Aboriginal women across Australia have been responding in many ways to the issues which have been mentioned in this essay - in particular to the issue of family violence. Such responses have varied from one community to another. For instance members of the Yuendumu Women's Centre in central Australia have established night patrols to conduct their own policing (Yuendumu Women's Night Patrol 1992). Women's elder groups in other communities have established refuges (Human Rights and Equal Opportunity Commission 1993). In New South Wales the Mygunya Aboriginal Corporation has established a women's support service across the north west of the State (Selfe and Thomas 1991: 8). Peak organizations such as the Aboriginal Co-ordinating Council have also taken on proactive work in the area by employing specialist workers and promoting community justice mechanisms (Human Rights and Equal Opportunity Commission 1993). Some Aboriginal women have been approaching the issues through working at the level of the federal government.

The purpose of this essay has not been to 'speak for' Aboriginal women nor has it been to simplistically paint indigenous women as 'victims'. Rather what we have attempted to do is to take-up the point made by Judy Atkinson at the beginning of this essay and to analyse the available empirical data on the relationship between Aboriginal women and the criminal justice system. We have tried to concentrate on what such an analysis tells us about how the justice system operates in relation to Aboriginal women rather than on how Aboriginal women experience that system. Aboriginal women have themselves been expressing and acting on their experiences of the white justice system since invasion.

However there are many questions relating to juvenile justice, and the use of police and prison custody which need to be explicated. In particular the extent to which the custodial forms of criminal justice are used against Aboriginal women need to be fully documented and understood. It still seems to us almost unbelievable that half of all women going into police custody throughout Australia are Aboriginal, yet there is a complacency on this issue among white criminal justice administrators. We are also of the view that analytically the concepts of race, class and gender are important for developing an understanding of how the justice system works vis-a-vis Aboriginal women. However equally important is an analysis that contextualizes the discussion within the framework of colonial and neo-colonial processes. Again it seems evident that an understanding of the specific function of criminal justice agencies within the history of Australian colonialism is necessary to explain why such a deliberately punitive approach is taken in regard to Aboriginal women.

References

Atkinson, J. (1990a) 'Violence Against Aboriginal Women', *Aboriginal Law Bulletin*, 2: 46 (October).

Atkinson, J. (1990b) 'Violence in Aboriginal Australia: Colonisation and Its Impact on Gender', *Aboriginal and Islander Health Worker Journal*, 14: 2 (Part 1) and 14: 3 (Part 2).

Australian Bureau of Statistics (1991) Census 86 - *Australia's Aboriginal and Torres Strait Islander People*, Cat No 2503.0, Canberra: Australian Bureau of Statistics.

Barber, J.C., Punt, J. and Albers, J. (1988) 'Alcohol and Power on Palm Island', *Australian Journal of Social Issues*, 23: 2.

Bolger, A. (1991) *Aboriginal Women and Violence*, ANU Casuarina: North Australia Research Unit.

Brown D., Kramer, H. and Quin, M. (1988) 'Women in Prison Task Force Reform', in Findlay and Hogg (eds) *Understanding Crime and Criminal Justice*, North Ryde: Law Book Company.

Carrington, K. (1990) 'Aboriginal Girls and Juvenile Justice: What Justice? White Justice', *Journal for Social Justice Studies*: 3.

Cowlishaw, J. (1986) 'Race For Exclusion', *Australian and New Zealand Journal of Sociology*, 22: 1.

Cunneen, C. (1988) 'The Policing of Public Order: Some Thoughts on Culture, Space and Political Economy', in M. Findlay and R. Hogg (eds) *Understanding Crime and Criminal Justice*, North Ryde: Law Book Company.

Cunneen, C. (1990) *A Study of Aboriginal Juveniles and Police Violence*, Report Commissioned by the National Inquiry into Racist Violence, Sydney: Human Rights and Equal Opportunity Commission.

Cunneen, C. (1992) 'Aboriginal Imprisonment During and Since the Royal Commission Into Aboriginal Deaths in Custody, *Aboriginal Law Bulletin*, 2: 55.

Cunneen, C. and Robb, T. (1987) *Criminal Justice in North West New South Wales*, Sydney: NSW Bureau of Crime Statistics and Research.

Dodson, P. (1991) *Regional Report of Inquiry Into Underlying Issues in Western Australia*, Royal Commission into Aboriginal Deaths in Custody, Vol.1, Canberra: Australian Government Publishing Service.

Edwards, C. and Read, P. (1988) *The Lost Children*, Moorebank: Doubleday.

Eggleston, E. (1976) *Fear, Favour or Affection*, Canberra: Australian National University Press.

Gale, F. Bailey-Harris, R. and Wundersitz, J. (1990) *Aboriginal Youth and the Criminal Justice System*, Melbourne: Cambridge University Press.

Goodall, H. (1990) 'Saving the Children', *Aboriginal Law Bulletin*, 2: 44, 6-9.

Howe, A. (1988) 'Aboriginal Women In Custody, A Footnote To the Royal Commission', *Aboriginal Law Bulletin*, 2: 30.

Huggins, J. and Blake, T. (1992) 'Protection or Persecution? Gender Relations in the Era of Racial Segregation', in K. Saunders and R. Evans (eds) *Gender Relations In Australia*, Sydney: Harcourt Brace Janovich.

Human Rights and Equal Opportunity Commission (1991) *Racist Violence*, Report of the National Inquiry into Racist Violence, Canberra: Australian Government Publishing Service.

Human Rights and Equal Opportunity Commission (1993) *Mornington. A Report by the Federal Race Discrimination Commissioner*, Canberra: Australian Government Publishing Service.

Hunter, E. and Spargo, R. (1993) 'Alcohol Use and Incarceration Among Aboriginals in the Kimberley Region of Western Australia', unpublished paper.

Johnston, E. (1990a) *Report of Inquiry Into the Death of The Woman Who Died At Ceduna on 18 February 1983*, Royal Commission into Aboriginal Deaths in Custody, Canberra: Australian Government Publishing Service.

Johnston, E. (1990b) *Report of the Inquiry Into the Death of Joyce Thelma Egan*, Royal Commission into Aboriginal deaths in Custody, Canberra: Australian Government Publishing Service.

Johnston, E. (1991) *National Report, 5 Vols*, Royal Commission into Aboriginal Deaths in Custody, Canberra: Australian Government Publishing Service.

La Prairie, C.P. (1989) 'Some Issues in Aboriginal Justice Research: The Case of Aboriginal Women in Canada', *Women and Criminal Justice*, 1: 1.

Langton, M. (1989) 'Feminism, What Do Aboriginal Women Gain?' *Broadside* (National Foundation for Australian Women Newsletter) 2.

Langton, M. (1991) 'Too Much Sorry Business', Appendix D(i), in E. Johnston *National Report, Vol. 5*, Royal Commission into Aboriginal Deaths in Custody, Canberra: Australian Government Publishing Service.

Langton. M. (1992) 'Too Much Sorry Business', *Aboriginal and Islander Health Worker Journal*, 2: 16 (March/April).

McDonald, D. (1990) *National Police Custody Survey August 1988*, Research Paper No. 13, Canberra: Royal Commission Into Aboriginal Deaths in Custody.

O'Dea, D.J. (1990a) *Report of the Inquiry into the Death of Christine Lesley Anne Jones*, Royal Commission Into Aboriginal Deaths in Custody, Canberra: Australian Government Publishing Service.

O'Dea, D.J. (1990b) *Report of the Inquiry into the Death of Nita Blankett*, Royal Commission Into Aboriginal Deaths in Custody, Canberra: Australian Government Publishing Service.

O'Dea, D.J. (1990c) *Report of the Inquiry into the Death of Faith Barnes*, Royal Commission Into Aboriginal Deaths in Custody, Canberra: Australian Government Publishing Service.

O'Dea, D.J. (1991) *Regional Report of Inquiry into Individual Deaths in Custody in Western Australia*, Royal Commission into Aboriginal Deaths in Custody, Vol.1, Canberra: Australian Government Publishing Service.

Payne, S. (1990) 'Aboriginal Women and the Criminal Justice System', *Aboriginal Law Bulletin*, 2: 46 (October).

Payne, S. (1992) 'Aboriginal Women and the Law', in C. Cunneen (ed.) *Aboriginal Perspectives on Criminal Justice*, Sydney: Sydney University Institute of Criminology.

Pettman, J. (1992) *Living In the Margins*, North Sydney: Allen and Unwin.

Read, P. (1984) *The Stolen Generations*, Sydney: New South Wales Ministry of Aboriginal Affairs.

Scutt, J. (1990) 'Invisible Women: Projecting White Cultural Invisibility on Black Australian Women', *Aboriginal Law Bulletin*, 2: 46 (October).

Selfe, J. and Thomas, C. (1992) 'Aboriginal Women and the Law', paper presented at the Australian Institute of Criminology Conference, *Aboriginal Justice Issues*, Cairns, 23-25 June, 1992.

Strang, H. (1992) *Homicide in Australia 1990-1991*, Canberra: Australian Institute of Criminology.

Thomas, C. (1991) 'Addressing the Concerns of Aboriginal Women', in *Local Domestic Violence Committees Conference, Papers and Proceedings*, NSW Domestic Violence Committee, Sydney: NSW Women's Coordination Unit.

Wootten, H. (1989) *Report of the Inquiry into the Death of Malcolm Charles Smith*, Royal Commission into Aboriginal Deaths in Custody, Canberra: Australian Government Publishing Service.

Wyvill, L.F. (1990a) *Report of the Inquiry Into the Death of Barbara Denise Yarrie*, Royal Commission into Aboriginal Deaths in Custody, Canberra: Australian Government Publishing Service.

Wyvill, L.F. (1990b) *Report of the Inquiry Into the Death of Fay Lena Yarrie*, Royal Commission into Aboriginal Deaths in Custody, Canberra: Australian Government Publishing Service.

Wyvill, L.F. (1990c) *Report of the Inquiry Into the Death of Barbara Ruth Tiers*, Royal Commission into Aboriginal Deaths in Custody, Canberra: Australian Government Publishing Service.

Wyvill, L.F. (1990d) *Report of the Inquiry Into the Death of Muriel Gwenda Catheryn Binks*, Royal Commission into Aboriginal Deaths in Custody, Canberra: Australian Government Publishing Service.

Wyvill, L.F. (1990e) *Report of the Inquiry Into the Death of Deidre Abigail Short*, Royal Commission into Aboriginal Deaths in Custody, Canberra: Australian Government Publishing Service.

Yuendumu Women's Night Patrol (1992) *Aboriginal and Islander Health Worker*

Journal, 16: 2, March/April.
Youth Justice Project (1990) *Kids in Justice. A Blueprint for the 90s*, Sydney: Youth Justice Coalition.

Notes

1. Chris Cunneen is a senior lecturer at the Institute of Criminology, Sydney University Law School. He is also a consultant to the Federal Race Discrimination Commissioner. His major areas of interest include juvenile justice, penal policy, policing and the relationship between criminal justice systems and indigenous people. Kate Kerley is a lawyer with the New South Wales Domestic Violence Advocacy Service. She specializes in providing legal representation for women in cases of violence. Her particular interests include feminist legal theory, policing and penal policy, and the relationship of indigenous women to the law.

2. Hereafter the word Aboriginal will be used to refer to both Aboriginal and Torres Strait Islander women.

3. The Australian government established the Royal Commission into Aboriginal Deaths in Custody in 1987 after a long campaign by Aboriginal activists to get the issue of indigenous deaths in custody on the political agenda. The Royal Commission issued an Interim Report to government in 1988 and the Final Report in 1991. The Commission also reported separately on 99 Aboriginal and Torres Strait Islander deaths in custody which occurred between 1 January 1980 and 31 May 1989.

4. The women who died in police custody were Barbara Yarrie (Wyvill 1990a); Fay Yarrie (Wyvill 1990b); Barbara Tiers (Wyvill 1990c); Muriel Binks (Wyvill 1990d); Deidre Short (Wyvill 1990e); 'Woman At Ceduna' (Johnston 1990a); Joyce Egan (Johnston 1990b); Christine Jones (O'Dea 1990a); Faith Barnes (O'Dea 1990c).

5. Eggleston (1976: 16) noted that in the mid 1960s 'Aborigines comprise 22% of the male prison population but 64% of the female prison population [in Western Australia] ... A similar pattern may be observed in South Australia'.

6. The maximum security women's prison in New South Wales.

V Race, gender, and the sentencing process in a New Zealand District Court

Heather Deane[1]

Introduction

For some time concern has been expressed around the world about the over-representation of black and indigenous people in criminal justice statistics when compared with their numbers in the general population. Despite many studies which have attempted to explain this phenomenon, the results have been mixed, and often contradictory. Some have found judicial discretion in sentencing has led to discrimination in the courts, while others have found that legally relevant factors can satisfactorily explain the disproportionate numbers in the criminal justice statistics.

Women compared with men are disproportionately under-represented in criminal justice statistics. Traditionally it has been assumed that women are treated more leniently than men; they are thought to be less likely than men to be arrested, convicted and sentenced to prison. If women are treated more leniently than men, is it because of their sex, or is it for other reasons? Recent feminist writers have suggested that women are not necessarily treated more leniently than men, but that they are treated differently from men and that factors such as various social characteristics play an important role in the sentencing of women but not of men.

The primary aim of this essay is to investigate whether the race and gender of defendants is related to sentencing independently of other variables. Firstly, some overseas literature which is relevant to this discussion is reviewed and secondly these issues are considered in relation to sentencing in one district court in New Zealand. The data used have been collected from court files and the results reported here are based on the first analysis of a small sample of a much wider study covering the Wellington area over a number of years.

The sentencing task is seen as one which is complex. When making a decision, the Judge usually takes into account a number of factors. Not only are such factors as the nature and seriousness of the offence and the offender's previous convictions to be considered, but also to be weighed and balanced are the competing purposes of punishment, the circumstances surrounding the offence and the characteristics of the offender. The Judge has wide discretion to select the sentence which, within the bounds of the law, best does justice to the offender, the victim and the community alike.

Different approaches to sentencing have developed over the years with different emphasis being given from time to time to a variety of factors considered important in reaching sentencing decisions. Distinctions have been drawn between the influence of legal and extra-legal factors in sentencing decisions (Hagan: 1973). Briefly, legal variables directly relate to those factors which are legally relevant to the case, such as the nature and seriousness of the offence and the prior criminal record. This is sometimes called the Justice or Tariff model. The penalty is determined in a fairly standard way to be commensurate with the degree of seriousness of the offence and the prior criminal record. Little attention is paid to the circumstances of the individual or to the role of extra-legal factors such as race, age, gender, occupation and personal circumstances.

In contrast is, what is sometimes called, the individualized approach to sentencing. Whilst not discounting the strictly legal factors, this approach also takes into account extra-legal offender-related factors, such as those mentioned above, which are thought to be relevant to the case. This approach is much more likely to be adopted when the court is considering a sentence of, for example, incapacitation or rehabilitation. This latter approach has been called into question by some writers because it is seen as a form of unequal treatment which can lead to disparity in sentencing decisions.

Historically, research into sentencing concentrated on male offenders and was based on official criminal statistics. Criminal statistics provide an aggregate overview of sentencing in relation to such basic facts as type of offence, age, sex and particular sentences. They do not explain, however, how sentencing decisions are made at the level of individual cases or the reasons behind apparent variations in sentencing.

Since the 1970's there has been a growing awareness of the need for more detailed information about the sentencing process and the factors which are taken into account by the court. As a result of increasingly sophisticated research methodologies, sentencing studies have begun to draw distinctions between legal and extra-legal factors in sentencing decisions and these studies have found that differential emphasis on extra-legal factors can influence sentencing outcomes[2].

Race and gender are two such issues and the focus on them has been sharpened by the awareness of the political disadvantages that can be experienced by blacks in white societies, by indigenous groups in countries that have been transformed by colonization, and by women compared to men. It is therefore not surprising that race and/or gender have become the focus of sentencing studies.

Race and sentencing

Race has been a major issue in American criminological research for some time. The concern has been centred on the severe disproportionality between blacks and whites in the composition of the prison population. Blacks make up approximately one-eighth of the general population compared with about 50% of the prison population. Consequently there have been many studies on sentencing in the USA and they have produced varying conclusions. Some suggest that legal factors relating to the offence can satisfactorily explain the over-representation of black people in the criminal justice system. See, for example, Green (1961) and Hagan (1974). However, more recent writers disagree. Unnever (1980) found that the race of the defendant had a marked effect on sentence and other studies[3] have shown that extra-legal variables can affect sentencing decisions.

Similarly, in Britain, earlier studies relating to racial factors in sentencing, all carried out in the 1980's and based on small samples, reached similar conclusions to the earlier American studies (Crow and Cove 1984, McConville and Baldwin 1982). Later studies offered a different view. A British Home Office Bulletin dated 10 March 1989 stated that 'differences in sentencing between ethnic groups, in particular the high use of custody for blacks, may be explained partly in terms of differences in the type of offences for which they are prosecuted'. It inferred, however, that other, unspecified, factors might also be important. In support, Voakes and Fowler (1989) in their West Yorkshire Probation Service survey found that the greater use of immediate custody for black offenders was partly due to the judiciary using custody more frequently for black offenders than white at all levels of offence seriousness. Hood's research (1992), which is the largest and most recent British study on race and sentencing to date, found that (in five Crown courts in the West Midlands) black (Afro-Caribbean) adult males were dealt with more severely than whites or Asians. The study, which tested and controlled for many different variables, also found that the over-representation of black men in prison could be attributed in part (80%) to legal variables, i.e. the number appearing in court for sentence and the nature and legal characteristics of the case; and 20% to differential treatment in the courts.

There have been comparatively few sentencing studies investigating the reasons why indigenous peoples are markedly over-represented in criminal justice statistics. However, a study undertaken by Feimer et al (1990) involving white and Native Americans in South Dakota prisons found prior felonies was the only common variable that accounted for differences in punishment severity although a variety of independent variables was tested. The writers thought it was unlikely that there was generalized disparate treatment towards Native Americans based solely on racial differences. They suggested that the reason for the disproportionate representation of Native Americans in prison may be related to different patterns of behaviour, such as problems connected with alcoholism, poverty and unemployment.

Lewis (1989) in Canada examined sentencing practices in summary conviction courts over a nine-month period in 1988. In contrast to the previous study he found that being single, unemployed, of Native ancestry and residing 'off-reserve' were factors which influenced sentencing. Unemployed individuals of Native ancestry, residing 'off-reserve' were sentenced to prison more often than those of non-Native ancestry, even when controlling for nature of the offence and previous convictions.

Gender and sentencing

Traditional research based on official statistics suggested that women were dealt with more leniently than men, for example, that women were more likely than men to be given probation or discharges and less likely than men to be given prison sentences (Mannheim 1965, Walker 1968). However, the statistics do not tell us why this occurs. Morris (1988) argues that they show not that women are being dealt with more leniently than men, but rather that women are being dealt with *differently* from men. Morris suggests that these differences may occur because of the sex of the defendants. However, they may also occur for other reasons: for example, women may be less criminally experienced than men, have fewer prior convictions than men or commit offences of different levels of seriousness than men. Any of these factors could explain differences in sentencing patterns between women and men.

The impetus and increasing interest in women's studies in the 1980's has brought with it a stream of feminist criminology. Writers such as Morris (1988), Carlen (1983, 1985), Eaton (1986) and Worrall (1990) in Britain, and Adler (1975) and Leonard (1982) in the USA are but a few who have made considerable contributions to our awareness of stereotypical conceptions of women and their impact upon the criminal justice system. They have shown that, in the sentencing of non-routine cases, it is essential to look beyond the variables of seriousness of the offence and prior convictions (legal variables) to other factors such as economic situation, drug and alcohol dependency and those described earlier (extra-legal variables). Such factors appear to be influential in explaining differential treatment between men and women.

Farrington and Morris (1983), using court records, examined 408 cases of theft which included 110 women to investigate whether the sex of the defendant was related to sentencing independently of other variables. They found that while some factors, such as previous convictions and the seriousness of offence influenced sentence severity for both men and women as expected, some other factors were influential only when women were sentenced. For example, marital security, stable family background and children were more important for sentencing of women than of men and resulted in more lenient treatment of women. In contrast, women who were divorced or separated received relatively severe sentences. Nagel (1981) and many other writers since, have also found that being married had more 'advantages' for a woman being sentenced than for a man and that married women were less likely than unmarried women to spend time in prison.

Race and gender

Daly's (1989) Seattle study considered the interaction in sentencing between race and gender and extra-legal variables (that is, the offender's work history, age, family situation, marital status and family ties). Rather than finding that the mitigating effects of family ties or dependents were similar for all groups of offenders, it was principally for black women that such effects were strong and consistent. In 1989 LaPrairie's study showed that the disproportionate involvement of Aboriginal women in the Canadian criminal justice system was related to the type of offences committed by the women. In Kingston Prison, Canada's federal prison for women, 70% of Aboriginal women were committed for violent offences, compared with 32% of non-Aboriginal women. The study also found that Aboriginal women were more likely to be arrested for non-payment of fines than non-Aboriginal women.

Hood (1992) devoted one chapter of his book on race and sentencing to women. Even so, his sample of women was relatively small. As he says, there are very few British studies on women and none so far comparing black and white woman. His study covered Crown courts in the West Midlands and found that there were no significant differences between the chances of a black woman compared with a white women receiving a custodial sentence. There was also no evidence to support the hypothesis that women are treated more leniently than men, rather it was found that the considerable over-representation of black women in custody was due entirely to the number appearing before the courts and the legally relevant characteristics of their cases.

New Zealand study

To date there has been little examination in New Zealand of the effect of race or gender on adult sentencing. Apart from a small study by Sutherland et al (1973) on the effect of a legal aid scheme for Maori offenders in the Nelson Court, the major contribution in the area of race has been Moana Jackson's (1987 and 1988) work. The results of his extensive survey provide a very important contribution towards the explanation and understanding of Maori offending.

The New Zealand official crime statistics show that the rates of imprisonment of Maori men and women far exceed those of Pakeha New Zealanders[4]. The 1986 census statistics taken from the *New Zealand Official Yearbook* 1990 (New Zealand Department of Statistics, 1990) show that there were then 3.3 million people living in New Zealand, of whom half were male and half were female. Of the total population, approximately 12% were Maori. These proportions can be compared with the District Court statistics for 1987, which show that, of the 5,000 Maori and European men and women sentenced to custodial detention, 53% were Maori and 7% were women. When we look at court sentencing statistics, similar trends are apparent. With respect to men, Maori are clearly over-represented, particularly in the custodial population where they make up 53%. Maori women are even more over-represented. They outnumber Pakeha women in all penal categories; for example, they make up 65% of those sentenced to custody, 59% of those sentenced to periodic detention, 51% of those sentenced to supervision or community service and 50% of those fined.[5]

How can such disproportionate numbers occur in a supposedly fair and equitable legal system? Previous overseas research has shown that the racial disparity is not simply a consequence of sentencing disproportionately. There are various points in the criminal justice system where racial minority groups may be disadvantaged, such as at the point of police arrest. Writers like Hood (1992) and Walker (1987) have suggested over-representation in prison may be the result of an accumulation of small 'race effects' at different stages of the criminal process. Nevertheless the simple statistics quoted above show a disparate representation of Maori among different types of sentences. Inevitably this leads to the question of whether or not sentencing itself plays a part in accounting for the disproportionate numbers of Maori in the criminal justice system.

Method

Information for this essay was collected from the court files of one District Court, the district of which covered a population of approximately 46,000 made up of 13% Maori and 18% Pacific Island people. In 1989, this court was presided over, in the main, by a resident judge who had been sitting there for several years.

The sample

Because of the intention to focus on gender as well as race, the sample was limited by selecting only those offence categories where women are most frequently convicted. The sample comprised every adult person, male and female, who was sentenced in 1989 for the following offences in the District Court selected for this study.

1. Unlawful taking of property. The following theft offences within this category were included: theft from the person; theft as a servant; other theft by persons in a position of trust; shoplifting; other theft; and receiving.
2. Fraud and false pretences.
3. All drug offences.

In 1989, in the selected District Court, a total of 362 individuals were sentenced for the above offences. The total was made up of 149 (41%) Maori, 149 (41%) Pakeha, 61 (17%) Pacific Islanders and 3 (1%) others.

Maori and Pakeha only were included in the analysis for this essay[6] and they numbered 298 (82%).

Because the offences were generally regarded as being of relatively minor seriousness it was not anticipated that many in the sample would be likely to be sentenced to full custody. The 1985 *Criminal Justice Act* encourages the use of non-custodial sentences for property offences, so that it was of considerable interest to investigate the use the court made of the various community-based sentences available.

Over the last five years in New Zealand many treatment programmes and community service placements have been developed and some have been developed especially by Maori for Maori. Thus the Court is offered an opportunity to utilize community-based Maori programmes if desired. Wellington city and its environs is well serviced with such programmes.

Table 5.1 sets out the number of men and women, Maori and Pakeha, that came into the sample.

Table 5.1 Race and gender of the sample; numbers and percentages

	Maori		Pakeha		Total N
Female	68	(46%)	54	(36%)	122
Male	81	(54%)	95	(64%)	176
Total %		(100%)		(100%)	
Total N	149		149		

The table above shows that the sample clearly replicates the findings of criminal justice statistics which show that Maori are over-represented compared with Pakeha (50% of the sample were Maori compared with only 13% in the population of the area) and that men are over-represented compared with women (59% were male compared with an expected 50%). It also shows that, among Maori, a larger percentage were womcen (46%) than among Pakeha (36%) but in this particular sample the difference does not reach statistical significance.[7]

Data collection

The data was collected by examining the full court file on each case. The court file contained the CRN Information sheet giving brief details of the charge(s), brief details of the defendant, (age, race[8], occupation and sex); the police summary of facts, the list of previous convictions and sentences, the pre-sentence report and other reports, such as medical reports; and how each case was dealt with by the court.

As well, information about the social background, personal characteristics, and any presenting problems of each defendant were recorded when available. In many cases files were incomplete, particularly with respect to personal information concerning family circumstances and lifestyle.

Analysis of data[9]

The offence

The dishonesty offences selected for this study were grouped as follows:
· Shoplifting
· Receiving
· Fraud and forgery
· Other theft

The drug offences were grouped into:
· Simple cannabis possession
· Cultivate or sell cannabis
· All class B drug offences
· Other drug offences[10]

More serious cases falling into the above categories are not sentenced in the District Court where the maximum penalty for an indictable offence may not exceed three years imprisonment or a fine of $4,000, or both. Instead, they are dealt with in the High Court. This further restricted the sample to more 'routine' offences.

Table 5.2 shows the frequency of convictions for the selected offences. Overall, shoplifting (38%) was the most commonly occurring offence, whilst the defendants with possession of cannabis convictions made up 25% of the sample.

Table 5.2 Frequency of convictions for selected offences; men and women; percentages: N = 269*

	Male	Female
Shoplifting	27	55
Receiving	8	4
Fraud and forgery	11	15
Other theft	11	8
Simple cannabis possession	34	13
Cultivate or sell cannabis	4	5
All B class drug offences	4	1
Other drug offences	1	0

*   Offenders committing more than one type of offence have been ommitted.

There were two important differences in the offending patterns for men and women. More men were charged and convicted with drug offences and more women were charged and convicted with dishonesty offences. Men were significantly more likely than women to be convicted of simple cannabis possession; 79% of those convicted were men and only 21% were women[11]. In contrast, women were significantly more likely than men to be convicted of shoplifting: 58% of those convicted of shoplifting were women and only 42% were men[12]. There were no significant differences between races.

Description of defendants

Age at sentence

Table 5.3 sets out the percentages of men and women in each age group. Most of the sample were under the age of 30 years; 73% of men and 69% of women. The largest group were between 20 and 24 (35% of both men and women). There was a tendency for more of the men to be in the under 20 age group and for more of the women to be over 25.

Table 5.3 Age and gender of the sample; percentages: N = 298

Age group	Male %	Female %	Total N
15-19	20	13	
20-24	35	35	
25-29	18	21	
30-34	16	16	
35+	11	15	
Total N	176	122	298
Total %	100	100	

There were no significant differences with respect to race for either men or women in age distribution.

Previous convictions

First offenders formed the largest group. Of the total sample, 22% had no previous convictions and as might be expected from overseas research, two thirds of this group were women and there were 18% more Pakeha men and women than Maori[13]. A further 10% had only one previous conviction while the remaining two thirds had at least two.

It was only in the range of ten or more prior convictions that Maori men outnumbered Pakeha men and then only slightly. By contrast, Maori women with two or more prior convictions outnumbered Pakeha women by almost double.

Employment

The employment status of the defendant is recorded by the police and at the time of arrest only about a quarter (26%) of the defendants were in employment[14]. A further 38% were unemployed, nearly a quarter (22%) were domestic purposes beneficiaries and the rest were on other welfare benefits, usually the sickness benefit.

There were considerable differences between men and women. Figures 5.1 and 5.2 and Table 5.4 set out the employment patterns and show that men were more than twice as likely to be employed as women, a difference which was statistically significant.[15] In addition, the type of beneficiary status was different for men and women; men were more likely to be on an unemployment benefit while women were more likely to be on the domestic purposes benefit (DPB) which is available to sole parents.

Figure 5.1 Employment patterns of sample

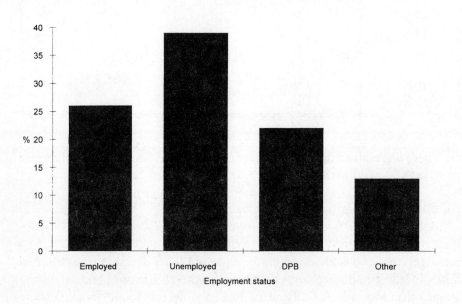

Table 5.4 Employment and gender; numbers and percentages:
N = 298

	Employed	Unemployed	DPB	Other[16]	Total N
Male	59 (34%)	88 (50%)	9 (5%)	20 (11%)	176
Female	17 (14%)	27 (22%)	57 (47%)	21 (17%)	122
Total	76 (26%)	115 (38%)	66 (22%)	41 (14%)	298

Figure 5.2 Patterns of employment and gender

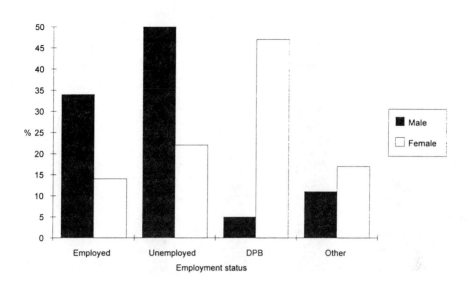

Table 5.5 and Figure 5.3 set out the employment patterns for Maori compared with Pakeha. Again there is a difference; more Pakeha than Maori were in employment and this difference is significant.[17]

Table 5.5 Employment and race;
numbers and percentages: N = 298

	Employed	Unemployed	DPB	Other	Total N
Maori	28 (19%)	65 (44%)	38 (26%)	18 (12%)	149
Pakeha	48 (32%)	50 (34%)	28 (19%)	23 (15%)	149

Figure 5.3 Patterns of employment and race

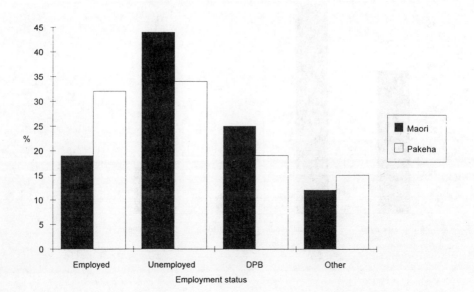

Marital status

The data on marital status are problematic as the Police record this
information at the time of arrest. It appears from pre-sentence reports and
court observation that it is not unusual for the defendant to have themselves
recorded as single, even if in a *defacto* relationship. Therefore, the number
of unpartnered defendants is likely to be over-represented. Further, the
marital status of a defendant can and does change by the time of sentence.
However, in cases where a pre-sentence report had been prepared for the
defendant it was possible to ascertain the correct marital status of the
defendant. Figure 5.4 sets out the marital status of the sample. Most have
been recorded as single; 60% of men and 40% of women. There were no
significant differences with respect to race for either men or women in
marital status distribution.

Children

Official data relating to children are not recorded on court files. However, nearly 50% of the women (compared with 5% of men) were recorded as receiving the Domestic Purposes Benefit, thus signifying that they were caring for dependant children. There was little difference in the proportion of Maori and Pakeha women who were receiving this welfare benefit.

Figure 5.4 Marital status of the sample; N = 298

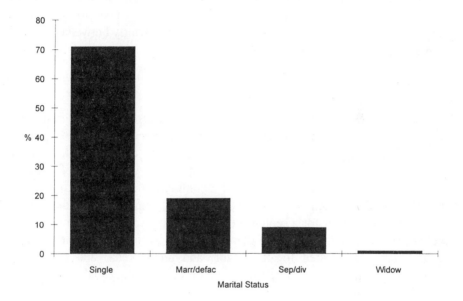

Pre-sentence reports

The pre-sentence report is the major source of objective information about each individual defendant available to the court. If it seems clear to the court that problems such as drug or alcohol addiction, gambling, family or other factors may be underlying the offending, then the judge may decide to order a report. It is also usual for a report to be written for any defendant facing a term of imprisonment.   Judges who are more inclined to take individual factors into account rather than simply using legal variables, are more likely to call for a pre-sentence report.

As well as giving background information to the court, pre-sentence reports also offer sentencing recommendations which may or may not be followed by the court.   Much has been written in the overseas literature about the effect of the pre-sentence report upon sentencing and this issue has been investigated in terms of race and gender with varying results (Eaton 1986; Jackson and Smith 1987; Gelsthorpe 1992; Mair and Brockington 1988 and LaPrairie 1990).

Full pre-sentence reports were requested in less that a quarter (22%) of the sample.   This was a relatively small number.   The probability of requesting a pre-sentence report did not differ significantly between men and women or between Maori and Pakeha.

Requests for other reports

In New Zealand, the court may also request shorter reports from Community Corrections (formerly known as the Probation Service).   These usually eliminate information about the background of the defendant and simply focus on, for example, the details of reparation and whether the defendant is in a position to pay; or the details of a community service or community care placement if such a placement has been found for the defendant. Reports on suitability for a sentence of community service were much more likely to be requested for women than men, with twenty community service reports being requested for ten Maori and ten Pakeha, and two being requested for Maori men.   Few 'other reports' were requested.

Impact of the recommendations of reports

There were 75 (25%) defendants for whom pre-sentence or community service reports were ordered by the court.[18]   The court followed the recommendations of the report for 48 defendants or 64% of the cases in which a recommendation was made.   However, overall, in this sample, the pre-sentence reports influenced a relatively small proportion of cases in this court in 1989.   There were no significant differences with respect to the likelihood that report recommendations were followed for either Maori or Pakeha, men or women.

The sentence

Table 5.6 shows clearly that more defendants were sentenced to a fine than to any other type of sentence. Fines represented 47% of the total number of sentences imposed. Fifty percent of those fined were men and 43% were women. Pakeha men were fined more often than Maori although Maori women were fined more than Pakeha.

Figure 5.5 Remand status of the sample; N = 298

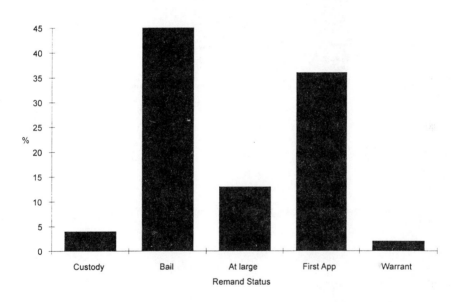

Remand status immediately prior to sentence

Figures 5.5, 5.6 and 5.7 refer to the remand status of the sample and show that more than one-third of the sample (37%) were sentenced on their first appearance in the court for the current offence. They appeared to be dealt with in a fairly routine way, usually by way of a fine and one-third of this group were female. Nearly half of the sample were on bail and most of the others were at large. Nine men had been held in custody, four of whom were Maori and five Pakeha, and one Maori and one Pakeha woman also had been held in custody. Thus men were more likely to be held in custody than women but there were no significant ethnic differences.

Figure 5.6 Patterns of remand by gender

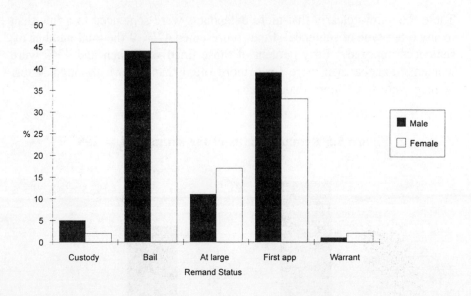

Figure 5.7 Patterns of remand by race

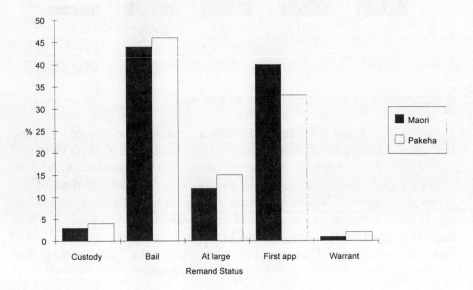

**Table 5.6 Frequency distribution of sentences;
numbers and percentages;[19] N = 298**

	N	%
Prison	20	6
Periodic Detention	63	19
Supervision (Probation)	26	8
Community Service Order	20	6
Reparation	34	10
Fine	140	41
Order to come up if called upon	29	9
Convicted and discharged	4	1
Discharged without conviction	6	2

Significantly[20] more men than women were sentenced to Periodic Detention. However, there were no significant differences with respect to race. Significantly[21] more women were sentenced to Community Service and 75% of the women were Maori. Slightly more men (14%) than women (8%) wereordered to pay reparation. There were no differences with respect to race. Ten percent of the defendants were ordered to come up if called upon (a type of conditional discharge). There were significantly[22] more women (14%) than men (7%) in this group and no race differences were found. Few defendants were sentenced to imprisonment and there was little difference found between Maori (8%) and Pakeha (5%). However, many more men than women were sentenced to imprisonment (75% to 25%) but given the small numbers in this particular sample the difference did not reach statistical significance.

In order to determine what variables were affecting the sentencing a stepwise multiple regression[23] was carried out on each of the most common types of offence, namely shoplifting and simple possession of cannabis. The variables included in the equation were race, sex, number of current convictions and number of previous convictions. The results showed that none of these variables had a significant impact in predicting the sentence for possession of cannabis. However, for shoplifting the number of previous convictions did make a significant contribution to predicting the sentence; the multiple correlation was 0.38.[24]

Discussion

The study examined sentencing of men and women, Maori and Pakeha, in one New Zealand district court. This was busy court, with a high volume of work, and for most of the period under study it was presided over by the same judge. Most of the sample were young, unemployed, and single and nearly one-quarter were first offenders.

The results show that the court generally dealt with the defendants in an equitable manner, and that in about 75% of the cases a justice/tariff model of sentencing was applied. At least one-third of the sample was sentenced in a routine way, that is, they were sentenced on their first appearance in the court. Relatively minor offences received relatively minor penalties by way of fines. Those in employment who were convicted of a more serious offence (such as a more serious drug charge or a serious fraud), tended to be fined and they received a heavier fine. One-third of the defendants were sentenced to community-based sentences. The unemployed men and women convicted of more serious offences and with several previous convictions tended to be sentenced to periodic detention. Significantly more men than women received this penalty. In contrast, significantly more women than men received a community service order. This could have been because the court considered it to be a more suitable sentence for women as it is less physically demanding. Community service is also an appropriate penalty for defendants who have little money to pay fines and it is suitable as well for those who may, in the court's view, benefit from a rehabilitative penalty.

This study found no evidence of discrimination between Maori and Pakeha. However there was some evidence that women may have been treated more leniently. This could have been reflecting the fact that a large proportion of the sample had been convicted of minor offences and that many of the female defendants were either first offenders or had only one previous conviction. Those men and women in the sample who received a more severe penalty had committed more serious offences and generally had more than one previous conviction. Their sentences were different for these reasons, irrespective of their race, gender, employment situation or marital status. In contrast with the overseas studies cited earlier, this study has not demonstrated evidence of differential sentencing based on extra-legal factors.

It is difficult to draw conclusions from the small sample and the limited court file data presented here. However, it is possible that if more defendant-related information had been available, for example, the details contained in pre-sentence reports, quite a different picture might have emerged. It is likely that other courts and others judges behave differently.

This is only the first data from a more extensive study which will include data from other courts in other years and information from court observations as well as court files. Already it is clear that no simple, single hypothesis about race and gender is likely to provide explanations in sentencing across different courts, times and judges.[25]

References

Adler, F. (1975) *Sisters in Crime*, New York: McGraw-Hill.

Carlen, Pat (1983) *Women's Imprisonment: a Study in Social Control,* London: Routledge and Kegan Paul.

Carlen, Pat (ed.) (1985) *Criminal Women: Autobiographical Accounts*, Cambridge: Polity Press.

Crow, Iain and Cove, Jill (1984) 'Ethnic Minorities and the Courts', *Criminal Law Review*, July, 413-417.

Daly, Kathleen (1989) 'Neither Conflict nor Labeling nor Paternalism will Suffice: Intersections of Race, Ethnicity, Gender, and Family in Criminal Court Decisions', *Crime and Delinquency*, 35: 1, January, 136-168.

Eaton, Mary (1986) *Justice for Women? Family, Court and Social Control,* Milton Keynes: Oxford University Press.

Farrington, David and Morris, Allison (1983) Sex, Sentencing and Reconviction, *British Journal of Criminology*, 23: 3, July, 229-248.

Feimer, S. and others (1990) Marking time: Does Race make a Difference? A Study of Disparate Sentencing in South Dakota, *Journal of Crime and Justice*, XIII: 1, 86-101.

Gelsthorpe, Loraine (1992) 'Race and Gender Considerations in the Preparation and Interpretation of Reports for the Court', *Home Office Research Bulletin*, 31.

Green, Edward (1961) *Judicial Attitudes in Sentencing,* London: Macmillan and Co.

Hagan, J. (1974) 'Extra-Legal Attributes and Criminal Sentencing: an Assessment of a Sociological Viewpoint', *Law and Society Review*, 8: 357-383.

Hagan, John and Bumiller, Kristin (1983) 'Making Sense of Sentencing: a Review and Critique of Sentencing Research, in Alfred Blumstein et al (eds), *Research on Sentencing: the Search for Reform,* 2, Washington, D.C.: National Academy Press.

Hall, Geoffrey G. (1987) *Sentencing in New Zealand*, Wellington: New Zealand: Butterworths.

Home Office (1989) 'The Ethnic Group of Those Proceeded Against or Sentenced by the Courts in the Metropolitan Police Districts in 1984 and 1985', *Statistical Bulletin 10th March,* Croydon, Surrey: United Kingdom Government Statistical Services.

Hood, Roger (1992) *Race and Sentencing,* Oxford: Clarendon Press.

Jackson, Hilary and Smith, Lorna (1987) 'Female Offenders: an Analysis of Social

Inquiry Reports', *Home Office Research Bulletin*, 23, London.

Jackson, Moana (1988) 'The Maori and the Criminal Justice System. A New Perspective: He Whaipaanga Hou. Part 2' *Department of Justice, Policy and Research Division* Study Series 18, Wellington, Government Printer.

LaPrairie, Carol (1989) 'Some Issues in Aboriginal Justice Research: the Case of Aboriginal Women in Canada', *Women and Criminal Justice,* 1: 1, 81-91.

LaPrairie, Carol (1990) 'The Role of Sentencing in the Over-Representation of Aboriginal People in Correctional Institutions', *Canadian Journal of Criminology*, July, 429-440.

Leonard, E. (1982) *Women, Crime and Society*, New York: Longman.

Lewis, Dave (1989) *An Exploratory study in Sentencing Practice in Summary Courts in British Columbia,* Vancouver: Legal Services Society, (unpublished).

Mair, George and Brockington, Nicola (1988) 'Female Offenders and the Probation Service', *The Howard Journal*, 27: 2 May, 117-126.

McConville, Michael and Baldwin, John (1982) 'The Influence of Race on Sentencing in England', *Criminal Law Review*, October, 652-658.

Mannheim, Herman (1965) *Comparative Criminology,* London: Routledge and Kegan Paul.

Morris, Allison (1987) *Women, Crime and Justice*, Oxford: Basil Blackwell.

Morris, Allison (1988) 'Women in the Criminal Justice System', *Prison Service Journal*, 70: 2-4, 22.

Sutherland, O. R. W. et al (1973) 'Justice and Race: a Monocultural System in a Multicultural Society', *New Zealand Race Relations Council,* Annual Conference.

Unnever, James D. (1980) 'Race Differences in Criminal Sentencing', *The Sociological Quarterly*, 21, Spring, 197-205.

Voakes, Rob and Fowler, Q. (1989) *Sentencing, Race and Social Inquiry Reports*, West Yorkshire Probation Service.

Von Hirsch, A. (1976) *Doing Justice: the Choice of Punishments*, New York: Hill and Wang.

Walker, John (1987) 'Prison Cells with Revolving Doors: a Judicial or Societal Problem?', in Kayleen M. Hazlehurst (ed.), *Ivory Scales: Black Australia and the Law*, Sydney: New South Wales University Press.

Walker, Nigel (1968) *Crime and Punishment in Britain*, Edinburgh: University Press.

Worrall, Anne (1990) *Offending Women*, London: Routledge.

Zatz, Marjorie S. (1987) 'The Changing Forms of Racial/Ethnic Biases in Sentencing', *Journal of Research in Crime and Delinquency*, 24: 1, February, 69-92.

Notes

1. Heather Deane is currently a Ph.D. student at the Institute of Criminology, Victoria University of Wellington, Wellington, New Zealand. Formerly a probation officer, she completed a MA in 1985 and her major research interests relate to prisons, drugs and crime and sentencing.
2. See, for example, Chiricos and Waldo (1975) for the influence of socio-economic status on sentencing.
3. See Hagan, J., Bumiller, K. (1983) and Zatz, Marjorie (1987).
4. 'Pakeha' refers to anyone of European origin.
5. In New Zealand there are a number of commmunity-based options. If ordered to serve a term of 'Periodic Detention', the offender must attend a work centre for up to 15 hours per week for a period no longer than 12 months. The work under the supervision of a warden is usually carried out on weekends. 'Supervision' (probation) is primarily for offenders who are considered to be at risk of further offending without some form of intervention. Under the supervision/guidance of a probation officer, the offender is offered assistance to address current problems identified by the court. The assistance can be in the form of, for example, counselling, drug and alcohol treatment, or a course in anger management. With the consent of the offender, the court can order the offender to undertake 'Community Service' for no less than 20 hours and up to 200 hours over a 12-month period. Community Service work is co-ordinated by a probation officer. The impact and severity of these sentences, all alternatives to imprisonment, can be severe and they ought not to be regarded as minor penalties.
6. Maori and European data only are used here. The remaining ethnic categories have not been included because of small numbers.
7. $\chi 2 = 2.72$; d.f. $= 1$; p $< .10$.
8. The definition of Maori was problematic. The ethnicity of the defendant is classified by the police who usually include as Maori all those who appear to be Maori or have a Maori name. Those Maori with European appearance and name will usually not be included and conversely, some who appear to be Maori but identify themselves culturally as European may be.
9. Statview package was used for the data analysis.
10. Those defendants convicted of an offence from more than one of the above offence categories were excluded.
11. $\chi 2 = 14.061$; d.f. $= 1$; p $< .001$.
12. $\chi 2 = 25.948$; d.f. $= 1$; p $< .001$.
13. $\chi 2 = 4.611$; d.f. $= 1$; p $< .05$.
14. This number is problematic as the defendant's employment status can, and frequently does, change by the time of sentence.
15. $\chi 2 = 135.4$; d.f. $= 7$; p $< .001$).

16. Other included retired, housewife, sickness beneficiary, student.
17. $\chi2=14$;   d.f.$=7$;   p$<.05$.
18. Discrepancies in numbers occur because more than one report was ordered for some defendants.
19. Multiple sentences of defendants have been included.
20. $\chi2=6.435$;   d.f.$=1$;   p$<.01$.
21. $\chi2=13.528$;   d.f.$=1$;   p$<.001$.
22. $\chi2=4.154$;   d.f.$=1$;   p$<.05$.
23. The stepwise multiple regression used here tries out each individual factor included in the analysis in turn as a predictor and then sorts out those which, in order, and uninfluenced by the other factors, are best predictors.
24. A correlation describes the amount of association between two factors. A correlation of 1.00 indicates complete agreement between two factors while a correlation of 0.0 indicates no association whatsoever. In this case the multiple correlation of 0.38 is only a moderate correlation and accounts for 14% of the variance.
25. **Acknowledgements:** I wish to acknowledge the assistance I have received from Dr Gabrielle Maxwell in relation to statistics and Professor Warren Young in commenting on the draft.

VI 'Striking a Balance': Lessons from problem-oriented policing in British Columbia

Gregory Saville and D. Kim Rossmo[1]

The police traditionally deal with the public the way many parents deal with their children. Armed with authority, they have cultivated an omnipotent air, hoping the threat of arrest and punishment would keep things under control. Their bluff has been called (Herman Goldstein, *The New York Times*, 1990a).
A lot of people in the outside community know that a small fragment of police time actually is spent on the adrenalin-churning pursuit of hot-off-the-burner crime. Most of it is devoted to routine patrols, service calls and follow-up investigations at cold crime scenes (Michael Valpy, *The Globe and Mail* 1990).

In the past few years, the police in Canada and in many other Western countries have been called to task for a number of traditionally unchallenged issues. Recently their role, function, and accountability have all been the subject of scrutiny. Changing immigration and demographic patterns, limited municipal and provincial or state resources, and a volatile political climate have all contributed to this increase in scrutiny. Furthermore, demands for police service have been increasing steadily over the past decade (Normandeau and Leighton 1990: 17). This has placed the police in Canadian society at a crossroads. Do they continue responding to calls for service through traditional police patrols or do they cultivate entirely new responses to social problems? This essay deals with the balance that police leaders must strike between these two extremes in our increasingly turbulent environment.
In 1990, Professor Herman Goldstein published *Problem-Oriented*

Policing (1990b) in which he provided practical substance for the current debate about community-based policing. His book documented a set of workable tactics that police officers across North America have been using to incorporate community resources in solving day to day problems with which the police must deal. Unfortunately, this new approach has not solved the organizational difficulties that police managers and line officers must face in implementing problem-oriented methods. This is primarily due to the newness of the approach (despite it's historical roots in policing). The programme described below outlines some of those difficulties, how to circumvent them, and some examples where solutions were actually found.

The state of affairs

The authors of this essay have worked as police patrol officers in central and western Canada and our experiences with problem-oriented approaches are quite different. Saville was assigned as a 'community officer' to a troubled neighbourhood in his city. Two previous officers had spent six months in that neighbourhood and had reduced problems through problem-oriented tactics. Afterwards, however, they were removed from this area due to a 'lack of available manpower'.

No follow-up assessment was conducted and no organizational support was provided to continue this process. This author found that there was no special training to explain how to use problem-solving tactics and, most importantly, no time away from radio calls. In fact, supervisors chastized community officers for taking time away from 'regular' duties and for neglecting to maintain monthly performance standards - standards based on numbers of traffic tickets issued, etc. As a result, this troubled area received little special attention and within a year the problems, and the police workload, had returned to its former level.

On the other side of the country Rossmo, with a partner, was assigned to a particularly troubled neighbourhood as part of a special problem-solving team. This team was provided with the necessary time and flexibility to address the special needs of the area. Members of the team spent a number of months setting their own work schedules and contacting a wide variety of community resources including media, urban planners, social workers, neighbourhood residents, city hall and community groups. They conducted an extensive analysis of both the crimes and the social problems in their area and fashioned tailor-made responses to the problems existing in that neighbourhood (Rossmo and Fisher 1993). Before long problems were being resolved in the area and calls for service dropped off.

Unfortunately the current experience for most police officers across Canada and in other western countries is closer to the former versus the latter. The reason that few inroads have been made with new initiatives, such as problem-oriented policing, relates to the organizational structure of police agencies. As Brown stated ten years ago, 'few municipal police forces have taken positive steps ... to institute and appraise over-all operating efficiency. It has been suggested for example that accountability and measurement of performance in future will not be the number of arrests made but the number of problems solved and the economic use of resources' (1981: 248). A decade later it seems little has changed within most Canadian police departments. We will analyse this structural problem in more detail later, since it is a critical factor affecting implementation.

This essay will first describe the problem-oriented approach and the SARA model.[2] It makes some clarifications that distinguish problem-oriented policing from more typical community-based policing programmes. We outline the British Columbia experience and also document two short case studies where officers from the problem-oriented policing course conducted problem solving projects in their communities. Finally we discuss the implementation hurdles facing police leaders and rank and file officers as they attempt to strike a balance between incident-driven policing and the problem-oriented approach.

A caveat is necessary at this point. The British Columbia problem-oriented policing programme developed and grew over the course of three years and was not, in reality, constructed as such from the beginning. Rather it took shape as it went along, first with the development and testing of a similar approach in Mount Pleasant, a neighbourhood in Vancouver, British Columbia. Lectures on the future of policing were later developed for senior constables in the Police Academy at the Justice Institite of British Columbia. Subsequently these lectures were turned into a day-long problem-oriented training seminar for police supervisors. Some of these supervisors went into the field to test the feasibility of this approach in their own departments and communities. They then brought the results of these problem-oriented projects back to be evaluated by seminar members.

The results of this preliminary work were developed, by the authors, into a two-week training course combining crime prevention and problem-oriented policing. Further, an executive training workshop was run for senior police administrators to explain the concept. Currently, problem-oriented training is being refined into a week-long course seperate from the standard crime prevention lectures. It will be available to a wider police audience, not just to selected crime prevention officers. For convenience, these initiatives have been called a 'programme' although some were coincidental, others were by design, and still others were modified from already existing courses. They are presented here as examples of the unpredictability in the implementation process. A key lesson is that, in spite of this unpredictability, there are still some things implementers can do to enhance the probability of success.

What is problem-oriented policing?

In contemporary urban policing, officers respond to incidents on an individual basis and attempt to solve problems at the scene. The incidents are phoned in by the public, dispatched over the police radio, and responded to by patrol officers. During the past 40 years the 'call for service' has become the mainstay of Canadian urban policing. Such incident-driven policing responds only to the symptoms of problems. The key concept underlying problem-oriented policing is that rather than attack the symptoms of a problem, officers work with a number of people in the community and employ a variety of approaches to deal with the causes of the problem. Many officers will recognize these problem-solving skills as good common sense. But the approaches in problem-oriented policing may have little to do with law enforcement or the *Criminal Code of Canada*. The people involved in problem-solving may not be connected to the criminal justice system.

In problem-oriented policing, officers utilize a four-stage approach to address recurring or serious community problems:

1. *Scanning* - officers identify the actual problem to be solved. The definitions in the *Criminal Code of Canada* may not be useful in this stage. Instead the problem might be a series of connected incidents and repeat nuisance behaviours that result in recurring complaints. Redefining the problem in this way, officers use community and police resources to attack the source of the problem;
2. *Analysis* - identifying the persons involved, the causes of the problem, information about the scene and the timing of the events, are all part of the analysis phase. This phase may be fairly simple, but may also involve a detailed investigation into the many sources of information that exist outside the police records system. Surveys, data analysis, questionnaires, and other forms of research can be included in this phase. This is the most crucial phase of problem-oriented policing and is not typical of the traditional police response;

3. *Response* - this involves tailoring a specific response to the problem situation. This might be a discretionary enforcement zone of zero-tolerance in a particular area or it might include traditional crime prevention programmes. It might involve a number of other inititatives such as environmental modifications to buildings, organizing community groups to tackle a specific issue, educational programmes in neighbourhood schools about the problem, media campaigns, creating recreational activities for youth, or a variety of other strategies. The key is that the response be tailor-made to the problem identified by the officers themselves;

4. *Assessment* - this involves an evaluation of the response to the problem. Unlike typical police actions, it should ideally be developed before implementing the problem-oriented response so that a before/after picture can be assessed. It is at this stage that officers determine if a new response should be developed, if the current response should be modified, or if the problem has been resolved or merely displaced to another area.

This four stage process - scanning, analysis, response and assessment - is frequently called the SARA model and it is a convenient way to envision the operation of a problem-oriented project. The problem-oriented approach does not need to be complex. Often a solution can be quickly developed on a simple problem with a brief analysis and a simple solution. What is important is that the root of the problem be addressed, not just the symptoms of it (Murphy 1992).

What's different about problem-oriented policing?

The most common critique raised during the programme in British Columbia, particularily by senior police administrators, was that problem-oriented policing is no different from other current community policing initiatives. This is incorrect for two key reasons: problem-oriented policing is situational and problem-oriented policing is 'smart' police-work that requires creativity and the time to do it.

1. Problem-oriented policing is situational

Community-based policing has been described as a philosophy for police agencies (Normandeau and Leighton 1990). In spite of this, many police departments claim that they are 'doing' community policing by establishing police storefronts or police/community liaison groups. Police foot patrols, bicycle patrols, Neighbourhood Watch/Blockwatch crime prevention programmes, and even victim services have been placed under the community-based policing umbrella (Normandeau 1991).

These initiatives may have value in themselves, however they *do not* represent a fundamentally different way of 'doing business'. These initiatives are conducted only by a few officers in the community relations section or crime prevention unit. Usually they do not involve the rank and file patrol officer whose job is still seen as responding to incoming calls for service. Additional evidence reinforcing this was provided by some of the police supervisors at the British Columbia executive training workshop. When asked about the 'primary police role', they described it as arresting offenders and enforcing laws, rather than preventing crime or proactively reducing recurring community problems.

Typically, community-based programmes are used in a generic fashion. If a break-in problem arises in a residential neighbourhood, the typical police response today is to dispatch patrol officers who file a report. The complaint is either investigated by the officer at the scene (who might canvass the neighbourhood or search for physical evidence) or is submitted to the general assignment detective office. The assignment detectives might return to the scene when time permits, usually long after any lead is cold. More likely the detective will simply telephone the victim to check for additional information.

This method of 'dialling-a-pinch' has minimal community involvement and is rarely successful. At best, the crime prevention officer might set up a Neighbourhood Watch/Blockwatch programme in that neighbourhood. Rarely is an arrest made. In fact, the average clearance rate for residential break-in's across Canada is less than 20%. In the past, anything higher than this has led to criticisms that police are taking 'creative' licence with their statistics. It is simply not believed by anyone who understands the limits of incident-driven policing that dispatching mobile patrols to break-in calls, along with a detective investigating cold leads long after the event, can effectively solve a majority of our residential break-in problems in urban areas.

Today the community-based approach represents the generic application of a neighbourhood watch or some other crime prevention programme. In the meantime, the uniformed patrol officers continue to return to their patrol vehicles and await the next call. This has become so ingrained in Canadian policing that that it has come to resemble an old police adage. Many officers use a radio code for arriving at the scene of an investigation called 10-7 ('out of service'). When they finish their investigation they report to the dispatcher that they are 10-8 ('in service'). In other words, when they're not available for radio calls they are out-of-service, in spite of the fact that this is where they are actually doing police work that is serving the public. They are in-service when they are available for radio calls but are not actively serving the public at all, other than waiting for the public to call. This is the current state of affairs. There is rarely a balance between alternative responses. It is a one-sided response that offers the community, the victim, and the attending police officer very little satisfaction.

In the problem-oriented approach it is the patrol officers themselves who are responsible for making an appropriate response to the recurring break-in problems in the neighbourhood. They decide whether generic crime prevention programmes are appropriate, or whether there is some specifically local dimension, such as poor lighting, truant students, etc., to the pattern of offences. The officers are given the time necessary to undertake research, to consult widely with the community, and to draw on resources of schools, local planners, lighting engineers, local vendors and neighbourhood groups, in formulating an appropriate crime prevention strategy specific to the neighbourhood. As Clarke points out, the key is small scale solutions applied to specific problem situations: 'in crime prevention, it pays to think small' (Clarke 1991: 5).

2. Problem-oriented policing is 'smart' police-work that requires creativity and time

Goldstein's work in developing the SARA system for problem-solving looks similar to other previously successful police activities. The reason for this is simple. Goldstein has taken the progressive and successful activities of police officers and has documented them. At the same time he states that police bureaucracies typically discourage many of these activies. They are considered 'soft' policing and are often relegated to special crime prevention or community relations units. Even in smaller towns where rural police officers have more oppportunities for flexible problem-solving, generally there is little organizational support or encouragement for rank and file officers to do this kind of policing.

Problem-oriented policing requires that police organizations give explicit support and encouragement for these activies, rather than just implicit permission to do them as long as they don't get in the way of 'real' police work. Goldstein doesn't consider the problem-oriented approach 'soft' policing - he considers it 'smart' policing. It is a sentiment now shared by many participants of the British Columbia problem-oriented policing programme.

During the various stages of the British Columbia programme, input was solicited from police leaders in seminars and workshops. The programme discussions highlighted some critical questions. From this we concluded that police leaders can determine if they are 'doing' problem-oriented policing by answering these five questions about their uniform patrol officers:

Do your officers get credit for it? Does your promotional system still use officer 'efficiency' based on case clearances, court convictions, files closed, quota systems, or performance sheets? In problem-oriented policing credit is afforded to officers who have the capacity to creatively solve problems, to maximize community resources, and to exhibit self-initiative in the solving of seemingly intractable community problems.

Do you have a way of evaluating solutions? Once a series of crimes or problems have apparently been solved, does your agency assess the problem six months or a year later to determine the effectiveness of the solutions? Are proper evaluations, community perception surveys, statistical analysis, and other forms of assessment the regular way of doing 'business'? Problem-oriented policing demands that this research be conducted in order to determine the appropriateness of the solution. Otherwise there is no way to know if the problem was ever actually properly addressed.

Do you focus on effectiveness versus efficiency? Is a thorough analysis conducted on a problem before a policing stategy is attempted? Does this analysis include comprehensive research using a variety of data sources outside of police records? Problem-oriented policing requires careful analysis to identify the root of the problem, otherwise the police response may simply continue to circle around the symptoms of the problem.

Do you give them some slack? Are uniformed officers provided sufficient time and encouragement to tackle the root causes of problems, rather than being told to do this between radio calls? Sufficient time in this context means that, while officers would still remain available to respond to priority 1 (emergency) calls, a concerted effort is made to use other resources to deal with priority 2 and priority 3 (non-emergency) calls. This will help free up officer time for problem-oriented policing since research has shown that most patrol officers in Canada (and in many western countries) spend less than a third of their time dealing with actual crime. A significant amount of their time is spent dealing with community problems or simply waiting for calls to happen (Bayley 1991; Ericson 1982).

Encouragement means that officers are supported in obtaining the necessary expertise and training in order to address their own neighbourhood problems. In problem-oriented policing, officers might seek out special training from urban planners or architects in order to determine what neighbourhood designs are contributing to opportunities for crime. It might mean that officers are working with traffic and road engineers, local driver trainers, auto associations, and the media to determine what factors are contributing to high rates of motor vehicle accidents.

Have you developed an organization where supervisors can participate in problem-solving? This is possibly the most problematic area for police leaders. Leadership qualities in problem-oriented policing do not focus on discipline or control; instead they focus on managing human resources to maximize skill, creativity and job satisfaction (Goldstein 1990b: 148-159). Many participants in the British Columbia programme felt that these were good leadership qualities for any job, but the point is that they are an *absolute necessity* if problem-oriented policing is to succeed. The support of line supervisors and middle managers is crucial, and retraining may be required in many police organizations (Goldstein 1990b: 167-172).

If the answer to any of the above questions is 'no', then it is doubtful that your police agency has made the necessary commitment to problem-oriented policing. With few exceptions, most urban Canadian police agencies have not yet struck this kind of balance between reactive and proactive approaches.

Another way of looking at this level of commitment is to consider the balance that police agencies must strike between their commitment to arrest on one hand (for the criminal justice system), versus community problem-solving on the other (for everyone else). As stated by the director of one Florida police agency committed to problem-oriented policing, 'Give a small boy a hammer and everything begins to look like a nail. So too with police departments ... give police arrest power, and everything begins to look like a crime' (Parker 1990: 22).

The British Columbia problem oriented policing programme

British Columbia has long had a history of innovation in policing and crime prevention. The province is the site of the Tumbler Ridge development, built in 1981 as Canada's first town constructed to the principles of crime prevention through environment design (CPTED).[3]   Additionally, the R.C.M.P. in British Columbia teach one of North America's most extensive training course in CPTED (Brantingham 1989).   This has created an environment where initiatives are frequently encouraged by progressive administrators and government officials.   The adoption of the problem-oriented policing training course for officers across the province is such an example.

In December 1986, the Vancouver Police Department set up the Mount Pleasant Liaison Team to tackle a series of problems in the neighbourhood of Mount Pleasant.   Not the least of these was a dramatic influx of street prostitutes which created an increase in complaints from citizens.   While not initially envisioned as a problem-oriented project, this approach eventually became the framework for the Liaison Team's work.   The lessons of this early project were subsequently incorporated into training lectures at the provincial Police Academy at the Justice Institute of British Columbia by the authors.

In 1990, a short lecture on the future of policing for a symposium on a government discussion paper, the *Policing 2000* report (Normandeau and Leighton 1990) was expanded into a day-long seminar in an advanced constables' course.   During this seminar, problem-oriented policing was introduced together with an assortment of other inititatives including community-based policing, regionalization, and organizational restructuring. In 1991, this was developed into a two-day training session on problem-oriented policing for patrol supervisors in a managers' course.   As part of their coursework, supervisors were required to spend a few months in their own police agencies attempting to apply this approach to problems in their communities.   The response to this project was extremely favourable, in fact, the second case study reported here is one product of that work.   As a result, the Police Academy decided to develop a two week course on problem oriented policing.

Concurrently, the Criminology Research Centre at Simon Fraser University and the Police Academy at the Justice Institute of British Columbia collaborated on a joint initiative to sponsor an executive training session - called the Police Studies Series - for Police Chiefs, senior police administrators, and senior managers from related agencies.   We felt that this format provided the ideal collaborative academic/practitioner environment for introducing the problem-oriented policing concept.   A day long workshop was scheduled as part of the Police Studies Series by the session co-ordinators for January, 1993 with Professor Herman Goldstein as the primary speaker. Professor Goldstein was keen to contribute and participate in this stage of the project and was received with enthusiasm by many of the workshop participants, who included about 70 senior police administrators from across the province, municipal officials and planners, members of the judiciary, media, and the academic community.

Finally, a problem-oriented policing course was conducted during January, 1993 and there was enthusiastic response by the attending officers who included crime prevention officers, storefront officers, community relations officers, and uniform patrol officers. It was intented to encourage this first group of problem-oriented trained officers to conduct projects in their own communities to demonstrate the effectiveness of the approach. Currently these efforts are underway and initial results are encouraging. Two of the projects presented by officers during the British Columbia programme are reported below.

It should be noted that the British Columbia problem-oriented policing programme has, so far, had a number positive outcomes. Within a month of the conclusion of the programme, some of the participants had gone back to their jurisdictions and successfully attacked problems with the new strategies. Others were planning on addressing more complicated situations over the course of the new year. Several of the participants were already in the process of setting up orientation and training sessions in their departments to pass along the ideas, concepts and tactics of problem-oriented policing. Such enthusiasm for the problem-oriented approach is clear evidence of the value seen in its strategies by experienced patrol officers.

In addition to these results, the authors disseminated an evaluation survey to participants after completion of the course. This survey examined the perceptions of officers after training was completed. Their responses provided additional insight into the potential of the problem-oriented approach in contemporary Canadian policing.

Perceptions of officers

Many police administrators, as well as course participants, felt it was crucial to avoid isolating problem-oriented policing practitioners from mainstream rank and file officers. There should not just be a problem-oriented policing 'bureau', or a specially-trained problem-oriented policing officer in each detachment/agency. It is important that every officer utilize this approach as part of his or her repertoire for day-to-day police work.

Furthermore, of approximately 50 officers who were exposed to problem-oriented training, only one officer felt that it was inapplicable in his police agency. But while officers felt the approach was appropriate and useful, it was interesting to note that half of those surveyed believed that problem-oriented policing was 'not the normal way of doing business' within their own police agencies. An additional 6% felt that a problem-oriented approach was never used at all in their agency. This seemed to dispel the myth that problem-oriented policing was 'the same old thing'.

There were a number of successful problem-oriented exercises presented by officers throughout the programme. In these exercises officers presented projects in which they had successfully incorporated many of the strategies taught during the course, or former projects in which they had worked previously that used some problem-oriented strategies (the first case study here is one example). Most importantly, in addition to the extensive Mount Pleasant project in Vancouver reported by Rossmo and Fisher (1993), course participants were also able to apply this knowledge to their own communities. When asked about 'the likelihood that you will have an opportunity to engage in problem-oriented policing upon your return', 78% of the course participants felt 'absolutely certain' or 'almost certain' that they would be able to implement problem-oriented policing. Clearly, many officers felt that there were ways they could find to overcome some of the implementation hurdles.

Two problem-oriented case studies

Case Study 1: Continuing Neighbour Disputes

During the year prior to the problem-oriented policing course, a local R.C.M.P. officer stationed in a community of 90,000 had an opportunity to tackle an on-going problem of recurring calls to a neighbourhood dispute. This officer applied tactics similar to problem-oriented policing and the incidents were presented as a successful example of problem-oriented policing during the course. It also demonstrated that, while these actions are rare in urban policing, they have great potential if they can be expanded in the future.

Scanning. In the scanning phase the officer identified that there were repeat disputes between neighbours of nearly a dozen residential homes. The traditional police and by-law responses to the problem had been incident-driven and ineffective. Continued threats, shouting, juvenile assaults, and assorted nuisance problems had been responded to on an individual basis. The problem was not being addressed.

Analysis. In his analysis the officer interviewed By-law Officers, neighbours in the area, victim services workers, other attending police officers, and he researched the police records system. The officer indicated that he could have been more thorough during this stage, but that he had not yet received problem-oriented policing training. He did, however, recommend that patrol reports from this area be 'batched' and forwarded to him in order to document the complete picture in the neighbourhood. He was able to identify quickly the underlying cause of this recurring problem. The root cause of many of the complaints was poor communication and a lack of dispute resolution abilities between a small group of neighbours.

One family had a young boy with on-going medical problems. This affected that family's ability to deal with other people. They would frequently react emotionally, blaming others for their son's medical problems. This family lived adjacent to another young couple whose lifestyle included regular loud parties, erratic driving, a large and noisy dog, and the inability to solve problems without resorting to confrontation. The members of these two households had banded together as friends and they did not get along with the remainder of the neighbourhood. Problems between the two groups escalated over the months to the point where some of the neighbourhood men had plans to confront, possibly physically, the two 'problem' families.

Response. For his response, the officer decided to have neighbourhood residents write out their own statements, to help clarify their specific concerns and get them involved in working towards a solution. It was determined that two opposing factions had formed and simply couldn't resolve disputes between themselves. A family from each side of the opposing factions, who were next door neighbours, had been identified during the analysis stage as frequent initiators of disputes. These families were focused on by the officer as a starting point for mediation.

The officer obtained mediation services from a municipal family services agency. He ensured that the local By-law Officer and other patrol members were made aware of the underlying cause of problems in this neighbourhood. The officer spoke to representatives of both factions to notify everyone of the steps being taken so that tempers would cool. Calls for services diminished as residents realized enforcement agencies were working together. No matter who they called, they were told that a mediation process was in place and would spread to them, once the conflicts among the two 'problem' families were addressed. The mediators were able to stop the erosion of trust which was present and settle the on-going disputes between various neighbours by preparing written agreements between them.

Assessment. At the time of this presentation to the problem-oriented policing course it appeared that a number of the recurring incidents in this neighbourhood had subsided. It seemed that the root cause of the problem had been correctly addressed. The mediator did a follow-up after three months with the two main families involved in this dispute and found that residents were getting along much better. The families expressed confidence in the mediator and were satisfied with the results of the mediation process.

This project, however, did not incorporate a complete SARA model and an after-the-fact assessment was missing. Although the police calls for service seemed to have subsided, without a complete evaluation it was unclear whether this was a long-term solution. However initial results were encouraging.

Case Study 2: Problem Billiard Hall

In another case, a police sergeant from a large city had tackled a series of recurring problems surrounding a local pool (billiards) hall. This project was initiated as a problem-oriented policing assignment in the police managers' course where supervisors were asked to identify and respond to real problems in their communities.

Scanning. The scanning phase identified complaints by residents of drug dealing, drinking in the parking lot, excessive noise, and assaults. The traditional police response had been to dispatch increasing numbers of patrol cars to the area, increase police surveillance, and apply more rigid law enforcement. Not surprisingly, these traditional responses did not affect the number of citizen complaints and the drug dealers and sellers merely became more aware of police activity.

Analysis. To analyse the problem, the sergeant then searched police records using the pool hall address as a parameter on the police records computer. He had conversations with residents and patrol officers about these recurring problems. Next, he searched and discovered the ownership and management history of this property.

This was followed by an investigation into the names of persons charged by police on previous occasions at this location. Just like a thorough criminal investigation, he followed a number of leads. But unlike a criminal investigation, his purpose was not a criminal conviction but rather the solution to a community problem.

The sergeant found that many of the pool hall patrons had criminal records, including the pool hall manager. Upon further investigation it was learned that this manager was rarely on site and employed a teenager to manage the premises. The property owner was discovered to be an elderly woman who had given up any responsibility for control of the premises. The underlying causes of this problem amounted to a poorly-managed pool hall, video games on site that attracted underage youths, a local turf that was controlled by drug dealers, and little effort by the pool hall management to control their clients effectively.

Response. The tailor-made response fashioned by this sergeant and his patrol team members included the following strategies: contacting the city By-law Office regarding licensing obligations of pool hall managers; informing city fire department officials about breaches of fire codes in the pool hall; notifying the provincial employee standards officials about improprieties with employment practices in the pool hall; requesting nearby liquor store staff to be especially vigilant about sales to minors and intoxicated persons; employing traditional police responses in conjunction with these other tactics; and speaking to the property owner, manager and the area residents to notify them of the situation and the actions being initiated.

The sergeant reported that initial response from neighbourhood residents and other agencies contacted was excellent. In fact, some of the area residents agreed to participate in these efforts and watch the pool hall to report futher infractions. Within a short time the property owner had expressed an interest in voiding her lease of the property. In initital meetings the property manager was uncooperative, however after these events he agreed to make some changes to the property including hiring a qualified on-site manager to monitor unruly patrons. He also agreed to implement controls on the property including the installation of adequate lighting in dark areas where many of his patrons were dealing drugs and causing disturbances.

Assessment. The sergeant indicated that a new manager had been hired and the complaints around this problem had subsided. In this case, as with the previous example, a complete assessment of the project was not possible as an evaluation had not been designed from the start. It did appear, however, that many positive results had emerged. Certainly police-community relations in this area had been positively affected, a variable that might also be included into any assessment.

Implementing problem-oriented policing: issues for leaders

Both case studies reported here involved straightforward solutions to problems. In both problems it was extremely important that the root causes be identified from the start. This is the importance of the scanning and analysis phases of SARA.

The responses in these cases, as in most problem-oriented policing projects, were well within the resources of creative rank-and-file police officers - constables, corporals, and patrol sergeants. But it is obvious that without encouragement and time, there are few reasons why patrol officers are likely to tackle problems in such a fashion. There must be an incentive. In many cases the officers involved in problem-solving indicate that there is considerable satisfaction in having time and opportunity away from routinely answering calls for service. Therefore, job satisfaction can be considered an important incentive, especially during this time of police career plateauing. This has recently been reinforced by a Halifax, Nova Scotia, study of police problem-solving which revealed a 20% increase in officer productivity, (one possible sign of higher job satisfaction) measured in this case by reduced sick days (Clairmont 1990).

However, at least in the initial stages, it is unlikely that job satisfaction alone will be sufficient for implementation. Successful implementation will more likely be based on striking a balance between reactive and proactive ap- proaches. This is another reason why commitment to the criminal justice system must be balanced with a commitment to problem-solving for everyone else. Striking this balance will be the challenge of police leaders in the 1990s.

Goldstein offers few solutions to the problems of implemention in his book (1990b). He suggests that the two most direct approaches to implementation are: the introduction of innovations throughout a police agency; or the introduction of innovations in a small unit (1990b: 172). Both approaches have been attempted throughout North America. For example the Calgary Police Service has been training the majority of their officers in problem-oriented tactics for the past year. The San Diego Police Department, perhaps the most committed police agency to the problem- oriented approach, has also attempted a system-wide adoption of the concept over the past six years.

Ideally in such approaches there exists a top-down commitment, the full training of officers, and the ability to provide the necessary time away from calls for service. While San Diego seems an especially successful case, the verdict is not yet in on the effectiveness of system-wide adoption elsewhere. Such an approach runs the risk of alienating important middle-managers who can get left out of the process. Furthermore, senior administrators and chief constables must still provide sufficient resources for emergency calls. It would be naive to expect these calls to simply disappear, though in many cases successful problem-oriented policing projects have dramatically decreased '911' calls from problem areas.

On the other hand, in striking a new balance it is incumbent on senior administrators and chief constables to analyse realistically the actual demand and required resources necessary for emergency calls, and to confront police boards and politicans with the need to reallocate lower priority calls elsewhere. These are the most demanding leadership decisions police administrators must make in the next decade.

The alternative is equally problematic. A special team of problem-oriented policing officers, as with the Vancouver example in Mount Pleasant, represents a more conservative approach which will not immediately draw resources away from general patrol. This does not, however, ensure system-wide acceptance. As the literature on implementation shows, expanding pilot projects without system-wide participation in each stage of implementation can mean alienating those who are supposed to carry them out - the rank-and-file police officers (Wasserman 1986; Bullock and Lamb 1984; Hyder 1984; Warwick 1982).

The key lesson from research in implementation is that there is no golden rule; there is no universal method to ensure successful adoption of problem-oriented policing. To this end, recent research in the implementation of new initiatives has been directed at developing a 'theory of situational implementation' (Hope 1993; Saville 1992). In this theory there are four general propositions, two of which are important for the discussion here:

1. the role of the implementer determines the potential for successful implementation; and
2. the social ecology, or the environment where problem-oriented policing is to be implemented, must be analysed by the implementer and incorporated into the implementation process.

The role of the patron officer

In the first proposition the implementer, the rank-and-file officer (for that is who inevitably does problem-oriented policing), must possess the necessary skills and training, must have or develop adequate knowledge about that problem, and must show the initiative and creativity to get the job done. This makes the rank-and-file officer's role crucial. For example, officers should be as aware of the latest tactics in crime analysis (eg. Brantingham 1991; Rossmo and Routledge 1989; Murdie and Saville 1988), as they are of new changes to criminal law. Expanding knowledge and training in this way will contribute to the personal resources that officers bring to bear on complex problems. Eventually it will be their own personal resources that can ensure successful implementation.

In a test of this theory, Hope (1993) has found that while implementing problem-oriented policing in St. Louis, rank-and-file police officers were more effective when they applied their own interpersonal skills to other community agencies rather than to the criminals themselves.

> The successes of the officers involved appeared chiefly attributeable to their mediational and negotiating skills in developing co-ordinated action ... the decentralized authority and local responsibility given to police officers - which problem-oriented policing places at the forefront of police-work - places them in a crucial and influential position as far as localized actions are concerned (Hope 1993: 24).

This is why operational police officers must be supervised with the greatest latitude, and must be encouraged to develop their own initiative and creativity in problem-oriented policing. It is at this level where solutions will likely be developed, including solutions to some of the implementation hurdles.

The role of organizational structure

In the second proposition of this new theory, the social ecology involves the environment where problem-oriented policing is to be implemented. This includes internal/organizational and external/societal environments. In this case, probably the most crucial factor for problem-oriented policing will be the internal environment of the police organizational structure. In the British Columbia programme, the police organizational structure was repeatedly mentioned as one of the main hurdles to be overcome if successful implementation is to occur. This is an environment where the organizational structure is based on chain-of-command and control of rank officers through regulation and discipline. In organizational theory these kinds of organizations are known as 'mechanistic'.

Implementation studies have shown that highly mechanistic organizations tend to be very susceptible to internal politics (Gullett 1975). As a result, new programmes such as problem-oriented policing can quickly become popular with one faction or another. The hurdle for implementation in this instance centres on the fact that popularity with one faction automatically means unpopularity with another. This has been called the 'paradox of popularity' (Grindle 1980) and problem-oriented policing is likely to face this paradox in many police organizations in Canada and elsewhere.

Ironically, turning a large portion of responsibility for problem-oriented policing over to patrol officers may be an effective way of defusing the paradox of popularity. If patrol officers are able to show positive results from problem-oriented demonstration projects, their success can become difficult to criticize regardless of who agrees or disagrees with problem-oriented policing. This has been confirmed in studies of public policy where Bullock and Lamb (1984) have found that turning implementation over to practitioners and clients had the effect of depoliticizing potential implementation hurdles. Such an approach may also work well with police agencies attempting to implement problem-oriented policing.

Conclusion

For the past few years the San Diego Police Department has held an annual problem-oriented policing conference for all levels of police officers and other community participants. They come together to discuss their experiences, successes, and failures with problem-oriented policing. This opportunity for building on the experience of others is the best means available to advance problem-oriented policing. It is an action-based form of collaboration that develops new approaches for implementation, new techniques of problem-solving, and new ways of cooperating with communities. The success of this action-based style of problem-solving is identical to a long history of research called 'action research', which is reported at length elsewhere (Chesler 1991; Trist and Murray 1990; Peters and Robinson 1984; Revans 1982; Susman and Evered 1978; Lewin 1946). It is important here to note that the *action-based style of problem-solving* has precedent and it is most effective in highly turbulent social and organizational environments - environments in which police officers are increasingly finding themselves. From this perspective, problem-oriented policing is clearly an action-based style of problem-solving. It has great potential in the future of policing.

As the British Columbia experience has shown, problem-oriented policing techniques develop as they are applied to the field. Although we incorporated some lessons of problem-oriented policing into the British Columbia programme, some of the initiatives arose independently. It was as if a critical mass was obtained and new opportunities and possibilities emerged on their own. Police leaders should not be alarmed at the unforeseen directions implementation sometimes takes. It points more to the illogic of the implementation process rather than to any weakness with problem-oriented policing. In fact, as illustrated here, such an action-oriented, flexible method of implementation is precisely the strength of problem-oriented policing.

In some cases, action can be taken immediately by astute police leaders and progressive police agencies. In other cases problem-oriented policing does not represent a significant departure from the current state of affairs, although officers in the British Columbia programme disagreed with this conclusion and most of the evidence supports them. Too often, police departments fall back on the line that they are a problem-solving or community-based agency because they are undertaking a few initiatives in these areas.

Finally, incident-driven policing may be the only police response that community residents in some areas can expect. But if police managers do not act in a proactive and progressive manner to change the traditional police response it's likely that some crisis will inevitably emerge in our increasingly turbulent society which will focus even greater public scrutiny on traditional police responses. In fact, during the writing of this essay the provincial government responded to a controversial police shooting and created a Royal Commission of Inquiry into Policing to make recommendations about, among other things, community-based policing.

Police leaders should take seriously the lessons being learned daily about problem-oriented policing. They should strike a balance between incident-driven responses and problem-solving approaches. Above all, they should provide the time, training, and encouragement for line officers to implement problem-oriented policing in neighbourhoods where such strategies might work. We are convinced that only these leadership decisions will signal a new way of doing the business of policing in the future.[4]

References

Bayley, David H. (1991) 'Managing the Future: Prospective issues in Canadian Policing', *User Report No. 1991-02, Ministry of the Solicitor General, Canada*, Ottawa: Ministry of the Solicitor General.

Brantingham, Pat and Paul (1991) *Environmental Criminology*, Prospect Heights, Ill: Waveland.

Brantingham, Pat (1989) 'Crime Prevention: The North American Experience', in D.J. Evans and D.T. Herbert (eds) *The Geography of Crime*, London: Routledge.

Brown, William (1981) 'The Future of Policing in Canada', in W.T. McGrath and M.P. Mitchell (eds) *The Police Function in Canada*, Toronto: Methuen, 243-269.

Bullock, C.S. and Lamb, C. (eds) (1984) *Implementation of Civil Rights Policy*, Monterey: Brooks/Cole.

Chesler, Mark (1991) 'Participatory Action Research with Self-help Groups: An alternative paradigm for inquiry and action', *American Journal of Community Psychology*, 19: 5, 757-768.

Clairmont, Donald (1990) *To the Forefront: Community-based Zone Policing in Halifax*, Ottawa: Canadian Police College.

Clarke, Ronald V.G. (ed.) (1992) *Situational Crime Prevention: Successful Case Studies*, New York: Harrow and Heston.

Ericson, Richard (1982) *Reproducing Order: A Study of Police Patrol Work*, Toronto: Butterworths.

Goldstein, Herman (1990a) 'Does Community Policing Work?', *The New York Times*, 30 December, e-1.

Goldstein, Herman (1990b) *Problem-oriented Policing*, Toronto: McGraw-Hill.

Grindle, M.S. (ed.) (1980) *Politics and Policy Implementation in the Third World*, Princeton: Princeton University Press.

Gullett, C. Ray (1975) 'Mechanistic versus Organic Organizations: What does the future hold?' in Keith Davies (ed.) *Organizational Behavior*, Toronto: McGraw-Hill.

Hope, Tim (1993) 'The Worst House on the Block: Problem-oriented policing and crime prevention', *Crime Prevention Studies*, 2.

Hyder, Masood (1984) 'Implementation: The evolutionary model', in D. Lewis and H. Wallace (eds) *Politics into Practice: National and international case studies in implementation*, London: Heinemann.

Lewin, Kurt (1946) 'Action research and minority problems', *Journal of Social Issues*, 2: 4, 34-46.

Murdie, Robert and Saville, Gregory (1988) 'Spatial analysis of Motor Vehicle Theft: A case study in Peel Region', *Journal of Police Science and Administration*, 16: 2, 126-135.

Murphy, Chris (1992) 'Problem-oriented Policing: A manual for the development and implementation of problem-oriented policing', *User Report No. 1992-19*,

Ministry of Solicitor General, Canada, Ottawa: Ministry of the Solicitor General.

Normandeau, Andre (1991) 'The Future of Policing and Crime Prevention in Canada: A review of some recent studies', paper presented at the 23rd Congress of the *Canadian Criminal Justice Association*, Victoria, British Columbia, 8-11 October.

Normandeau, Andre and Leighton, Barry (1990) *A Vision of the Future of Policing in Canada: Police-Challenge 2000 - Background Document*, Ottawa: Ministry of the Solicitor General.

Parker, Pat (1990) 'Contributions to the Concept Police, *The Law Officer's Magazine*, November, 22-25.

Peters, Michael and Robinson, Viviane (1984) 'The Origins and Status of Action Research', *Journal of Applied Behavioral Science* 20: 2, 113-124.

Revans, Reginald (1982) *The Origins and Growth of Action Learning*, Bromley, England: Chartwell-Bratt.

Rossmo, D. Kim and Fisher, Doug (1993) 'Problem-oriented Policing: A cooperative approach in Mount Pleasant', *Vancouver RCMP Gazette* 55: 1, 1-9.

Routledge, R. and Rossmo, D. Kim (1989) 'Estimating the Size of Criminal Populations', *Journal of Quantitative Criminology*, 6: 3, 293-314.

Saville, Gregory (1992) 'The Rational Crime Preventer: Towards a theory of situational implementation', paper presented to the *Seminar for Criminological Analysis*, Montreal, University of Montreal, 27-29 May.

Susman, G. and Evered, R. (1978) 'Assessment of the Scientific Merits of Action Research', *Administrative Science Quarterly*, 23: 582-602.

Trist, Eric and Murray, Hugh (1990) *The Social Engagement of Social Science: A Tavistock Anthology, Volume 1*, Philadelphia: University of Pennsylvania Press.

Valpy, Michael (1990) 'Is Hunting Bad Guys Good Use of Police?' *The Globe and Mail*, 23 November 3.

Warwick, D.P. (1982) *Bitter Pills*, Cambridge: Cambridge University Press.

Wasserman, Robert, et al (1986) *Directing the Implementation of a Differential Police Response System: Participants Manual*, Professional Conference Series of the National Institute of Justice, Washington: U.S. Department of Justice.

Notes

1. Gregory Saville is a research criminologist with the Royal Commission of Inquiry into Policing in British Columbia. He spent eight years as a police officer and is currently completing his Ph.D. at the School of Criminology, Simon Fraser University. He is also director of the Action Assessment Group, a crime prevention consulting firm. D. Kim Rossmo has been a Vancouver police officer for twelve years and is currently Vice-President of the Vancouver Police Union. He teaches policing at Simon Fraser University and at the Police Academy, Justice Institute of British Columbia. He is

currently completing his Ph.D. at the School of Criminology, Simon Fraser Univeristy.

2. The S.A.R.A. model is the strategy used to attack problem situations on the street. It stands for 'Scanning, Analysis, Response and Assessment'. These are stages that officers go through in the process of tackling day-to-day problems.

3. C.P.T.E.D.: The 'Crime Prevention Through Environmental Design' model was initially developed by C. Ray Jeffery in his 1971 book, *Crime Prevention Through Environmental Design* (Beverly Hills: Sage). It represents a programme where officers collaborate with planners and architects to attempt to reduce opportunities for crime by modifying the built environment. The programme has seen considerable development in British Columbia.

4. This article was made possible partly through the financial support of the Canadian Police College, Ottawa.

VII   Achieving the 'Good Community': A local police initiative and its wider ramifications

D.B. Moore and J.M. McDonald[1]

The debate about community policing in the Anglophone common law democracies appears to have waned. A peak of excitement was reached towards the end of the 1980s. Many of the programmes advocated by enthusiasts have been implemented. Some of these programmes have been seen as reasonably successful.

In the 1980s the debate saw an inevitable division into enthusiasts and cynics, optimists and pessimists. The optimists have suggested that the effects of community policing, and of a more general collective response to crime, might eventually prove much broader than had originally been anticipated. 'Could it be', asked Jerome Skolnick and David Bayley in one influential study, 'that crime, like war and other disasters, might turn out to be America's best antidote to *anomie*?' (1986: 214). Can communities be enlivened, social networks strengthened, in the process of providing a collective response to crime? Skolnick and Bayley's fellow optimists think so, and they think that what is true for the United States will hold true for other wealthy industrialized liberal democracies such as Britain, Canada, Western European nations, and Australasia. The pessimists think that this dream of regenerated, cohesive communities is utopian; sadly, they say, the dream cannot become reality. Neither police nor any other government agency can solve the problems of civil society in this era of industrialization (Greene and Mastrofski 1988). Such persuasive pessimism has tended to close the academic debate.

If the debate about community policing has quietened down in the 1990s this is not necessarily because the optimists have lacked practical suggestions, or because the pessimists have produced overwhelming arguments. A better explanation of the changing focus of debate is to be found in the nature of the reform process within police departments and other agencies of the justice system. A philosophy of community policing - vague though that philosophy often is - has prompted some significant changes to the recruitment and training of police in New South Wales. That same philosophy of community policing has also influenced reforms to the organizational structure of Australia's police departments. Although the officers and the organization have been changed, however, the biggest change of all still lies ahead (Walker 1989). Government departments with an interest in the justice system are now engaged in a broader debate with the justice agencies themselves - police, courts, and corrections. Departmental officials and their colleagues in other agencies are considering how best to change the environment in which police operate. The biggest question is not: what sort of police officers do we need to maintain order in the community? Nor is it: what type of police organization best keeps the peace? *The question is: what sort of community do we want, and how do we best achieve that community?*

This is a very broad question that crosses party political boundaries. It takes us well beyond some earlier debates about reform of the justice system. Nevertheless, key points from the more specific debate about community policing ought not be forgotten when seeking an answer to broader questions about the good community and how to achieve it. The optimists in the more specific debate about policing were right to suggest that the community policing movement may yet produce far-reaching changes such as had not originally been anticipated. The movement may indeed help to change communities in ways of which their members approve. The pessimists were, nevertheless, right to suggest that far-reaching social changes would not be brought about by neighbourhood watch schemes, beat policing programmes, or community consultative committees - not, at least, while these continue to operate in their current form and with their current rationale. Admirable though they may be, none of these initiatives represents a really significant break with past procedures. Each initiative has produced a means by which the police might more efficiently go about their existing tasks. For example, information gathering is improved; members of the public venture information that would not otherwise have been forthcoming. Much of that information is used to prevent property crimes, and to secure the arrest of some of the people who commit these property crimes. Nevertheless, none of these initiatives represents a means of addressing a different set of tasks.

Reducing the level of property crime is an important goal. Many current initiatives in community policing represent better means of achieving this traditional police goal. But the real significance of neighbourhood watch, beat policing, and community consultative committees may lie in the fact that they suggest new ways to approach problems of public safety and public order. All three initiatives encourage a focus on the causes rather than the symptoms of crime. All three initiatives not only ask citizens for information; they also encourage a modest degree of citizen involvement in the task of achieving and maintaining good order. And it is these two developments - a concern both to solve underlying problems and to foster the participation of the general public - that may prove to be the most significant aspects of contemporary reform in the name of community policing. It is in this dual commitment to problem solving and to popular participation that the link between the goal of a better police service and the goal of a better community may be found. But what practical form will such goals take?

It is our contention that certain schemes involving a new approach to juvenile justice may already be forging the link between better policing and a better community. The schemes we have in mind seek the active involvement of anybody affected by the offending and illegal behaviour of a young person or a group of young people. All of those affected - victims, offenders, and the supporters of both - are involved in finding an appropriate response to an offence. All are involved in the collective process of achieving restitution, reparation, and reconciliation in the aftermath of that offence. Both of the present authors have been closely associated with one particular version of this juvenile justice model, and it is this version of the model that we wish to discuss here. The model in question was established in the southern New South Wales city of Wagga Wagga in 1991. Adapting the Family Group Conference process from New Zealand, the designers developed what was originally called an 'Effective Cautioning Scheme'. After two years of operation, however, alternative terminology was being proposed. Changing perceptions about the aims and possibilities of the scheme were encouraging the use of the phrase 'Comunity Accountability Conference'.

As we see it, the model that has emerged in Wagga encourages police to think differently about their response to juvenile crime, about their response to the needs of victims, and about the most just, most effective means of preventing crime. The scheme offers police a new way of responding to victims, to offenders, and to the community of people supporting either or both. At the same time as it offers something new to police, the scheme encourages people affected by offensive, illegal behaviour to consider how they might minimize the harm caused by that behaviour. The scheme offers to those affected a way of minimizing the harm. It offers constructive ways to deal with the anger and resentment of victims, families, and friends. The scheme also offers to reduce the likelihood that more harm will be caused by the same offenders. It does this by encouraging local communities to find better ways of providing care, support, and guidance to young offenders. At the same time, however, it sends a very clear, very strong message that the behaviour was unacceptable. A civilized community will seek to learn from the mistakes of its members but it will not abide the subjugation, or victimization, of one person by another.

If the scheme functions as we have described it, then it is indeed significant. First, it furthers the process of police reform, but it also contributes to the larger task of changing the environment in which police operate. That is to say, it not only encourages police and the rest of the community to think carefully about how best to respond to juvenile crime; it also provides police and the general community with a new way of responding to that crime. Second, the scheme is concerned to address not only the symptoms of juvenile offending - symptoms which include hurt and angry victims - but also the causes. These causes will vary from case to case, but the scheme is well suited to address many of them. And if the scheme is addressing the causes of juvenile offending, it follows that it is simultaneously addressing the causes of potential adult offending, since the passage of time turns many juvenile recidivists into young adult offenders. Finally, the scheme represents a significant move to a fuller, more participatory form of democracy. Earlier initiatives in community policing emerged within an understandably more narrow framework.

In this narrower, liberal democratic framework, officials who are overseen by parliamentary representatives regulate the lives of citizens. The latter vote from time to time, and they more or less passively accept the services provided by agencies of education, health, welfare and justice. In contrast, within the broader framework of participatory democracy, citizens are not passive consumers of public services. They take an interest in health, education, welfare and justice. Indeed, they are encouraged not only to take an interest, but to participate in decisions that affect them and those who are close to them.

Local public participation in debate about the provision of government services in education, health, and welfare is now accepted. Indeed, government policies expect and even encourage participation. The developing juvenile justice model in Wagga offers to put the same theories about participation into practice in at least one part of the justice system. People who would normally be required to accept the judgements of court and welfare officials are instead given the opportunity to determine collectively their own responses to offending by young people and to the grievances of victims. These responses must not, of course, transgress any existing laws: nor do they. But the evidence of the first two years since the scheme's inception in Wagga does suggest that the scheme achieves much that the traditional formal legal response to crime cannot achieve. Victims, offenders, their friends, and their families consider the Family Group Conference process preferable to both traditional police cautions and to court. Participation in the process seems to strengthen the existing social bonds between people - and often to establish new bonds. The process may thus represent a means of 'regenerating communities through crime prevention'. To understand how such a scheme evolved, and to estimate the likelihood of its continuing success, one needs first to understand the origins of the scheme. These are to be found across the Tasman.

Aotearoan origins

At the core of the new juvenile justice scheme in Wagga Wagga is a process known as the Family Group Conference, a process adopted from New Zealand (Aotearoa) and adapted to fit local requirements. The use of Family Group Conferences in New Zealand's official juvenile justice system was provided for in legislation passed by the New Zealand Parliament in 1989. The phrase 'Family Group' is a rough translation of the Maori 'whanau' - the extended family, and the process itself derives from the traditional Maori practice of meeting on the marae to seek a collective response to wrongdoing. *The Children, Young Persons, and their Families Act* 1989 sought to use this collective process as a way of responding to the misdeeds of any young offender, regardless of ethnic background. The potential success of the process was seen to derive from the active involvement of family members and, where possible, the involvement of victims. The Family Group Conference seemed to offer a solution to the recognized problems of the existing system, a system which was operating according to legislative guidelines framed fifteen years earlier. That 1974 legislation, and the system it produced, had failed to achieve its stated objectives. Young offenders were not being diverted from the formal justice system; there was still an excessive reliance on the decisions of courts; families and victims were excluded from the process of responding to the offence (Maxwell and Morris 1992: 19). New legislation was required.

The juvenile justice legislation passed by the New Zealand Parliament in 1989 has increased the discretionary power of state officials to decide an

appropriate course of action in response to juvenile crime. In addition to
warning young offenders, or arresting them and thus sending them to court,
police now have a third option; they may refer a matter to specialist police
colleagues called 'Youth Aid Officers'. These officers may decide simply
to warn a young offender. Alternatively, they may decide to arrange a
Family Group Conference. If a Youth Aid Officer decides that attendance
at a Family Group Conference would be appropriate, discretionary power
then passes to the Department of Social Welfare's 'Youth Justice
Coordinators'. These coordinators are entitled to convene Family Group
Conferences. A range of options might be agreed to during such
conferences. Sanctions involving material reparation and community service
are available. Another option is to pass the case on to a third agency - the
Youth Court. This is where the young offender would have been sent, had
the police initially made a decision to arrest rather than to divert. However,
the availability of the intermediate option of a Family Conference is designed
to make it more difficult for young offenders ever to reach the stage of
court, let alone detention.

In summary, New Zealand police have a new option for dealing with
young offenders. They also have two new classes of official with whom they
are required to negotiate when dealing with young offenders. Police must
negotiate with Police Youth Aid Officers and Youth Justice Coordinators.
These officials have at their disposal a modified version of a traditional
Maori process, a process that offers an alternative way of dealing with young
offenders. The Youth Court has also acquired an additional sanction.
Judges can refer young offenders back to a Family Group Conference for
further *après*-court conferring. The model, in other words, interposes a new
layer of welfare officials between police and the courts. Ultimately, the aim
of the model is to prevent as many young offenders as possible from filtering
through this intermediate layer to the most costly part of the system - the
courts and detention centres. From the legislators' point of view, this is a
smart exercise in cost-reduction, as well as a more effective process for
dealing with young offenders.

The design of the new model in New Zealand is precisely what one would
expect when central government politicians and bureaucrats seek to translate
a successful and sensitive local initiative into a national model. The New
Zealand model has incorporated social welfare workers into the process in
the form of Youth Justice Coordinators.

Traditionally, and quite appropriately, welfare departments have defended
the rights of young offenders. In the process, welfare departments have
checked the power of police departments and courts over young offenders,

and have thereby performed a valuable political and social duty. They have maintained a balance of power in the justice system. But if the values and objectives of the welfare department become dominant in one part of the justice system, the balance of power in that part of the system is threatened. Thus, it might have been predicted that certain objectives of the new model of juvenile justice would be overlooked under the new arrangements after 1989. Officials of the welfare department maintained their traditional and appropriate focus on the defence of young offenders' rights. The department, now split into two administrative divisions, was nevertheless expected to broaden its focus overnight. It was now to be concerned with the rights of victims, the rights of communities, and the collective obligations of communities towards their members.

It was a lot to ask, and hardly a surprise, therefore, when a review of the Act - a review completed early in 1992 - found that the rights of victims have not been widely respected in the new system (Mason 1992). Many victims have, in effect, been used as a means to the end of achieving a better outcome for young offenders. The choice of venue for Family Group Conferences has been made by offenders. They have been surrounded by supporters; most victims have not. What is 'culturally sensitive' to the needs of offenders can sometimes be distressing or intimidating to victims of different cultural backgrounds. In addition to these concerns about victims, police have a range of concerns about their own ability, under new arrangements, to protect the general community from that minority of offenders who continue to offend, are predatory, sometimes violent - and who are well aware of their rights under the new Act.

These problems have not overshadowed the successes of the new model, and the potential of Family Group Conferences to deliver better outcomes for all involved has been recognized by practitioners in Australian criminal justice systems. The model offers a responsible alternative to court and detention. It involves local communities in decision-making (Maxwell and Morris 1993). It gives victims some opportunity to participate in the process of deciding on appropriate sanctions or recompense. It offers indigenous peoples the opportunity to be something other than the passive subjects of imported criminal justice systems. The model draws on untapped community resources. For all these reasons, a procession of Australian officials has visited New Zealand on fact-finding missions since the new legislation was implemented. The first of these visits was undertaken in October 1990 by members of the Youth Justice Coalition of New South Wales.

The political centre

With fortuitous timing, the Law Foundation of New South Wales provided a group called the Youth Justice Coalition with a grant in 1990 to examine the state's juvenile justice system. The coalition - a group of lawyers, youth workers and academics - used the grant to fund an inquiry, and the results of that inquiry were published the following year under the title *Kids in Justice*. One of the present authors, John McDonald, was a member of that inquiry. As a former teacher, and now adviser on juvenile justice to the state Police Service, McDonald was already well familiar with the key issues in debates about juvenile justice. Researching for the *Kids in Justice* report nevertheless gave him a renewed interest in the justice arrangements of other jurisdictions. The recent changes in New Zealand struck him as sufficiently important to warrant a visit to that country. Accordingly, he travelled to New Zealand during October 1990 with three colleagues - a sworn officer of the New South Wales Police Service, a member of the Police Minister's staff, and an officer from the state's Public Interest Advocacy Centre.

Impressed by what was seen in New Zealand, McDonald wrote, with one of his fellow fact-finders, a paper entitled *Can It Be Done Another Way?* (McDonald and Ireland 1990). The paper proposed alterations to the state's juvenile justice system, the most significant of which would be the introduction of the Family Group Conference process for dealing with young offenders. The Police State Executive Group - the Commissioner and Assistant Commissioners - endorsed the report's proposals in 1991, and it was circulated widely to relevant agencies and individuals. Many expressed their support. Few acted. Developments since that time have provided a fascinating contrast between the central bureaucratic path to reform and the local, communitarian alternative.

In Sydney, the central path to reform proceeded. The Law Week Forum held at state Parliament House in May 1991 addressed problems of the juvenile justice system. Guest speakers included Judge Michael Brown, Principal Judge of the Youth Court in Auckland, and Justice Michael Kirby, President of the New South Wales Court of Criminal Appeal. Judge Brown, who had played a significant role in the reform process in New Zealand, offered a forceful argument in favour of the Family Group Conference Process. The process, he argued, offered more humane outcomes and treated all parties with respect. Justice Kirby found these arguments persuasive, but declared the process a possible threat to the fundamentals of the British justice system. The print and electronic media, found Judge Brown interesting but not threatening. He received a good deal of favourable exposure. The Police Minister likewise found Judge Brown's proposals interesting.

The Police Minister at the time was Ted Pickering, an influential member of the Liberal Party. He discussed the scheme with the Police Commissioner and his policy advisers on several occasions. He liked the scheme. But frankly, he could not sell it. Having earlier lambasted the Labor Government from the opposition benches about softness, criminality, and the need for a bit of pain, he could hardly devalue his political currency with a system that placed little value on punishment as an end-in-itself. Furthermore, Pickering's colleague, the Corrective Services Minister, Michael Yabsley, was busy 'putting the value back into punishment'. The scheme would be politically unacceptable in New South Wales at this time. Instead, Pickering opted for Community Aid Panels. The value of Community Aid Panels was to be found, first, in their name, and secondly, in the fact that representatives from various government and community agencies could be associated with them.

The idea of 'community' contained in the title of the panels has much the same dual meaning as the idea underlying the philosophy of 'community policing.' 'Community' here means, first, that group of people with whom we can do business. Second, and more broadly, the term 'community' refers to that mass of citizens who are about to receive improved services from us. And this is how Community Aid Panels operate. Instead of a warning from a police officer or a magistrate, a young offender can be given the benefit of a firm but understanding caution from several other public officials or identities who have no place in the young person's life and who, in emotional or interpersonal terms, mean nothing to them. Prior to the 1991 state election, the Police Commissioner was informed by the state Premier, Nick Greiner, that the government had a new policy on juvenile justice. That policy was Community Aid Panels. This having been decided, the Police Service was told to abandon their interest in Family Group Conferences. It appeared that, so long as Pickering remained Police Minister, New South Wales was not going to go down the New Zealand path of juvenile justice reform. But there have been some significant changes in New South Wales over the last decade or so. The political system has become more open and the Police Service has become more accountable to, and involved with the community.

Back in 1976, when the Labor Party gained a majority of Legislative Assembly seats in the New South Wales state election, the Premier, Neville Wran, assigned the police portfolio to himself. The governance of police in New South Wales had already been a controversial issue for several years, with allegations concerning corrupt police and politicians playing a part in the political demise of Robert Askin (Hickie 1985). Wran appointed a commission of inquiry into the administration of police. Justice Edwin Lusher found endemic corruption, and urged major reforms. Lusher's proposed reforms were delayed until 1983, but they had a profound effect on policing in New South Wales thereafter. The Police Board established in that year was responsible for policy development and for the appointment of senior commissioned officers. The new policies proposed by the Board included promotion by merit, improved recruitment and training, and simplified lines of accountability. Putting their own proposals for promotion by merit into effect, the Board appointed Chief Superintendent John Avery to the position of Commissioner. Following Avery's appointment, the reform process entered a new stage, as plans he had already outlined in a text on policing were put into practice (Avery 1981). The most important of these proposals was for a process of regionalization. With the aim of improving police governance, the state was divided into four regions, each region divided into six or so districts, each district divided into patrols, and each patrol into sectors. More responsibility was given to officers at lower levels of the organization. Clearer lines of accountability were supposed to ensure that this greater freedom was not abused.

Many of the problems experienced during the phase of implementation were predictable. Others came as a surprise. None will be discussed here (see Moore 1992). For our purposes, only one aspect of this long process of reform needs to be emphasized: By the early 1990s, district and patrol commanders in the New South Wales Police Service had a good deal of autonomy to experiment with new programmes that conformed with the philosophy of community policing. Not all of them chose to do so, but one who experimented with enthusiasm was the patrol commander for Wagga Wagga, Chief Inspector Kevin Wales. And the officer to whom Wales had given the task of putting the community policing philosophy into practice was unusually well-placed to do the job properly, bringing academic and industrial perspectives to the task. Senior Sergeant Terry O'Connell was just completing a Bachelor's degree in social science when he was asked to establish the Beat Policing programme in Wagga. He was also Deputy President of the New South Wales Police Association. Here was an opportunity. Given the apparent impasse at the political centre, John McDonald went to the local level and raised the issue of Family Group Conferences with Terry O'Connell.

Local variations

The idea was put to the Wagga Wagga Community Consultative Committee and to a small number of police, academics, lawyers, and professionals from justice and welfare agencies. The meeting, held in Wagga in mid-1991, evinced a positive response from most of those present. The point was made by one of the participants that what the New Zealanders had designed, and what McDonald was proposing, was a means of putting into practice the theory of reintegrative shaming, a theory developed by John Braithwaite of the Australian National University. McDonald agreed. Indeed, he had already made that connection. Earlier in the year, he had read Braithwaite's important work *Crime, Shame, and Reintegration* (1989). Realizing the book's significance, he had contacted Braithwaite and pointed out the similarities between the latter's general theories and emerging specific practices in juvenile justice. From the outset, then, any changes to the juvenile justice system in Wagga could be debated in the light of a clearly articulated social and criminological theory.

Meanwhile, members of Wagga's Community Consultative Committee were already pressing on with practical matters. A sub-committee agreed to compare Community Aid Panels and Family Group Conferences with the current offerings of the juvenile justice system. Marie Thompson, head of the Community Consultative Committee, travelled to New Zealand with Terry O'Connell to look at the new arrangements. Both returned convinced that some version of the New Zealand juvenile justice system could not fail to be an improvement both on the current New South Wales system, and on the proposed Community Aid Panels. After consultation with her fellow committee members, Marie Thompson wrote to newly appointed Police Commissioner Tony Lauer, informing him of the Community Consultative Committee's decision to approve the use of Family Group Conferences in Wagga. This correspondence put the Commissioner in a difficult position. On the one hand, he was faced with members of a police patrol and a Community Consultative Committee who had done just what Lauer's recently retired predecessor John Avery had long advocated. They had got together, consulted vigorously, and produced constructive proposals, which they now planned to implement in their city. On the other hand, Lauer had to consider the relationship between the Police Service and the Government. It wasn't long before Chief Inspector Kevin Wales received a memorandum to the effect that his Wagga patrol was to have nothing to do with Family Group Conferences.

The Patrol Commander found himself in a difficult position. Kevin Wales had earlier asked his Beat Police to come up with some alternative strategies for dealing with young offenders. The current system, as he saw it, was arbitrary, unfair, and ineffectual. It left victims angry, police cynical, and did little for offenders or their families either. Thus prompted, members of the Beat Police had begun to take a broader perspective on the problems of young people. They were working more closely with Education Department officials such as the Home School Liaison Officer, as well as with members of various welfare agencies. They were proposing alternative educational programmes for school refusers. Now, just when Kevin Wales' officers and community representatives were proposing a new and apparently workable scheme for his patrol, direction from above appeared to want to put a stop to such local initiatives.

Marie Thompson and other members of the Community Consultative Committee went to the local media. The police in Wagga, they said, were their police. No Minister was going to force the Police Commissioner to force the Regional Commander, to force the District Commander, to force the Patrol Commander, to force the Beat Police and the Community Consultative Committee to bail out at this stage. Provided with strong local support, the Patrol Commander was able to resist the pressure from above.

Beat Police proceeded with their plans. Terry O'Connell, familiar as he was with the creative use of industrial loopholes, now found an entirely legitimate way to run Family Group Conferences in Wagga under existing legislation. Conferences could be run according to the Commissioner's Instructions on the cautioning of young offenders. O'Connell had discovered a different interpretation of standing procedure.

Police in New South Wales had been cautioning young offenders for decades as an alternative to arrest (Seymour 1988: chs 3 and 6). The traditional caution involved a sergeant at the station asking young offenders whether they realized the full extent of their wickedness. When this question was answered in the affirmative, the young person was free to go. Some would offend again. Most would not. All of them would think the police a little silly. A police caution was generally considered a soft option by all parties. Not that most police necessarily considered the juvenile court system to be more effective. Rather, the juvenile court was considered a tough option. And there were two good reasons why the majority of police, in the majority of patrols, across the state preferred - indeed, still prefer - to send young offenders to a tough court rather than to administer a soft caution.

The first reason for this preference is bureaucratic, the second we might call emotional. The bureaucratic reason is that many police decisions are taken according to a technical, procedural rationale. Dealing with young offenders becomes process work. Surrounded as they feel themselves to be with internal and external watchdogs, officers are concerned that the forms are filled out correctly and they are relieved of unnecessary responsibility as quickly as possible. Under current arrangements, and in a system that is still more inclined to punish mistakes than to reward initiative, passing the young person on to the next agency - courts, welfare, or corrections - makes a good deal of sense. The second, related reason for preferring courts to cautions is that officers are regularly confronted by the anger of victims - anger which is heightened when a victim perceives the offending behaviour to be condoned by the lightness of the sanction. A light sanction is read as an affront to the victim's dignity. By passing to courts all responsibility for dispensing sanctions, police are able to plead their own case to aggrieved victims. Police have done all they can. They hope that this plea will help them to deflect the victim's anger. That leaves police to contend only with the tirades of tertiary-educated professionals about police boorishness. Eventually these tirades just become background noise.

A survey of officers in Wagga confirmed this rationale for the way police were dealing with young offenders (O'Connell and Moore 1992; Moore and O'Connell 1994). Yet the surveyed officers did agree that the soft option of cautions and the hard option of court had two significant features in common. Neither achieved their objectives for offenders, and neither did much on behalf of victims. Starting from this position, O'Connell suggested a third alternative to his colleagues. With an eye to political acceptability, and to draw the contrast with existing procedures, he proposed that the new model be called an 'Effective Cautioning Scheme'. At the heart of the proposed scheme would be a procedure that bore a marked resemblance to the Family Group Conference. A working party was established to consider the details of the scheme. How could it best achieve the hastily formulated objective of 'maximizing the impact of juvenile cautioning'?

It was soon decided that the stated objective was both too vague and too narrow. Certainly, the scheme should aim to ensure that a young person who had committed an offence was able to understand the impact of that offence, able to accept responsibility for the offence, was given another chance, and would be less likely to offend again. But simply focusing on the offender was only half of the picture. Those Beat Police who had been using a diagram called the 'crime impact grid' in their school-based crime prevention programme understood this very well. At the centre of their diagram was a blotch - reminiscent of those 1960s Batman fight scenes - labelled 'offence'. On one side of the offence was the offender, on the other side was the victim. Both were connected by relational lines to family, friends, and colleagues from school and work. Other links were drawn to church or sporting groups, and to professionals such as doctors, educators, counsellors, and officials of the justice system. All of these people were affected when a crime was committed. It would be myopic to construct a new model of justice which overlooked these basic social facts. To focus on the offender alone would be to repeat the mistakes of the past. A broader approach would be needed.

In August, four months after McDonald had first proposed the use of Family Group Conferences in Wagga Wagga, O'Connell convened his first 'Effective Cautioning Conference'. He invited the enraged victim of a motorcycle theft to discuss the matter with the recently apprehended offenders and their families. The victim took some persuading, but eventually attended the police station, ready for retribution. An hour later, he and the offenders left with their supporters, unharmed and on good terms, having arranged for the repairs to be effected, and discussing their mutual interest in bikes. This was an easy business. But when the end of year festivities of some local high school students went awry, causing several thousand dollars worth of damage, matters looked a little more complicated. Again, following initial investigations and straightforward admissions of culpability, a meeting was convened. It was attended by students, families, teachers, and the owner of the damaged property. Agreements for compensation - partly monetary, partly involving unpaid work - were quickly reached. But the parties were themselves more impressed by the process by which the agreement had been reached, than by the outcome. The incident and its aftermath received wide and extremely supportive publicity, not only in the local media, but also in Sydney. The credibility gap was crossed at this point. Sceptics were now prepared to concede that there might be something in this 'Effective Cautioning Scheme'.

O'Connell himself was more than convinced. What most impressed him as he convened his first half-dozen or so conferences was not the ease with which a just agreement was been reached between parties. Rather, it was the extent to which opinions changed. Instead of having their contempt, anger, or shame fuelled by the process, victims, offenders and their supporters experienced the restoration of a degree of respect and trust. Victims did not seem to want offenders to be punished. They wanted to have their say, they wanted any damage repaired or goods returned, they wanted an apology. Above all, most victims wanted to 'get through' to the offender. They wanted the offender to see things from their point of view. O'Connell was observing a dramatic confirmation of John Braithwaite's theory of reintegrative shaming.

Theoretical interlude

Crime, Shame, and Reintegration was first published in 1989, appearing around the same time as a number of other general theories of crime and legal compliance (Gottfredson and Hirschi 1990; Tyler 1990). In his book, Braithwaite sought to explain the fact that most people obey the law most of the time. This formula, of course, turns the traditional concern of criminology upside down. The classical school of criminology asked why some people break the law. Their answer was that criminals weighed the advantages and disadvantages of committing an offence. If the advantages - such as pleasure or wealth, outweighed the disadvantages - such as pain or loss of liberty, then the decision was taken to offend. The logical solution for the authorities was to devise tougher sanctions. Critics of this view asked the same question as the classical criminologists - why do some people break the law? But they arrived at different answers. One school of thought suggested that some people were born into criminality, predestined by their genetic inheritance. Later variations on determinist theories included theories of psychological or social determinism. People were driven to criminality by their psychological profile or by their socio-economic circumstances. Punishment as an end-in-itself might therefore be too simplistic a response.

Modern criminal justice practices have been influenced by these criminological theories. There is an element of truth in most of them, but there are also many flaws. Recent attempts to deal with some of the flaws in criminological theory have led to a reversal of the basic question about law-breaking. The focus of late has been on compliance rather than transgression. If we can better understand why most people abide by the law, why most people respect the rights of their fellow citizens most of the time, then we might find better ways of responding to those people who do break the law, who do violate the rights of others. Rather than address any alternative theories here, we will concentrate on Braithwaite's answer to these questions (Moore 1993; Moore and O'Connell 1994).

The basic argument of *Crime, Shame, and Reintegration* (Braithwaite 1989) is that most people obey the law not simply or even mainly because they fear the formal penalties of the state. Rather, they obey the law, first, because their own conscience tells them to and, second, because they fear disgrace in the eyes of those who matter to them. The phenomenon common to private conscience and public disgrace is shame, and this makes shame an important regulator of social life. When a feeling of shame is evoked by public exposure of inappropriate behaviour, this feeling might be called 'disgrace shame' (Schneider 1977). When the threat of potential shame warns people not to complete an action that they might have been contemplating, then shame has encouraged discretion. Conscience might, therefore, be called 'discretion shame' (ibid). Unlike disgrace shame, however, discretion shame is not necessarily an unpleasant feeling. It is essentially a private means of intuiting what is publicly appropriate. It is an internal reminder of one's bonds with others. Those who have an active conscience, those who are regularly reminded of their bonds with relatives, friends and colleagues - such people should generally be able to avoid the more painful feeling of disgrace shame that is evoked by inappropriate behaviour. Discretion shame helps people to avoid disgrace.

When a person acts inappropriately, violates the rights of another person, breaks the law, how do modern criminal justice systems respond? Do they have means of fostering consciences, strengthening an offender's ability to feel discretion shame, strengthening bonds between offenders and their supporters? On the contrary, modern criminal justice systems seek to punish an offender with a 'ceremony of degradation' (Garfinkel 1956). They seek to stigmatize offenders, to set them apart from the community. Offenders may be set apart symbolically, through public denunciation. They may be set apart quite literally, in prisons and detention centres that physically remove offenders from the community. Where an offender represents an immediate physical threat to other citizens, their physical removal helps to ensure the safety of others. But how can this be justified in other cases? If Braithwaite's explanation of offending is correct, then the policy of severing an offender's links with their community is counter to all logic. Those social links need to be strengthened, not severed and, where they are absent or weak, new links need to be nurtured.

According to Braithwaite, this process of strengthening rather than severing a person's links with their community could begin in a 'ceremony of reintegration'. In the traditional ceremony of degradation - such as criminal court - an offender is castigated, symbolically degraded and stigmatized as part of the process of punishment for a crime. A ceremony of reintegration, in contrast, makes a clear distinction between unacceptable behaviour, on one hand, and the person responsible for that behaviour, on the other. Having expressed remorse, and having accepted responsibility for their offending actions, a person may be forgiven and accepted back into the community. This is the basic pattern of a ceremony of reintegration - shame and remorse for the act, followed by reacceptance or social reintegration of the person who committed the act. Of course, such ceremonies occur daily in informal settings. Children are shamed by their parents for inappropriate behaviour, and then accepted again moments later with some appropriate gesture. In the same way, apology is followed by forgiveness - shame by reintegration - between relatives, friends, and colleagues on a small scale, and on a daily basis. Social life is regulated this way. People make mistakes, and are given an opportunity to learn from them. The boundaries between acceptable and anti-social behaviour are drawn and redrawn. Why then does the formal response to offending behaviour use the opposite strategy? Why are punishment and stigmatization valued for their own sake?

These questions can only be answered with reference to the history of criminal justice systems, and space permits no such exercise here (see Garland 1990, Friedman 1993). We can, however, address a related question: If ceremonies of reintegration are used daily in informal settings in response to inappropriate behaviour, can such ceremonies be used by officials of the justice system? Can this subtle informal method of maintaining social order be used as the basis of a formal process? This is precisely how the Family Group Conference has been interpreted in Wagga Wagga. The phrase 'reintegrative shaming' was used frequently during the developmental phases of the programme. Use of the phrase had the political effect of linking Braithwaite's respected theory with the emerging practice of bringing victims, offenders, and their supporters together to seek restitution, reparation, and reconciliation. The theory also provided some further guidelines, as the effective cautioning model developed during 1992.

Back to Wagga

The first few Family Group Conferences convened in Wagga by Terry O'Connell proved more than successful. Participants were enthusiastic when asked to compare the process with the available alternatives. None felt aggrieved. Some of O'Connell's colleagues thought the scheme deserved a decent trial. The Community Consultative Committee were impressed. Accordingly, some careful thought was given to the question of how the conference process might operate formally within the police patrol. It was decided that a panel of sergeants should meet weekly and review all of that week's cases of young offenders - those aged between ten and seventeen - who would otherwise go to court. In cases where the offender's guilt was not an issue (which were the majority of cases) the Sergeants could now consider the alternative of a Family Group Conference as an effective caution. In cases involving multiple offenders, all of them would attend the one conference. As the 'crime impact grid' of the Beat Police illustrated graphically, the heart of the problem was an incident that turned ordinary citizens into offenders and victims. Conferences would, therefore, focus on the incident. This decision had the additional advantage of halving the total number of conferences required.

The effects of establishing a Sergeants' Review Panel were several. First, panel members were obliged to consider the relative merits of court appearances and conferences. The extent to which they were prepared to have matters dealt with in a Family Group Conference would be a measure of their confidence in the developing scheme. This was a sensible, gradualist approach. The confidence of the Sergeants' might wax or wane on the basis of feedback about the conferences. As it happened, however, the feedback was almost entirely positive. Confidence waxed. Consequently, the ratio of court appearances to cautions was reversed in Wagga within the first six months of 1992. Where three-quarters of juvenile cases had previously gone to court, only a minority now did so.

A second effect of the Sergeant's Panel was to alter the way in which officers on the street or at the station assessed cases. The charge books for the first half of 1992 show a significant decline in the number of charges for minor public order offences, many of which amount to the charge of failing to show respect for the blue uniform. Officers charging for public order offences knew that these charges would be reviewed by senior colleagues and that frivolous charges would not be well received. Having to second-guess the response of the Sergeants to a given case appeared to have shifted the rationale employed by officers when charging offenders. Knowing that the Family Group Conference involved victims in the process, officers now appeared to be assessing cases differently. The most important underlying question was no longer procedural or technical. Police were now encouraged to think about the purpose of their work and to make appropriate, sensitive use of the discretion which was an inevitable part of that work. The most important question was now social; it concerned people, rather than rules. Was the offending behaviour directed at, and affecting a victim? If so, then the victim had a right to be heard. Law enforcement secured that right. The offence could be dealt with in a Family Group Conference. Having the option of dealing with matters in a conference seemed to have altered the way police in Wagga Wagga assessed the purpose of their interventions. Increasingly, the perceived aim of intervention was to minimize the harm caused by the offence.

By the middle of 1992, then, it was clear that the new model was having a transformational effect upon police. It had caused them to reassess the nature of their involvement with young people who had transgressed the law. It was also earning them a good deal of *kudos* around town. Local newspaper and television coverage of the new initiative was generally positive.

But what effect were conferences really having on participants? Reports by many participants were positive. Unsolicited letters of praise arrived at patrol headquarters. How could this apparent ability of conferences to achieve their stated aims be explained? What could be said about the after-effects of the conferences? To address this question, O'Connell contacted colleagues at Charles Sturt University's Riverina campus, including one of the present authors, David Moore. The latter had taken an interest in the scheme from the time it was first proposed by John McDonald. Having for several years done part of his teaching in the university's justice studies programme, Moore had worked with police from most states, and was familiar with many of their concerns. Like McDonald, he considered that Braithwaite's theories offered a way to resolve the stand-off between criminological theorists and criminal justice practitioners. And like McDonald, he considered the Family Group Conference to be a way of putting the theory of reintegrative shaming into practice. Accordingly, he was more than happy to work with Terry O'Connell in order to examine what was happening in and after the conferences. The evaluation began with Moore sitting at the back of the room during conferences - with the full permission of participants and the University's ethics committee - and comparing notes at the end of proceedings with the coordinator, O'Connell.

At the same time as this evaluation was beginning - in the winter of 1992 - a group of four final year students from the university's social welfare programme undertook their own independent evaluation of the scheme, especially in relation to the police role in it. None had been associated with the scheme, but all had previously worked in some part of the justice system. Their report was not expected to be entirely favourable. Some of their lecturers had strong reservations about the scheme, especially in relation to the police role in it. The students themselves had of course been subjected to a good deal of colourful literature on justice. Much analysis of modern criminal justice systems could be said to be written in the metaphors of a morality play. The tale of the battle for people's souls is full of the language of 'coercion', 'net widening', 'empowerment' and - thanks to Saint Foucault - 'the collective gaze'. Police are rarely allocated a positive part in these scenarios. Nevertheless the students' unpublished report, completed a year after the first Family Group Conference was held in Wagga, proved an exception of this general rule.

Based on detailed interviews with thirty participants chosen at random from a larger, unbiased sample, the report noted that participants had found conferences to be 'positive, effective, and an appropriate way of dealing with the first offence committed by a juvenile' (Dymond et al 1992: 1). The authors of the report admitted that, in the course of the interviews, their own preconceptions about family type, socio-economic conditions, and lack of success at school had been 'turned on their head' (ibid: 6). Most young offenders already had quite strong networks of social support, but these had been strengthened in the wake of a conference. The involvement of young people with sporting and other associations increased after conferences. Young people and their parents reported improved communication; parents perceived real behavioural changes in their children (ibid: 7, 8). The report concluded that any follow-up to the conference programme should be optional, not mandatory. In most cases, the authors felt, subsequent follow-up would be superfluous at best. What would be required, if the programme were to be expanded or introduced in other patrols, was a thorough training programme for coordinators. The skills of the founding conference coordinator could not be taken for granted or underestimated.

At this point, O'Connell and Moore decided that their own study of the conference process should concentrate on building a large body of knowledge about the dynamics of the process itself, and about participants' perceptions of the process. They could not hope to obtain methodologically defensible statistics on recidivism rates from the relatively small sample available in the Wagga patrol, and in the absence of any control groups. Such statistics could only be obtained from a larger study conducted in several patrol groups over several years. John Braithwaite agreed, and began to investigate the possibility of arranging such a study for metropolitan Sydney or for the Australian Capital Territory. O'Connell and Moore - now with the support of the Criminology Research Council [2] - would concentrate on attempting to explain exactly why Braithwaite's predictions appeared to be correct, why the conferences appeared to be so effective, and why the victim satisfaction rate measured in two surveys by students was as high as 90%.

There was still much about the process that was not understood. Nevertheless, by September 1992, when the Australian Institute of Criminology convened a national conference in Adelaide on juvenile justice, Braithwaite, O'Connell and Moore - together with their colleagues from New Zealand - had a good deal to say on the issue of Family Group Conferences (Gerrull and Atkinson 1993). Accusations about class-gender-ethnic bias - such as one must routinely expect in response to any positive initiative in the justice system - were rather more subdued than usual. Traditional alliances appeared to be shifting. The Family Group Conference process was given eloquent support by several Aboriginal and Maori women, leaving a few delegates confused about where to direct their standard-issue accusations concerning middle-class values and insensitivity.

Understanding the process

After the first full year of operation, and thus after several hundred cases had been dealt with, some basic facts about the Effective Cautioning Scheme had come to light. Aware of valid concerns about sample size and the length of the period of data collection, O'Connell and Moore were nevertheless able to work with some rough approximations. Agreements for material reparation had been reached by consensus. Around 95% of all property had been replaced or damage repaired, despite the fact that agreements reached in conferences were not legally binding. Victim satisfaction with the process was measured by survey at around 90%.[3] The number of young people who offended again after a conference appeared to be a little over 5%.

With these figures, of course, anyone predisposed to criticism could rightly argue that full compensation was not achieved in every case, that not every victim was entirely happy with the procedure or the outcome reached, and that the process had not prevented some recidivism. It has been suggested that the scheme engages in widening the net of state control, of wasting police resources, of allowing police to play the role of social workers. A second group of critics is concerned that the scheme might undermine the rule of law. A third express some concerns about the 'republican' or 'communitarian' impulse which underlies both Braithwaite's theory and the practice of Family Group Conferences. Some have even produced convoluted arguments that reduce to a warning not to let police near young people (Sandor 1993) or not to let police take funds that should rightly go to schools (Polk 1994). And if the latter argument were relevant to the scheme, we would, of course, agree.

The Wagga Wagga model has benefited from these criticisms, most of which have been addressed elsewhere (Braithwaite 1993; Moore 1993 and Moore and O'Connell 1994). In response it has been pointed out that a scheme successfully diverting young offenders at the first point of contact with the justice system could not properly be accused of dragging people into the system. One must also ask: can a scheme be seen as a waste of public resources when it draws on the resources of the community - of civil society - to address problems that professionals cannot hope to address? Should a department responsible for keeping the peace, enforcing the law, and providing emergency and miscellaneous services, be told to stick to reactive law enforcement when Royal Commissions, Parliamentary Committees and academic treatises regularly decry the self-defeating nature of such simple-minded reaction to complex social problems?

The Wagga Wagga police have not been hugely concerned with meeting these criticisms (Alder and Wundersitz 1994). They were more interested in understanding what was *right* with the scheme, in understanding why and the extent to which it appeared to work. One of the points that struck them most forcibly was the underlying similarity of the conferences. Judge Mick Brown, in discussing the many conferences that he had observed in New Zealand, had described with his usual eloquence a standard sequence of emotions encountered in any properly prepared conference. In a diagram labelled 'Crime and Damage to Victims', Brown describes victims as proceeding through an emotional sequence of fury, hurt, loss, understanding, and forgiveness. Offenders proceed through a matching sequence of acknowledgment, remorse, shame, reparation, and expiation. The sequence ends for both parties with healing. And healing corresponds here closely to the phenomenon that Braithwaite calls the 'social reintegration' of victim and offender.

A similar sequence had been observed in the Wagga conferences, although what most struck the Wagga Wagga police - as it struck those few outside observers who had been granted permission by participants to observe a conference - was the apparent sharing of emotions by all of those present at a conference. Certain emotions appeared to be 'contagious'. Mick Brown's observations about a regular sequence of emotions matched what was being observed in Wagga, as did the specific emotions he had listed. The expression of the same emotions by individuals in different conferences was striking. But even more notable was the frequency with which all the people attending a given conference would *simultaneously* express the same emotion, regardless of each person's role in the conference. If one person expressed shame, all did. If one person sighed with relief, the mood in the whole room lightened. One person's willingness to forgive spread rapidly to all present.

Comparison of several dozen conferences yielded a related observation: the strength of this emotional reciprocity was influenced by the configuration of conferences. It tended to be strongest: where there was a rough parity between the number of people who had come to the conference to support the victim(s), and the number of people who had come to support the offender(s); where community members who supported both or neither party attended as witnesses and then contributed to the discussion; where siblings - particularly younger siblings - attended conferences; where larger numbers -

from eight to about twenty - were involved. The level of emotional reciprocity also seemed to increase during the course of a conference.

Both of the researchers felt that there was some connection between these observations and a further observation concerning the small number of repeat offenders. The researchers and several other observers had independently predicted with confidence, after certain conferences, that the young person would be back within six months - having at least, one hoped, committed a less damaging offence. The key indicator - for everyone who made such a lugubrious prediction - was not the young person's social circumstances. Certainly, the nature of the paternal relationship - or the lack of it - seemed to be one common theme, but that was no explanation. Well-adjusted children of single parents are common enough. No, what struck Moore, O'Connell and a few others was the almost eerily similar expression on the faces of those few young people whom we correctly predicted would offend again within six months. The facial expression of affect was proving an accurate predictor of behaviour after conferences. And these were the conferences where victims would say afterwards: Look, I think this is a great process, and I am grateful for the opportunity to have come here, but I don't think I got through to him/her. (S)he just didn't seem to register.

What theory, the researchers were forced to ask, could account for all of these observations? The participants at nearly every conference, regardless of their relationships to each other, and regardless of the nature of the offence, express a remarkably similar sequence of emotions. They seem to experience these emotions collectively and almost simultaneously. And in the case of those few conferences that are perceived to be less than successful, though not a failure, the perception of limited success is explained by all observers in terms of the offender's facial expression. An expression which suggests an apparent inability to experience the same emotional sequence as the rest of the group. Some comprehensive psycho-social theory was required to explain these phenomena. But let us first review the dynamics of a Family Group Conference as conducted in Wagga.

There is, of course, no such thing as a 'typical' conference. Numbers in attendance will vary from perhaps five to twenty or more. (The numbers reported from some New Zealand Conferences have been larger still.) The nature of the offence will vary. The number of offenders will vary - usually from one to three - as will the number of victims: one chap has concussed another with a piece of wood; two kids have stolen the clothes of three flatmates from their washing line; three kids have broken into a car and stolen money that happens to have been raised for a local charity - the victims are numerous; the damage from an attempted school arson affects the daily lives of dozens. Despite such differences, most conferences follow roughly the same sequence. The coordinator begins the conference by greeting and than introducing all present, emphasizing their relationship to offender(s) and/or victim(s). The point is made that people are there to discuss an incident, and to determine whether the problems arising from that incident can be resolved. People are made aware of their formal right to request an end to proceedings and to have the matter proceed to court. (No one has exercised that right to date.) The conference proper then begins. The offender's version of events is requested first. This is usually followed by versions of events as perceived by the offender's supporters - parents, siblings, neighbours, colleagues. Offenders are often a little surprised at the extent to which their supporters actually perceive themselves to be victims of the incident. But if they are surprised at these accounts of 'indirect victimization', they are frequently astonished and often shocked to hear of the impact that the offence - say, a burglary, theft, or assault - has had on the person most directly affected.

To mark this transition in the conference to the victim's version of events, the coordinator will usually ask the offender: What were you thinking about at the time of the offence? or: How do you think the victim felt about that? Here one can talk of a typical response to the question. Almost invariably, the offender was thinking about 'nothing' at the time of the offence and 'didn't know' what the victim felt. Indeed, this is the common theme uniting most offences across the spectrum, from those of small consequence to those that threaten the victim's liberty, dignity or life. The offender reports simply not seeing things from the victim's point of view (Damon 1988; Wispé 1991). And when victims of offending behaviour are given an opportunity to put their version of events to the offender, the result is usually clear on the offender's face: the blank look of surprise is rapidly followed by the lowering of the face in shame. That shame is shared by everyone at the conference. It is most pronounced in those who are there to support the offender - although none of them are in any way culpable for the offence. Their shame seems to be felt not for the offender's legal guilt. Rather, they seem to be ashamed about the transgression of social norms by a person with whom they are associated. Bonds between people have been threatened by the offending behaviour.

And yet, as soon as this shame and remorse are expressed, a process of reintegration begins, just as Braithwaite's theory predicts. Not only does the offender begin to see things from the victim's point of view; rather more surprisingly, victims often begin to see things from the offender's point of view. The community of people at the conference then to discuss general questions of appropriate and inappropriate behaviour. Someone - often a younger sibling - makes the distinction between the unacceptable behaviour and the still acceptable offender. A younger brother or sister will exclaim: I hate what he did but I don't hate him!

Victims usually agree with this assessment. The offence is not being excused, condoned, or justified. The behaviour is strongly rejected, but the way is open for the social reintegration of the offender. The ensuing discussion of reparation continues the process. Almost invariably, it is the offender, and sometimes the offender's family, who call for the tougher penalties at this stage. They feel that the right to be reaccepted has to be earned. Offenders propose substantial amounts of community work or some other form of tariff that will demonstrate their willingness to atone for the damage they have caused. The bargaining that ensues - victims argue the case for leniency, for understanding that this mistake can and has been learned from - such bargaining runs counter to much of the received 'wisdom' about what victims do and do not want. The bargaining is one part of the process of forgiving and it may, in turn, start the long process of restoring trust.

It is in those rare cases where the offender remains impassive, where the victim's point of view has not 'got through', that conferences are felt to be less than successful. Here there is no apparent shame and remorse, even though some agreement for material reparation has been reached and is later honoured. How can these observations to be accounted for? The theory that would explain them will have to draw strongly on psychology. Braithwaite's theory of reintegrative shaming, in contrast, is derived explicitly from sociology. Its predictive power has been repeatedly confirmed, but the theory doesn't really account for the emotional power of these 'ceremonies of reintegration'. In order to account for that powerful emotional reciprocity and to explain why it is apparently possible to predict with some accuracy that certain young offenders will offend again when they do not experience the key emotions, we require an exploration of what shame is, rather than what it does. This may help us to understand why victims are able to predict reoffending and to acknowledge their prediction with sadness. Early theoretical work in the area has produced some interesting hypotheses which later research might test (Moore 1994a, 1994b).

Discussion

There is still much about these processes which is not fully understood. A lengthy study of participants' perceptions and experiences needs to be completed, and the findings need to be compared with the important work already done in New Zealand by Gabrielle Maxwell and Allison Morris (1992, 1993). Only larger longitudinal studies will provide trustworthy statistics, comparing rates of reoffending after conferences with those after a court hearing. Two such studies are being planned for Canberra and for parts of Sydney.

It must, of course, be continually stressed that even if conferences produced no net change in rates of reoffending, they would still offer significant advantages over other procedures. The family group conference model involves victims in the response to the offence. It gives them an opportunity to deal with their anger and resentment. It also arranges material reparation, which is paid -in our opinion - precisely because there is no legal obligation on people to meet agreements reached in conferences. The currency of conferences is ethical rather than legal, social rather than administrative. Fulfilling agreements is a matter of maintaining honour, regaining dignity, restoring trust. People understand this. They honour their agreements.

In addition to the better deal offered to victims, conferences appear to offer a number of other benefits which were not originally anticipated. They appear to foster networks of support between parties at the conferences, such as parents of offenders. Less than a year after he had convened his first conference in Wagga, Terry O'Connell was speaking to the mother of a young fellow who had attended a conference some time earlier. The boy's mother had rung O'Connell to thank him and to ask his advice on another matter. She referred in passing to a support group. When asked what she meant, she explained that a group of parents, having discovered in casual conversation that they had in common the experience of a conference, had formed an informal network of support - more for each other than for their children. This is a fine example of what the social theorists mean when they talk of *building social capital* - though no one associated with the scheme anticipated that it would happen quite so quickly or spontaneously (Coleman 1990).

For a surprising number of offenders as well, the conferences bring more direct benefits than might have been predicted. Our New Zealand colleagues like to report anecdotes of victims offering employment to offenders. The same surprising outcome has not been uncommon on this side of the Tasman. Neo-classical criminologists might see a disturbing trend here. Clearly, young folk will get wise to this and commit crimes in order to be offered employment at the conclusion of their conference. We think not. Anyone calculating the ratio of pleasure and pain with that degree of perspicacity is likely to understand the value of interpersonal bonds with friends and relatives.

This short list of benefits for victims, families, and some lucky offenders has been offered in order to defend the use of conferences, even if they were to achieve no reduction in rates of reoffending. We are nevertheless confident that a larger study will show more clearly what our rough statistics and our small-scale evaluation in Wagga already suggest: successful social reintegration of young offenders does occur during and after most conferences. And where successful reintegration has occurred, reoffending is unlikely.

The model really does seem to offer, then, the prospect of *'regenerating communities'* - of creating more cohesive family and community life. It seems to offer a better outcome for victims, offenders, their families and friends. It also offers a better outcome to police, many of whom consider themselves to be victims of the inadequacy of current arrangements. The model that has been developed in Wagga has the additional advantage of being gradualist. It has not been imposed from above, but rather, developed as a result of consultation, debate, and persuasion on the ground. Being gradualist, the scheme may continue to evolve smoothly. The age range of eligible offenders might eventually be extended upwards - say to twenty-one, or twenty-four - giving more people the chance to minimize the harm caused by crime through a process of collective negotiation. (This would, however, almost certainly require legislative changes.) The range of offences which are considered appropriate to have dealt with in conferences might also be extended. Here any decision must depend on the willingness of victims to participate, and on the preparedness of the decision-making panel to extend the range of offences being sent to conference. The admission of officials from other agencies to what is currently the Sergeants' Panel might encourage further debate about how offences should best be dealt with.

The geographical reach of the scheme could certainly be extended. That prospect has already alarmed some critics. It has been suggested that the scheme would not work in big cities. These critics may not have heard that Wagga, for all its charms, ranks eleventh of one hundred and sixty nine patrols in the state in its rate of recorded juvenile crime. It has been suggested that the programme won't work for Aboriginal people. Aboriginal people, as it happens, have shown more interest in the programme than many other groups in the community. They recognize the place of shame in healing wrongs committed against others.

Many of these criticisms are indicative of the vested institutional interests and half-disguised prejudices confronting anyone who seeks constructive change in the justice system. But the real obstacle to change will possibly be lethargy. Perhaps the current juvenile justice system, for all its faults, is relatively stable. People know their place. Police officers, welfare workers, legal aid solicitors, magistrates, judges, and corrections officials continue their tough and usually thankless work as best they can.

However, those who have taken the time to change one part of this dolorous system in a modest city in southern New South Wales have found that change to part of the system has a catalytic effect upon the rest of it. The local court already has a more manageable load, as do the still overburdened social workers. Relations between police and young people are improving. Local teachers are beginning to reassess their approach to discipline. Some local schools have stopped suspending offenders and are looking more intelligently at how they might better deal with troublesome students. Teachers are discussing at conferences the link between education and reintegration. They have suggested that the term 'Community Accountability Conference' would better reflect the central purpose and complexity of the process. The term implies that community members are active decision-makers, not recipients of well-polished services.

The success of a reform should not, however, be measured in terms of its impact on officialdom. The real success of social reform must be measured in terms of its impact upon the general citizenry. And as we have argued, this reform appears to be achieving what it was designed to achieve. It is not a reform whereby the state offers kinder welfare or tougher punishment to young offenders. This is a reform whereby the state arranges and coordinates a collective response to crime by the community of people who have been most affected by it. That response is designed to minimize the harm caused by the crime. The process occurs at the very first point of contact with the justice system, seeking justice for victims and offenders within a community that will be strengthened by its collective response to the incident. The Family Group Conference, or Community Accountability Conference, is fundamentally a democratic process. It respects people's rights while reminding them of their duties. So we commend the scheme to members of any community with the collective will to arrange a better system of justice for its young people.[4]

References

Alder, J. and Wundersitz, J. (1994) *Family Conferencing: The Way Forward or Misplaced Optimism?* Canberra: Australian Institute of Criminology.

Athens, L.H. (1989) *The Creation of Dangerous Violent Criminals*, London: Routledge.

Avery, K. (1981) *Police: Force or Service?* Sydney: Butterworths.

Braithwaite, J. (1989) *Crime, Shame, and Reintegration*, Cambridge, Cambridge University Press.

Coleman, J.S. (1990) *Foundations of Social Theory*, Cambridge, MA: Harvard University Press.

Damon, W. (1988) *The Moral Child: Nurturing Children's Natural Moral Growth*, New York: Free Press.

Dymond, K., Jamieson, J., Coates, B., and Couling, N. (1992) *Report on Young Offenders who have been subject to the Wagga Wagga Police Cautioning Process*, Wagga Wagga: School of Humanities and Social Sciences (unpublished).

Friedman, L. (1993) *Crime and Punishment in American History*, New York: Basic Books.

Garfinkel, H. (1956) 'Conditions of Successful Degradation Ceremonies', *American Journal of Sociology*, 61: 420-424.

Garland, D. (1990) *Punishment and Modern Society: A Study in Social Theory* Chicago: Chicago University Press.

Gerrull, S. and Atkinson, L. (eds) (1994) *Proceedings of the National Conference on Juvenile Justice*, Canberra: Australian Institute of Criminology.

Gottfredson, M.R. and Hirschi, T. (1990) *A General Theory of Crime*, San Francisco: Stanford University Press.

Green, J.R. and Mastrofski, S.D. (eds) *Community Policing: Rhetoric or Reality?* New York: Praeger.

Hickie, D. (1985) *The Prince and the Premier* Sydney: Angus and Robertson.

McDonald, J. and Ireland, S. (1990) *Can it be Done Another Way?*, Sydney: New South Wales Police Service (Internal Report).

Mason, K. (Chair) (1992) *Review of the Children, Young Persons, and their Family Act 1989*, Report of the Ministerial Review Team to the Minister for Social Welfare, The Hon. Jenny Shipley, Wellington.

Maxwell, G. and Morris, A. (1992) *Family Participation, Cultural Diversity and Victim Involvement in Youth Justice: A New Zealand Experiment*, Wellington: Victoria University.

Maxwell, G. and Morris, A. (1993) *Kids in Trouble*, Wellington: Daphne Brasell and Assoc.

Moore, D.B. (1992) 'Criminal Justice and Conservative Government in New South Wales (1988-1992): The Significance of Police Reform', *Police Studies* 15: 41-54.

Moore, D.B. (1993) 'Shame, Forgiveness, and Juvenile Justice' *Criminal Justice*

Ethics 12:1, 3-25.

Moore, D.B. (1994a) 'Evaluating Family Group Conferences: Some early findings from Wagga Wagga', in D. Biles and S. McKillop (eds) *Criminal Justice Planning and Coordination*, Canberra: Australian Institute of Criminology.

Moore, D.B. (1994b) 'Pride, Shame, and Empathy in Children's Peer Relations', in K. Rigby and P.T. Slee (forthcoming).

Moore, D.B. and O'Connell, T.A. (1994) 'Family Conferencing in Wagga Wagga: a Communitarian Model of Justice', in C. Alder and J. Wundersitz (eds) *Family Conferencing and Juvenile Justice*, Canberra: Australian Institute of Criminology.

O'Connell, T.A. and Moore, D.B. (1992) 'Wagga Juvenile Cautioning Process', *Rural Society* 2:2,16-19.

O'Neill, J. (1993) 'Highway Robbery', *The Independent Monthly,* October: 36-41.

Polk, K. (1994) 'The Family Conference: Theoretical and Evaluative Questions', in C. Alder and J. Wundersitz (eds) *Family Conferencing and Juvenile Justice*, Canberra: Australian Institute of Criminology.

Sandor, D. (1993) 'The Thickening Blue Wedge in Juvenile Justice', *Alternative Law Journal* 18:3.

Scherer, K. (1992) *Justice: Interdisciplinary Perspectives* Cambridge: Cambridge University Press.

Schneider, C.D. (1977) *Shame, Exposure, and Privacy*, Boston: Beacon.

Seymour, J. (1988) *Dealing With Young Offenders*, Sydney: Law Book Company.

Skolnick, J.H. and Bayley, D.M. (1986) *The New Blue Line*, New York: Free Press.

Tyler, T.R. (1990) *Why People Obey The Law*, New Haven: New Haven: Yale University Press.

Walker, S. (1989) 'Paths to Police Reform', in D.J. Kearney (ed.) *Police and Policing: Contemporary Issues*, New York: Praeger.

Wispé, L. (1991) *The Psychology of Sympathy*, New York: Plenum Press.

Wundersitz, J. (1992) 'The Netwidening Effect of Aid Panels and Screening Panels in the South Australian Juvenile Justice System', *Australian and New Zealand Journal of Criminology* 25: 115-134.

Youth Justice Coalition (NSW) (1990) *Kids in Justice: A Blueprint for the 90s*, Sydney: Youth Justice Coalition.

Notes

1. David Moore teaches history, politics and justice studies at Charles Sturt University, New South Wales. John McDonald is Adviser to the New South Wales Police Service on youth affairs and juvenile justice.

2. The Criminology Research Council is the external research arm of the Australian Institute of Criminology, Canberra.

3. This high level of satisfaction in victims was recorded both immediately after the conferences and up to four months later.
4. The views expressed in this essay are those of the authors alone, and do not necessarily reflect the official position of institutions with which they might be affiliated.

VIII   Native policing in Canada: A critical enquiry

Tonio Sadik[1]

Introduction

This essay examines the development of Native policing in the Canadian context. It explores the relationship which has existed between Native peoples and the policing institutions utilized to achieve social order in their communities. By combining an examination of Native policing at the national level with field research in one specific Native community, this inquiry provides a broad overview of national issues with a sensitivity to concerns as they emerge in the micro-context. Hence, a focus on the Walpole Island First Nation serves to highlight one community's struggle towards autonomy and self-sufficiency in this regard. In the final analysis, however, the most significant achievement in regard to Native policing has been the replacement of 'regular' police officers with those chosen by a Band Council.[2] Although this had been a primary objective of many Native communities, it was hardly envisioned as the *only* one.

There is little evidence to support the supposition that Native peoples have been struggling to re-assert their autonomy merely in an effort to replicate the policies and institutions they have attempted to shed in the first place. Indeed, there is considerable evidence to suggest that the earlier aspirations of some of these communities may have been more ambitious. As it stands, Natives have been empowered only to the degree that they have been willing to establish institutions which correspond to those which already exist in the wider society. This has prevented the assumption of a more active and creative role in the establishment of an autonomous policing structure, let alone a system of self-governance. Moreover, contemporary policing practices have increasingly been criticized, both in Canada and the United States, for their high cost and relative ineffectiveness. Hence, it may not only be in their interest, but rather prudent of Native communities to examine, and actively pursue, alternatives which offer more tenable results.

This research cannot hope to discern, or even review, such alternatives. For the most part, such a task would best be carried out by each community itself; since the needs of each community tend to differ, so too do the initiatives meant to appease those needs. Rather, this research attempts, *first*, to establish the degree to which autonomy in Native policing has only been achieved through replication, and *second*, to underscore the need for Native communities to find alternatives to the contemporary policing model which, in many respects, does not adequately meet their needs. In no way is this research meant to appear as an indictment of police officers in general or specific police departments. Indeed, many of the deficiencies in the policing model which are explored have been identified by police officers and legal administrators themselves. Hence, while this research does challenge some aspects of contemporary policing, it does so with constructive intent.

Methodology

The Walpole Island First Nation is an Indian Reserve[3] located in south-western Ontario, near the town of Wallaceburg. Comprising five islands, the largest of which is 'Walpole', this community consists of 200 square kilometres of land, water, and marsh, and has a population of 1700 (Van Wyck 1992). By virtue of being an island, Walpole has enjoyed a relatively high degree of geographic independence. However, because of its location in what has become both an agricultural and industrial *mecca*, the Walpole Island community has a long and intensive history of interaction with its surroundings. It lies between the Canadian and American borders, and has its 'front' on one of North America's busiest international shipping lanes. Indeed, it is useful to recognize at the outset that this community cannot be distinguished from a non-Native community on the basis of superficial stereotypes which attempt to assert idyllic cliches about 'Indian country'.

Having been the first Native community in Canada to achieve a form of self-governance,[4] this community has experienced significant development under the guidance of an active Band Council. Indeed, Walpole Island has maintained a research facility since the mid-1970s, and this has facilitated the development of a cooperative research programme between Walpole Island and the nearby University of Windsor. This programme, called

Nin.da.waab.jig ('those who seek to find'), arose as a reflection of complementary interests between these two parties, and provides Walpole Island with an alternate source of research to those of the provincial and federal governments (Hedley 1986). It is through this programme that this research has been made possible.

The findings of this research are the result of personal interviews, field observation, and archival and literary research. A total of fifteen formal, and three informal, interviews were conducted over a period of five months in 1992. However, this entire research project will have spanned almost two years by the time of its completion. While every effort has been made to be accurate and complete in this research, it is necessary to state its limitations. Because this research examines policing only in communities defined as 'Native', its applicability can only be extended to Natives who have chosen to live within such communities, and who are recognized 'Band Members'.[5] Furthermore, although this research purports to examine the development of Native policing, it cannot be expected to incorporate adequately all relevant Native and policing issues. Hence, discussions with regard to many related issues (e.g. crime, self-government, etc.) remain peripheral to this research.

Theoretical framework

The development of clear policies in regard to Native policing have been doubly inhibited through the withering of a Native self-identity, and a corresponding growth of policing institutions. Among other things, pronounced advancements in transportation and telecommunications, throughout this century, have had a profound impact on the ability of Native communities to maintain culturally specific and cohesive community structures. Moreover, an ideological shift in the strategy used to inhibit criminal activity in the 1970s, termed 'crime control', has spurred a fantastic growth in North American police institutions (Williams and McShane 1988). These two trends can be seen to have merged in recent decades whereby Native communities have come, increasingly, to rely upon the contemporary model of policing to curb crime and maintain social order.

This conclusion, in itself, is relatively unproblematic as there is no explicit reason to suggest that Natives *should not* have come to rely upon the contemporary policing model. However, with hindsight, several matters come to light which suggest that there may have been other alternatives available to Native peoples. This observation is particularly relevant in the present context for two reasons; not only has there been a recent resurgence of what has been called Native 'pride' or 'awareness', but governments and researchers alike have been finding that recent developments in policing are falling short of their mark (Solicitor General 1991 and 1990; Normandeau and Leighton 1991). These findings suggest that Natives may be prudent in pursuing alternative strategies for the resolution of community problems which the police have not been able to resolve (e.g. youth crime, alcoholism, drug abuse, etc.). Moreover, by taking this lead, Natives may find this to be a prime opportunity to assert solutions which are more 'community' and/or 'culturally' specific.

However, a difficulty emerges in regard to the degree to which conditions and features in contemporary Native communities can be attributed directly to some discernible facet of that which may be deemed to be authentically 'Native'. Indeed, two perspectives arise from this dilemma and serve, in a negative way, to establish a basis for this research. The first perspective holds that Natives have no grounds from which to assert claims of autonomy, while the second attempts to assert idyllic cliches about Native peoples (typically in the context of 'tradition') which are in contrast to the reality of the Native situation. This research refutes both of these perspectives, maintaining the *emergent* status of Canada's indigenous cultures (Carstens 1991; Mooney 1979), while rejecting the rhetoric of *traditionalism* which tends to mystify an understanding of contemporary Native issues (Brodeur 1992). Hence, this research examines Native policing in a context which recognizes the inherent sovereignty of contemporary Native cultures, without either minimizing, or mystifying, them.

The police: a critical profile

Manning (1971) argues that the police's self-proclaimed area of expertise (over crime) is inherently vast and unmanageable and, as a result, that the police have resorted to a 'manipulation of appearances'. Indeed, there is significant irony in the use of 'crime control' as the criterion to assess not only, but 'sell', this institution to the public (Ericson 1982). Only a fraction of the time an officer spends on 'patrol' actually relates to anything 'criminal' (e.g. criminals, criminal law). For example, McCabe and Sutcliffe (1978) found that the time spent on incidents defined as 'criminal', in England, were on average only 6% of a patrol officer's work. Moreover, Reiss (1971), in the United States, found this figure to be only 3%.[6] This leads one to question the rationale which justifies the assessment of police work in this way.

Corresponding to a conception of 'police work' as relating primarily to crime is the emphasis which these institutions put on requiring more resources in an effort to adequately inhibit criminal activities. This element of police work was emphasized to such a high degree, beginning in the 1970s, that we saw a fantastic increase in the resources used to 'fight crime' (Williams and McShane 1988). Statistics from 1962 to 1977 show that the number of police personnel (including civilians) per 1000 citizens increased by more than 60% during this period,[7] and that spending on policing over a similar period increased by more than a factor of ten.[8] More recent data, from 1986, suggests that the number of police officers has levelled off,[9] while costs have continued to soar.[10] Although these figures speak for themselves, they do not show what effect, if any, these changes have had on the level of crime.

Consequently, the critical question in this regard is whether more police officers, more police cars, more sophisticated equipment, and more access to firearms in fact reduce the level of crime. Although the public has been led to believe that there is an inverse correlation between these resources/procedures and the level of crime, the connection is, in fact, much more tenuous (Stahura and Huff 1979). There is no doubt that the police do provide an essential service in our society. The more significant point to be drawn out, however, pertains to which services the police are most suited to provide. In this regard, one must determine if there are services currently provided by the police which may be better met in other ways, or by other institutions. While it is not my intention to undertake an evaluation of the various services provided by the police, it is essential to underscore the inherent unsuitability of a traditional police response - which is concerned primarily with being fast and potentially forceful (Solicitor General 1991) - to situations which require more sensitivity and extended care. The inappropriateness of organizing an entire police force on this basis is shown most clearly by the finding that less then 4% of all calls for service pertain to life-threatening incidents or events in progress (Solicitor General 1991).

Indeed, violent crimes are of the sort which the public are most concerned about. Yet, what proportion of crimes fall into this category?[11] Police statistics indicate that violent offences represent only 5.8% of all the crimes reported in Canada (Griffiths and Verdun-Jones 1989). Hence, one must re-assess the basis on which policing is organized and, moreover, attempt to determine which sorts of activities the police are *ill-suited* to resolve.[12] Do we really expect the police to solve a person's drug problem (e.g. possession)? Are the police actually going to resolve alcohol-related offences (e.g. under-age drinking)? Can we really expect the police to eliminate homelessness (e.g. loitering) and poverty (e.g. theft)? Or, is it these problems, which relate more closely to other conditions (e.g., socio-economic status), which keep the 'crime rate' ever-inflated? The definition of many problems, with which the police deal regularly, as 'crimes' has made the police task an insurmountable one, while, at the same time, it has allowed these problems to persist.

One such problem, particularly relevant in this context, is that of racial discrimination. Not only is racial discrimination a significant problem in the larger Canadian society, but it is one which is reproduced at an alarming rate by the contemporary institution of policing. This is because not only has racial discrimination become an institutionalized part of the entire criminal justice system (i.e. it has become 'systemic'), but because police officers, in general, exercise a higher degree of discretion than any other criminal justice official. Indeed, the general problem of discrimination is quickly revealed in an examination of criminal justice statistics. Keeping in mind that Natives make up less than 4% of the national population, they constitute approximately 10% of the federal penitentiary population (Canadian Bar Association 1988), including 15% for incarcerated women (Department of Justice 1991). For Native males over the age of fifteen and considered to be 'status' Indians,[13] compared to their non-Native counterparts, they are thirty-seven times more likely to be incarcerated (Hylton 1981). And for Native women this figure is a staggering one hundred and thirty one times more likely. A study in Saskatchewan (Hylton 1981) found that a Native male turning sixteen had a 70% chance of at least one stay in prison before he turned twenty-five. Figures this high indicate that in such places as Manitoba and Saskatchewan, where Natives represent 7% of the population, but make up 46 and 60% of prison admissions respectively, for young Native males prison may have become the equivalent of what high school is for non-Natives (Jackson 1989).

There are, however, many problems which arise in any attempt to pursue solutions to these problems, particularly when they are framed as alternatives to the contemporary policing model. In some respects, this institution has become so ingrained in our society that such a quest seems formidable. Yet, developments in recent years have lent support to such a position. This is reflected most clearly in the development of 'community policing'; a strategy which is attempting to shift the focus of policing from 'reacting' to crime to a 'proactive' approach.[14] This revised method of policing has arisen during the last decade, and is currently being implemented throughout Canada in an attempt to address problems which have not been addressed in the 'crime control' model of policing. Most generally, it involves two changes; a transition from a hierarchic para-military type of organization to one which is more civilian oriented, and, the development of a structure which is integrated into a broader context to form a social service network more apt to provide a long-term response to problems (Solicitor General 1991).

Community policing is an approach which should be lauded for its identification of problems which exist in the crime control model of policing. However, it has also been criticized, particularly in regard to its implementation as a panacea (Leighton 1991). Essentially, community policing attempts to counter those developments which have made policing increasingly technical, but have not made it any more effective. Some describe this as a 'back to the future' approach. This phrase refers to a growing awareness in regard to the illusory benefits of a technologically-oriented society. Although the achievement of this awareness is important, in the context of community policing, it has done little more than romanticize the past. It has attempted to import past practices into the present context with little regard to their current suitability. Moreover, while community policing has allowed police officers to inquire into the nature of their roles in this institution *without threatening the positions which they hold* - a significant point - it has also been threatened by officers who are unwilling, or perhaps unable, to make this broad transition (Solicitor General 1991). To the degree that the police operate with an implicit mandate to exercise discretion in a way which conforms with dominant community attitudes, and which may include discrimination based on race, community policing may not render any improvement at all. Hence, while community policing can be identified as a step in the right direction, we should not be led to believe, as its implementers seem to suggest (e.g. the Solicitor General), that it is a solution in itself.

The development of native policing

Loree (1985) notes that relations between the police and Natives have been of concern since before Confederation. The North West Mounted Police (N.W.M.P.), the precursors of today's Royal Canadian Mounted Police (R.C.M.P.), were in fact established to control Native and Métis populations of North-Western Canada (Brown and Brown 1973). While there is an indication that some Native groups were grateful to the N.W.M.P. for suppressing the worst aspects of the whisky trade[15] (Aboriginal Justice Inquiry, Vol. 1, 1991), more commonly, the N.W.M.P. are recognized as the main instrument employed by the government to carry out its repressive policies (Brown and Brown 1973). The early period marks the beginning of a dilemma which is at the root of the Native struggle for autonomy in policing. On the one hand, the police are mandated to perform a protective function for civilian (including Native) communities, while on the other hand, they represent the coercive means with which the government was able to impose control over Native peoples in the first place.

As a result of this dilemma four general models have emerged which attempt to alleviate some of the friction between the police and Native peoples. The first two models include 1) providing legal education for Native peoples, and 2) emphasizing cross-cultural training programmes for police forces. Both of these assume that enhanced (access to) information can help to address problems in the criminal justices system, but, ultimately, have had little effect due to their focus on the 'individual' and their denial of a problem at the systemic level. The latter two models, 3) the inclusion of Native constables in police forces,[16] and 4) the establishment of tribal policing programmes, attempt to address these problems at a more substantive level. Although tribal policing, in particular, has shown some promise, it is the model most reluctantly pursued by the Canadian government(s). Harding (1991) stresses, however, that none of these models were created in a way which complemented the notion of self-governance for Native peoples. He points out that from the beginning the models were implemented in a way which was to reinforce the underlying political assumptions of the day, and have maintained an ideology of assimilation (Harding 1991). In this respect, these models were initiated with a cross-purpose: addressing problems with regard to policing Natives, but only to the degree that the *status quo* was not being significantly challenged. The dialectic which emerged from this situation underscores the inherent limits of each of these initiatives.

Policing on the Walpole Island First Nation: a case study

Little is known about policing on Walpole Island prior to the twentieth century. In part, this is due to a fire in a federal storage facility, in 1897, which destroyed many of the materials pertaining to this early period. Although there had been *some* police activity on Walpole Island prior to the turn of the century, Burton Jacobs, a highly respected Native Elder, suggests that policing did not become relevant until the beginning of this century. This observation provides the starting point for this examination, and underscores the relatively recent arrival of policing in this community. Indeed, it should be kept in mind that, prior to the advent of regular policing services, this community must have relied on its own resources to maintain public order.

However, even before the police became significant on Walpole Island, it was customary for Agency Offices[17] to maintain a prison cell; and this was indicative of the Indian Agent's inherently authoritarian role (Hawthorn-Tremblay 1967). The first explicit record of police activities on Walpole Island comes in 1910, and pertains to a Police Magistrate holding court in 'Indian (Council) Hall'. The case in question involved a school teacher who had brutally beaten a Native pupil, and Walpole Island's Indian Constable was given the responsibility of taking this teacher away the following day. At least two further 'Indian Constables' worked on Walpole Island during the first two decades of this century, under what was known as the Dominion Police. However, in 1919, the Dominion Police was absorbed into what had become known as the *Royal* North West Mounted Police (R.N.W.M.P.), and the name of this newly formed conglomerate was changed to the Royal Canadian Mounted Police (R.C.M.P.). Hence, the R.C.M.P. received authority over Walpole Island in 1920.

At this time, R.C.M.P. officers did not live on the Island, and when a problem arose, if they were not already there, they would have to be summoned. This would have been one of the duties of the respective Indian Constable. There is an indication that such Constables may have had the authority to make arrests and to go to court, but even then, their activities were limited by their dependence on the R.C.M.P. By the 1950s, legislative overlap had created contradictions in the jurisdictions of the police, and led the R.C.M.P. to establish a detachment on Walpole Island in 1953. Although an informal relationship of co-operation had begun to develop between the Ontario Provincial Police (O.P.P.) and R.C.M.P., it broke down with the development of further jurisdictional complications (O.P.P. 1987). The main problem which was to emerge related to the three levels of government which had developed: federal, provincial, and Band. The *Indian Act*, which was federal, was enforced by the R.C.M.P., while provincial laws were enforced by the O.P.P. But with the growth of Band by-laws, a new controversy arose. Because the power to enact by-laws stemmed from a provision in the *Indian Act*, and because by-laws superseded all provincial legislation, it was the R.C.M.P.'s responsibility to enforce them. However, as the number of by-laws began to grow, so too did the R.C.M.P.'s reluctance to provide resources to these communities.

For this reason, Indian Constables were hired to carry out the leg-work involved in by-law enforcement and, more generally, in keeping the peace. Although their authority to keep the peace extended beyond the enforcement of by-laws, the exercise of formal power was always carried out by, or in

conjunction with, the R.C.M.P. Hence, in the event that an Indian
Constable wanted to issue a fine, he would always have to get assistance
from the R.C.M.P. In this respect, an Indian Constable's authority was
largely symbolic, and relied upon his ability to make people believe that he
in fact did possess sufficient powers. However, an Indian Constable's role
continued to be hampered by one of two circumstances. Either he was
increasingly forced to call upon the R.C.M.P. to process a charge,[18] or, there
simply were not enough by-laws to warrant the cost of appointing an Indian
Constable in the first place.[19] Initially, in an attempt to resolve this problem,
Indian Constables were hired at a more productive level, full-time.

However, even with the establishment of a local R.C.M.P. detachment and
a full-time Indian Constable, Walpole Island's by-laws were not being
enforced, and the Band Council was becoming discouraged. Part of the
problem at this time pertained to the 1951 revision of the *Indian Act*. This
revision required that all by-laws be revised to correspond to its new
mandate. Coupled with the original problems of by-law enforcement, this
proved to bring their enforcement to a virtual standstill. By 1960, not much
had changed, and Councillors were anxious for solutions. During this period
a transformation began to take place on Walpole Island. In 1959, Walpole
Island became only the second 'Indian Reservation' in Canada to handle its
own revenue funds, and the election of Burton Jacobs as Chief, in 1960,
became the turning point for Walpole Island's shift into a new political era.

The 1960s were characterized by an increase in the political self-reliance
of the Walpole Island Band. This is reflected in the growing number of
initiatives which this community attempted to undertake. However, rather
than pursue conventional avenues for the resolution of community problems,
Walpole Island's Council began to exercise some of its powers vis-a-vis the
revised *Indian Act*. In this regard, the 1951 revision of the *Indian Act*
altered the status of Natives from that of 'complete disempowerment'[20] to
that of *limited* re-empowerment. Although many revisions had been made
to the *Indian Act* of 1951, opinions differed as to the degree of real
improvement which had been achieved (*Nin.da.waab.jig.* 1989). Indeed,
there was little doubt that assimilation remained the primary goal of this
legislation and, more recently, its insidious undertones have become more
fully recognized. While the new *Indian Act* did give Native Bands more
powers, it did so within a framework which necessitated that they establish
themselves in a way which paralleled the wider society. One of the new
provisions contained within the *Indian Act* had given Native Bands the
opportunity to hold a referendum on the issue of alcohol in their
communities.[21] In 1959, the Walpole Island Band voted in favour of

acquiring liquor privileges which, unwittingly, precluded the R.C.M.P. from enforcing liquor and liquor-related offences.

Although the consumption of liquor by an adult on the Reserve was no longer an offence under the *Indian Act*, the tendency for criminal acts to be defined as 'involving liquor'[22] necessitated that 'liquor-related' offences be enforced by the O.P.P. Hence, the R.C.M.P's jurisdiction on Walpole Island was severely constrained which, in turn, served to further complicate the by-law issue. In addition, although the R.C.M.P. had, for the most part, already abandoned by-law enforcement on Walpole Island, a new policy was being pursued by the R.C.M.P. which eliminated any hope of having them resume this responsibility. It stated that the force's policy did not provide for the enforcement of by-laws under the *Indian Act*. The reason given by the R.C.M.P. was that because most by-laws had to do with civil and property rights, they could not be considered proper subjects of attention for a force concerned primarily with the enforcement of criminal law.

In this regard, residents of Walpole Island, and many other Native communities, were put into a predicament which rendered by-law enforcement in particular, and law enforcement in general, unviable. Indeed, this angered many Native communities, and Walpole Island's Council responded by asking that the R.C.M.P. be removed from the Island entirely. Council's difficulty, however, was that they had not been empowered to the degree that they could simply *replace* the R.C.M.P. Hence, when these services were found to be ineffective, no mechanism existed to allow this community to institute new services. They had been considered passive recipients of such services, and now that these services were in jeopardy, it left open the question of who would fill this vacancy. Although the R.C.M.P. remained on Walpole Island until 1968, the events which preceded their ultimate removal were an attempt on the part of the Band to assert control over law enforcement.

Two main initiatives arose at this time; first, consistent with a recommendation of the R.C.M.P. was an increase in the use of Native Constables; and second, was an increased reliance on the O.P.P. However, progress in the areas of policing and by-law enforcement remained ambiguous. Nevertheless, Walpole Island's Council continued to pursue the more general goal of increasing its level of self-sufficiency. For example, in 1961, consistent with a provision in the 1951 *Indian Act*, Walpole Island received control over its welfare programme under the *Ontario General Welfare Assistance Act*. Such achievements served to re-affirm this Band's ability to assert administrative control over its affairs, and could only have positive implications for similar pursuits in other areas (e.g. policing).

Indeed, it was likely the success in these areas which led the Chief and a group of Councillors to pursue the removal of the Indian Agent. One incident is particularly revealing in this regard. Although it would be difficult to substantiate, Burton Jacobs, and a few of the Councillors who supported him, all felt that they were being subject to unusual police attention at this time. Jacobs, specifically, indicated that he had encountered a series of episodes of harassment by the police, and while he admitted that they *could* have been coincidental, he suspected that they were related to his campaign for the removal of the Agent (Taylor 1984). These incidents underscore the dilemma which many Natives face in regard to the role of the police. Nevertheless, by 1964, Council had attained what it believed to be majority support for the removal of the Indian Agent, and in September, 1964, the Indian Agent announced that he had a transfer pending, which took place early in the following year. However, with the removal of the Indian Agent there emerged a new problem for Councillors. Although they no longer needed to consult an Agent when making decisions, they were by no means free to act on their own behalf.

It was in June, 1966, that Walpole Island received control over its affairs under a uniquely established form of self-governance. After a one-year period without the Indian Agent, a new precedent had been set among Native communities. Moreover, the commencement of work by Walpole Island's first Band Constable, later that year, also contributed to the growth of locally controlled Native policing. He was appointed as a 'Supernumerary Special Constable' with the R.C.M.P., and was vested with the full authority of a 'Peace Officer'. His official/legal title, however, was not 'Police Officer', nor did he receive an appointment with the O.P.P. as had initially been desired. His duties were limited to the enforcement of certain terms of the *Indian Act*, and all Band by-laws. However, while it was clear that the R.C.M.P. could assist the Constable in enforcing sections of the *Indian Act* (e.g. laying charges and prosecuting), no one knew what procedure would be followed when a charge was being laid in respect to a by-law. While he could adequately lay a charge and act as a witness in court, he could not be expected to also act as a Prosecutor. This problem was to continue to inhibit the effective enforcement of by-laws, and maintained an element of uncertainty in regard to this Constables actual authority.

In 1968, the R.C.M.P. announced that it was removing its detachment from Walpole Island. As a result, the O.P.P. in Sombra began to take a more active role in the policing of Walpole Island. The O.P.P. did not set up a detachment on the Island but, in conjunction with the Native Constable, began to conduct regular patrols. However, only months later, changes were announced by the O.P.P. While there was to be no direct change to Walpole Island, the O.P.P.'s Sarnia detachment was being relocated, which, as a consequence, affected the jurisdiction of the O.P.P. in Sombra; Sombra was to continue to police the Island, but patrols were to be less frequent. This, in turn, increased the need for a local police detachment. It was determined that Walpole Island's police force should be enlarged to four persons. In part, this was due to the anticipated opening of a bridge which was to connect Walpole Island and the Canadian mainland. Opened in May, 1970, the community recognized that this bridge was going to have a profound impact on the Island. Not only could anyone now commute to and from the Island, but the amount of traffic which was to enter Walpole Island was going to increase dramatically. Hence, the effectiveness of the police was perceived to be of paramount importance.

Burton Jacobs, who had been Chief for ten years, was replaced by Don Isaac in 1970; an incumbent who was particularly keen on establishing a locally controlled police force. Later that year, the Superintendent of the O.P.P. addressed Council to explain a move which was being planned for the establishment of a local Native police force with *three* officers. Its most significant feature was to be that this force was to work under the auspices of the O.P.P. rather than the R.C.M.P. This would enable it to enforce provincial legislation, in addition to by-laws and the *Indian Act*, and its officers would have the authority to pursue individuals beyond the confines of the Reserve. While the O.P.P. continued to patrol the Island, it was not in a position to enforce either by-laws or the *Indian Act*.

With the election of Chief Isaac, the focus of Band Council shifted from enhancing this community's self-sufficiency in accordance with the *Indian Act*, to more far reaching reforms. Indeed, policing was to become a major focus for this Council, and plans were under way to have the Walpole Island Police Force become self-sufficient. There were two ways in which this could be achieved: Walpole Island could allocate sufficient resources to policing to make the O.P.P. unnecessary, or, they could join together with other Native communities to establish an autonomous Native police force. Although it was the first alternative which had initially been favoured by Isaac, the prohibitive cost of supplanting the O.P.P. proved too much for this community. Hence, Walpole Island began to contact other Native groups in regard to the formation of a (provincial) Native police force.

The idea of such an initiative did not take long to catch on. The Association of Iroquois and Allied Indians (A.I.A.I.) began to represent the various Native communities who were interested in such a project, and initiated negotiations with the government. The germination of this initiative should not be understated: the development of an autonomous Native police force represented a radical departure from the types of reforms envisioned in earlier decades. In the face of increasing uncertainty with regard to policing, and increasing disenchantment with the willingness of the government to resolve long standing problems, this impetus underscores the growing commitment of Native peoples to resolve their own problems. While Walpole Island was a focal point for this initiative, many other communities had become involved, and similar movements had also begun to operate in other parts of the country (Harding 1991). From a pragmatic perspective, this initiative contained a multitude of redeeming features. The formation of a (provincial) Native police force could resolve many of the difficulties which both Walpole Island, and other Native communities, were experiencing.

The atmosphere seemed very optimistic and, at one point, there was even a report suggesting that Walpole Island would provide the training ground for this new provincial Police Force. However, while the planning of this initiative continued to receive support from Native communities, little had changed in the area of policing. Indeed, it seemed that the government was reluctant to give in to such a proposition, but was hard pressed to come up with alternate solutions to difficulties which had developed in regard to the policing of Native communities. In February, 1974, the government did finally respond to Native demands with the issuing of a report which had been produced by the Provincial Solicitor General. Entitled the 'Task Force on Policing in Ontario', it recommended that Ontario initiate what was to become the (Ontario) 'Indian Constable Programme'. The main impetus of this report was to bring Native Constables under the jurisdiction of the O.P.P. rather than the R.C.M.P. (O.P.P. 1987). Although this had been identified by Native Bands as a necessary step for over a decade, such a change was to have Native Constables come under the partial jurisdiction of the (Ontario) *Police Act* which, in turn, would *preclude the development of an autonomous Native police force.*

With the implementation of the Indian Constable Programme over the latter part of 1975, and into 1976, attempts by Natives to implement their own initiatives were increasingly displaced. This programme had been implemented on a grand scale and, as a result, had the effect of suppressing all other initiatives. Although 100% of the funding was now to be provided by the provincial and federal governments, a significant degree of control had shifted from the Band to the province. Indeed, funding had not been provided without strings attached. This programme is best characterized as a 'basket of goods': Native communities were only in a position to receive full funding in the context of this programme. Hence, they received little opportunity for input into policing, and were compelled to abandon their own initiatives in favour of one for which they would not have to pay. The implementation of this programme on Walpole Island was to be the final 'reform' which this community would see, and was to establish the framework around which all other developments in policing would emerge.

In the contemporary period, the reforms and initiatives sought by this community have become more mainstream. Critical to developments in this regard has been the institution of the Indian Constable Programme, and the degree to which Native communities have been made to rely on the funding of this programme. Although Walpole Island had always received partial funding for its Constables, the extent to which funds have been specifically allocated under this programme has eliminated the ability of Native communities to develop their own policing programmes. Rather, the Walpole Island Band is involved in policing primarily at a *managerial* level, and has had little say in what shape developments will take. Although several modifications have been made in regard to the arrangement of policing in this and other Native communities, including: the development of a five year 'policing agreement';[23] a renewed cost sharing agreement;[24] and the development of a tripartite negotiation process;[25] these changes continue to occur within the constraints of the (Ontario) 'Indian Constable Programme'.

Discussion

We have seen that the trend on Walpole Island, ultimately, and perhaps inadvertently, has been towards the replication of the common policing model. Although 'Native policing' is not *identical* to that in non-Native communities, it has been premised on the same 'crime control' model and, if the trend we have observed continues, no doubt, will be 'identical' at some point in the future. As a result, like its non-Native counterpart, it is plagued both by high costs and relative ineffectiveness. Although we have seen that recent actions taken by the Solicitor General have attempted to alter the fundamental basis of policing (i.e. community policing), we have also seen that these changes are relatively short-sighted and operate within a political, as well as practical, framework. It is in the culmination of all of these factors that we are able to narrow the focus of this research on to 'Native' policing.

For a large part, it is the strength of the messages which suggest that policing (as we know it) is not only necessary, but the only means by which public order can be maintained. While this is equally true in Native and non-Native communities, the police have had a more ambiguous role in Native communities, and, as a result, are not as firmly ingrained in these communities. Moreover, we saw that on Walpole Island, in the early 1970s, this Band attempted to institute its own police force to the exclusion of any other. Hence, unlike in the non-Native context, Natives have been quite willing to explore alternatives to the current policing model. However, thus far, such attempts have maintained their focus on the repudiation of mainstream police authority, rather than on the implementation of alternatives to the contemporary policing model.

It is within this context that I have attempted to illustrate the degree to which 'Native policing' has been defined by the contemporary policing model. Moreover, it is as a result of this finding that I have challenged the practicality of this model, and, in turn, have attempted to underscore the need to implement alternatives to this model. Indeed, problems with the contemporary model of policing have been interpreted as a *necessary evil* in the further implementation of this model (e.g. in Native communities). This has only been achieved, however, as a result of the 'sell job' which has been undertaken to make us believe that policing *is the only alternative*. Apart from the practical advantages which Native communities may have in regard to the implementation of alternatives to policing, there are further criteria which serve to highlight the desirability of taking such actions.

Native communities find themselves in a complex position in the contemporary context. The recent rejection of the Charlottetown Accord by Native peoples, which would have entrenched their sovereignty in the Canadian Constitution, while also eliminating the *Indian Act*, epitomizes this complexity. To a significant degree, the viability of Native claims is tied to the support which they receive from the Canadian population at large. It is through the mobilization of such support, through such groups as the Assembly of First Nations, that Native peoples have been able to bring their concerns to the forefront of the political agenda. The continued mobilization of such support remains an integral ingredient for the ultimate recognition of Native sovereignty.

Critical to such support is the perceived validity of the claims which Native peoples make. In this regard, Native groups have been asserting their sovereignty on a variety of fronts to strengthen their own positions, but also to receive public exposure and support. Although the assertion of sovereignty in policing was inspired by the profound inability of the judicial system to provide 'justice' to Native peoples, it has also operated to provide legitimacy to more general calls for sovereignty. In this regard, there is no reason for Natives to pursue autonomy in policing only in an effort to replicate the institutions which they are shedding. Rather, by exploring potential alternatives available to them, Natives may find more constructive means of dealing with problems in their communities, while at the same time strengthening their claims of sovereignty.

In an earlier section, I cautioned against the superficial imposition of 'traditional' alternatives to policing. Native communities are in a precarious situation, and it is unlikely that oversimplified 'traditional' solutions will be able to deal effectively with their needs. In an effort to ensure the viability of alternatives which are, in fact, deemed appropriate, communities could begin to institute alternatives *along side* current structures of policing. It is unlikely that policing, as it is known today, will be done away with entirely. After all, communities will continue to need a minority of services meant to address the most serious of crimes (e.g. violent crimes), and in some cases, will continue to require a rapid, and in some cases forceful, response to some situations. The emphasis of this research, however, has been on the degree to which such services are *not* necessary, and as such, on the implementation of initiatives which are better able to deal with a wide variety of situations.

A primary concern for all Native communities inclined to pursue alternatives to policing is the degree that such alternatives will have to continue to correspond and interact with the Canadian judicial system. In the long run, this problem may resolve itself as more and more Native communities develop their own resources, and, in this way, are able to rely upon and assist one another. Nonetheless, these are problems which will have to be dealt with, but which should not preclude the development of alternatives in this regard. For the time being, it is individual communities which must act on their initiative, recognizing that the contemporary policing model offers few solutions and little hope for reform.

Conclusion

This research has examined the development of Native policing. It has explored the relationship which has existed between the Native peoples and the institutions used to police their communities. Through archival and academic research, as well as a focus on the Walpole Island First Nation, I have attempted to illustrate the degree to which 'Native policing' has come to be synonymous with 'regular' policing. Although this, in itself, was not a problematic finding, a critical examination of the contemporary policing model served to underscore some of the difficulties in this regard. The goal of this research has been to identify, and where possible to address, some of the deficiencies inherent in the 'crime control' model of policing to achieve social order within communities. This was undertaken in the hope that such an examination might renew a search for more creatively-based alternatives better able to deal with the problems afflicting the contemporary Native setting.

References

Aboriginal Justice Inquiry of Manitoba (Report of the) (1991) *The Justice System and Aboriginal People*, Vol. 1, Manitoba: Queen's Printer.

Brodeur, Jean-Paul (1991) 'Justice for the Cree: Policing and Alternative Dispute Resolution', Quebec: The Grand Council of Crees/ Cree Regional Authority (unpublished).

Brown, Lorne and Brown, Caroline (1973) *An Unauthorized History of the RCMP*, Toronto: Lewis and Samuel.

Canadian Bar Association (1988) *Aboriginal Rights in Canada: An Agenda for Action*, Canada: Canadian Bar Association.

Carstens, Peter (1991) *The Queen's People: A Study of Hegemony, Coercion, and Accommodation Among the Okanagan of Canada*, Toronto: University of Toronto Press.

Department of Justice (The) (1991) *Aboriginal People and Justice Administration: A Discussion Paper*, Ottawa: Department of Justice.

Ericson, Richard V. (1982) *Reproducing Order: A Study of Police Patrol Work*, Toronto: University of Toronto Press.

Griffiths, Curt T. and Verdun-Jones, Simon N. (1989) *Canadian Criminal Justice*, Canada: Butterworths.

Harding, Jim (1991) 'Policing and Aboriginal Justice', *Canadian Journal of Criminology* July-Oct, 363-83.

Hawthorn, H.B. and Tremblay, M.A. (1967) *A Survey of the Contemporary Indians of Canada* (two volumes), Canada.

Hedley, M. J. (1986) 'Community Based Research: The Dilemma of Contract' *The Canadian Journal of Native Studies* VI: 1, 91-103.

Hylton, John H. (1981) 'Locking Up Indians in Saskatchewan', in Thomas Fleming and L.A. Visano (eds) *Deviant Designations: Crime, Law and Deviance in Canada* (1983) Canada: Butterworths and Co., 61-70.

Jackson, Michael (1989) 'Locking Up Natives in Canada', *University of British Columbia Law Review* 23, 215-99.

Leighton, Barry N. (1991) 'Visions of Community Policing: Rhetoric and Reality in Canada', *Canadian Journal of Criminology* July-October, 485-522.

Loree, D.J. (1985) *Policing Native Communities*, Ottawa: Canadian Police College.

Manning, Peter K. (1971) 'The Police: Mandate, Strategies, and Appearances', in Jack D. Douglas (ed.) *Crime and Justice in American Society*, United States: Bobbs-Merrill Company, Inc., 149-93.

McCabe, S. and Sutcliffe, F. (1978) *Defining Crime: A Study of Police Decisions*, England: Basil Blackwell.

Mooney, Kathleen A. (1979) 'Ethnicity, Economics, the Family Cycle, and Household Composition,' *Canadian Review of Sociology and Anthropology* 16, 387-403.

Nin.da.waab.jig (1989) *Walpole Island: The Soul of Indian Territory*, Windsor: Commercial Associates/Ross Roy Ltd.

Normandeau, Andre and Leighton, Barry (1991) 'Police and Society in Canada,' *Canadian Journal of Criminology* July-October, 251-5.

Ontario Provincial Police (O.P.P.) (1987) *Indian Policing: History of the Indian Constable Programme*, Canada: O.P.P.

Reiss, Albert J. Jr. (1971) *The Police and the Public*, New Haven: Yale University Press.

Shearing, Clifford D. (1984) *Dial-A-Cop: A Study of Police Mobilization*, Toronto: Centre of Criminology, University of Toronto.

Solicitor General (Ministry of the) (1991) *Community Policing: An Introduction to the Community Policing Philosophy and Principles*, Ottawa: Queen's Printer.

Solicitor General Canada (1990) *A Vision of the Future of Policing in Canada: Police-Challenge 2000 (Discussion Paper)*, Ottawa: Solicitor General.

Stahura, John M. and Huff, Ronald C. (1979) 'Crime and Police Employment: A Structural Model,' in David M. Petersen (ed.) *Police Work: Strategies and Outcomes in Law Enforcement* (1979) United States: Sage, 79-95.

Taylor, John Leonard (1984) *Indian Band Self-Government in the 1960's: A Case Study of Walpole Island*, Ottawa: Treaties and Historical Research Centre, The Department of Indian Affairs.

Wanner, Richard A. and Caputo, T.C. (1987) 'Punitiveness, Fear of Crime, and Perceptions of Violence', *Canadian Journal of Sociology* 12:4, 331-44.

Williams, Frank P. and McShane, Marilyn D. (1988) *Criminological Theory*, United States: Prentice-Hall.

Williams, Paul C. (1972) *The Oneidas and the Canadian Legal System: Middlesex County*, Canada: unpublished.

Van Wyck, Sheila M. (1992) *Harvests Yet to Reap: History, Identity, and Agriculture in a Canadian Indian Community*, Toronto: University of Toronto: Ph.D. Dissertation.

Notes

1. Tonio Sadik, B.A. (Hons) (Carleton), M.A. (Windsor) is a doctoral candidate in the Department of Sociology, Simon Fraser University. His main area of interest lies in the examination of Native issues, but also includes crime and social (in)justice, the sociology of law, and the social construction of gender relations. He is committed to enhancing sociology's efficacy in the area of policy formulation and has presented his research at a variety of academic conferences.
2. A 'Band Council' is a body of up to twelve 'Councillors' and one 'Chief' elected to represent the members of a respective Native community.
3. An 'Indian Reserve' is a piece of land, defined both geographically and politically, set aside by the Canadian government for Natives to live on. There exist more than six hundred 'reserves' in Canada, all of which are organized in accordance with a comprehensive piece of legislation, enacted in 1876, entitled the *Indian Act*. This piece of legislation was, and continues to be, the primary instrument used by the government to assert control over Native peoples in Canada.
4. Walpole Island has maintained a form of 'delegated authority' since 1965.
5. A 'Band Member' is an individual who, through ancestry and/or bureaucracy, has been defined as 'Indian' in accordance with the *Indian Act*, and who belongs to a specific Native Band.
6. American and English data are used where Canadian data are not readily available. Although such data are often not directly applicable to the Canadian context, in many cases they remains the most accurate means for estimation. Unless noted otherwise, data are always Canadian.
7. This corresponds to 1.7 police personnel per 1,000 population in 1962 to 2.8 in 1977 (Ericson 1982).
8. From 1961 to 1978, provincial spending on policing increased from $34 million to $404 million, while federal spending increased from $49 million to $556 million (Ericson 1982).
9. From 52,000 in 1977 (Ericson 1982) to 55,000 in 1986 (Normandeau and Leighton 1991).
10. The annual budget for police services in Canada in 1986 was approximately $5 billion (Normandeau and Leighton 1991).
11. Typically, the proportion of violent crimes is greatly over-estimated (Wanner and Caputo 1987).
12. For example, Shearing (1984), conducting research in Toronto, found that calls to the police broke down as follows:
    - 23.6% - internal police business
    - 16.3% - accidents, collapses, illness
    - 8.9 % - suspicious circumstances
    - 8.7 % - traffic problems

- 7.4 % - public nuisance
- 7.3 % - other calls
- 7.2 % - services
- 6.7 % - reports of theft
- 5.5 % - disputes
- 3.4 % - response to fire or ambulance service
- 2.5 % - report of injury to person or property
- 2.2 % - returning calls
- 0.3 % - robbery or hold-up

13. The distinction between 'status' and 'non-status' Indians was created by the *Indian Act*, and although both are in fact 'Indians', only the former are recognized as such under this Act.

14. 'Reactive policing' refers to a model of policing which is based on 'enforcement', whereas 'proactive policing' is grounded in 'prevention'.

15. Culminating with the 'Cypress Hills Massacre' (1872), Native communities of the West were increasingly disrupted by the actions of whisky traders; so much so that Sir John A. Macdonald formed the N.W.M.P. two years earlier than planned. His greatest fear, however, related not to the traders but to the possibility that Natives might initiate an 'Indian war' against all Whites (Brown and Brown 1973).

16. This was done, primarily, through a federal program, initiated in 1973, entitled the 'Native Special Constable Program'. In Ontario, a similar programme was adopted in 1975, entitled the 'Indian Constable Program', which is explored in more detail in the following section.

17. 'Agency Office' refers to a structure, typical on most Reserves, which housed an office in which the 'Indian Agent', a non-Native male appointed by Indian Affairs to take charge of a Reserve, would carry out his duties.

18. This could reflect an increase in the denial of an Indian Constable's authority, or an increase in the severity of offences committed.

19. Although this was not the case on Walpole Island.

20. Under the pre-1951 *Indian Act*, Natives were defined as 'wards' of the State.

21. The original *Indian Act* had made the possession and consumption of any alcohol by a Native person an offence.

22. For example, in Middlesex County (which borders Walpole Island in Lambton County to the east), Williams (1972) found that of all Natives sent to county jail in July and August of 1965, 87% were committed there for offences defined as 'liquor-related'.

23. The most significant feature of this 'policing agreement' is that it allows (Ontario's) Native communities to develop their own parallel agreements after receiving approval from the province.

24. Currently the federal government contributes 52% of the costs while the province contributes 48%. The previous arrangement had been 60:40 respectively.

25.   Currently, Native communities are required to negotiate for limited policing resources in a tripartite forum.   They are represented by First Nations Policing, and negotiate with the federal and provincial governments under the auspices of the Indian Commission of Ontario.

IX Urban policing and Aboriginal social health: Research and action

Graham Brice[1]

Introduction

One aim of this essay is to aid the 'self-analysis' of police about which Chief Superintendent Owen Bevan (1991: 51) proposed:

> To have any chance of improving our national and collective performance, people in positions of power, authority and influence must be self-analytical and purposeful enough to acknowledge shortcomings, deficiencies and mistakes ... When people and organizations convince themselves of ... infallible perfection they precipitate huge problems. Such phenomena have not been unknown in Australian policing circles to date.

Despite acknowledged improvements, it seems common for Aboriginal householders and community leaders in Adelaide to perceive relations with police as a very stressful and problematic element in their urban lives, a view unquestionably endorsed by two historic national reports. The first inquiry into the extent of racist violence against Aboriginal and Islander people, the National Inquiry into Racist Violence (Human Rights and Equal Opportunity Commission 1991:121, 209) concluded that the problem was 'endemic' ... as it 'permeates the day-to-day lives of Aboriginal people either through direct acts of violence, intimidation and racist abuse, or through ... more insidious processes'. Secondly, the final report of the Royal Commission into Aboriginal Deaths in Custody (RCIADIC 1991) proclaimed (not merely 'alleged') that all Aboriginal people labour under a racism which 'is institutionalized and systemic, and resides not just in individuals or in individual institutions but in the relationships between the various institutions'.[2]

This essay presents a local and regional, urban perspective on an aspect of this daunting issue, bringing police, academic, and Aboriginal, views to bear on the question of 'where to from here'?

Discussion amongst Aboriginal groups in the wake of the ABC Documentary 'Cop it Sweet' on the policing of Redfern in New South Wales portrayed no element of surprise. Locally, allegations of racist violence and/or intimidation or harassment by some police officers seem to continue - even if not through formal channels of complaint.[3] Reportedly, spokespersons for the South Australian Police Force regard all allegations that such violence is widespread as either, lacking substance: 'perceptions ... being passed off as fact';[4] or, at most, concerned only with 'isolated incidents' which are dealt with swiftly and consistently - hence there is 'no problem'. Thus, to the extent that there is a problem, it is predominantly constructed as individualistic according to this perspective - in stark contrast to that of these two major inquiries.

The official police response to these inquiries seems to have been primarily one of denial. Rather than being 'objective and value-free' they have been seen as highly opportunistic and/or, inherently biased. Clearly, resolution of such conflicting views remains impossible without agreement that there is an underlying reality of disturbing proportions. Remarkably in Adelaide, this seems to have been forthcoming on both sides despite such official comments.[5] One systematic research project in Adelaide seems to have been central to this 'self-analysis' and in the open and constructive, albeit embryonic, discussion which has emerged. A further project, has corroborated the former. Together, these two recent studies of urban Aboriginal experience and perception seem vital to the consideration of such opposing views.

The main study in this regard, a National Health and Medical Research Council funded, population-based research project with a public/social health focus, was jointly conducted by the Aboriginal Education Foundation of South Australia (AEF) and The Flinders University of South Australia (FUSA). From here on this will be referred to as the 'AEF/FUSA' study. As such, it constituted a rare example of an Aboriginal-initiated, cross-cultural study using a methodology jointly constructed with Aboriginal people. The research approach primarily utilized in-depth, semi-structured interviews conducted by Aboriginal people or others well known and respected by the Adelaide Aboriginal community.[6] We will turn to the second study later.

This essay not only examines select, comparative (Aboriginal and non-Aboriginal) data from the final stage of that research, it also reports on a subsequent Aboriginal initiative to bring police to a discussion table in order to calm what have historically been recognized as 'troubled waters' between police and Aboriginal people. Despite having been regarded as 'historic' by Colin Tatz (Professor of Politics, Macquarie University), who formally launched the forum in July 1990, this event has received little recognition. Later it will become clear why a re-examination of this event seems warranted.

'Taking control': the AEFF/FUSA project

Taking Control (Radford et al 1990),[7] the research report of stage one of the AEF/FUSA project, gained wide publicity. It highlighted the experience of 88 randomly-chosen Aboriginal household-heads in state housing in Adelaide, focusing on issues of stress, self-harm, and social structure in this urban Aboriginal population. One of the wide range of social and health-related topics investigated concerned perceptions of police interaction with Aboriginal households. Results included the following:

Police: household visits: Three-in-five of all participants (54 participants, or 62%) reported police had visited their households in the last two years without having been called; 24 had the police 'call' at their homes at least four times in the last two years.

Police: household entries: One-in-four (20, or 24%) reported that police had 'entered their houses without invitation or a warrant, and without proceeding to arrest someone'.

Police: physical abuse: One-in-five (16, or 19%) claimed someone in their household had been 'physically abused by police'. One half of people allegedly abused were children of respondents.

'Persistent disturbance /unreasonable attention' (commonly regarded by Aboriginal people as 'harassment') outside the household: Two-in-five (35, or 40%) of all household-heads reported someone in their household had been subjected to some form of 'harassment'. Of these 35, 20 were personal experiences described in some detail to interviewers. Some

involved allegations of specific incidents of violent behaviour. Others did not. Some resulted in official complaints. Most did not.

Forms of alleged 'harassment'

The 'persistent disturbance/unreasonable attention' ('harassment') took two main forms: both with and without allegations of physical violence. The latter consisted mainly of property ownership questions and assumptions.[8]

The findings could hardly have been unexpected, as Aboriginal people themselves greatly contributed to the question-framing and were responsible for most of the interviewing. In essence, this research comprised (perhaps for the first time in South Australia) a 'black study' of 'black people's perceptions of white people in situations of power', at least in certain important, but limited ways. In other words, while this project was conducted according to rigorous scientific principles, it did not set out to demonstrate scientific 'objectivity' as such, but it provided a 'view from below'.[9] Furthermore, much of the research took place during a period of heightened Aboriginal awareness associated with Bicentennial Celebrations. Interestingly though, Radford et al (1990: 64) reported no simplistic, anti-police thread in these data. Of the 35 who reported experiences or events of 'persistent disturbance /unreasonable attention' ('harassment'), closer investigation revealed they were 'not particularly anti-police in comparison with those who did not report such police "attention"'. Rather, allegations of harassment seemed quite consistently to be reported in conjunction with other aspects of police action. The report continued (Radford et al 1990: 64-65):

> In addition, 'harassment' outside the household was not associated with particular 'targeting' of participants with legal histories, but it was significantly statistically associated both with allegations of past experience of physical abuse by police (by a member of the respondent's household), and with the number of times police had called at the house. It would seem that participants from frequently-visited households are especially (that is, significantly more) likely to also be subject to 'harassment' outside the home - usually in the streets.[10]

It is important to note that some 53 participants (60%) made no allegations of this particular kind. It seems equally important that the Royal Commissioner in his final report (Johnston 1991: 125) quoted a Commissioner's elevation of the 'view from below' to the status of 'fact', as he referred to the 'grotesquely disproportionate amount of contact' with police and the ensuing 'deep-seated and debilitated feelings' of 'powerlessness' expressed by 'many articulate Aboriginals'.

Stressful life events

Besides the major interviews and discussions, participants were also asked to sort cards on a table-top representing their perceptions of major stressful events in their lives. These 34 topics had been developed over months of negotiation with Aboriginal care-givers. Results show that perceived major stressful events included:

a) *Frequency of contact by police.* One quarter of the interviewees (22, or 26%) regarded 'frequency of contact with police', as one of the most stressful matters of their lives.

b) *Gaol-term.* Nearly one half (39, or 46%) ranked 'gaol-term' as a highly stressful matter of life, representing the fourth most stressful factor overall, behind issues of death/loss, and health.

Events subsequent to 'Taking Control'

Over 400 copies of *Taking Control* were distributed to the South Australian Police Department, Department of Social Security, and other relevant government agencies including many Aboriginal organizations, which received them without charge. It has since been reprinted. Several police officers attended the public launching at Tandanya Aboriginal Cultural Institute in Adelaide. Television news covered its release on several stations there, and it received some national, and a little local, newspaper attention. As far as the AEF is aware, police have responded positively to *Taking Control*, as a few superintendents have kept in contact with AEF staff since its release, and have attended several important Aboriginal events in response to invitations sent to them.

On 3 July 1990, in response to both an apparent resurgence of concern in the Aboriginal community over Aboriginal/police relations in Adelaide, and the impact of *Taking Control*, Aboriginal community leaders initiated a 'historic'[11] meeting - also at Tandanya. More than 20 (mostly very senior) police representatives sat with approximately the same number of Aboriginal leaders in a round-table conference. In the words of a participant, the meeting aimed to 'clear the air' and to discuss future strategies of working

together. The AEF invited Professor Colin Tatz[12] to address the gathering.
Ms Marj Tripp, an Aboriginal leader with many years experience of working
closely with police, chaired the meeting which was taped and later
transcribed by the AEF.

Six key propositions were presented by Professor Tatz:

1. That 'institutionalized racism is rife' in 'a lot of bureaucracies, not just
   police or medical ones' (p.2 of the meeting transcripts);
2. That police need to espouse a clear 'absolute ideology of non-
   discrimination' which 'must be steered into being' rather than waited for,
   and which must come from the top, and be 'pinned to the mast-head'
   (p.2);
3. That in Redfern, New South Wales, it was just one unit out of many
   which gave the police a particularly bad name (p.2);
4. That the aim to change prejudicial *attitudes* was likely to be ill-founded
   as it is more realistic to increase both the life-experience and the broad
   awareness of police officers, together with their skills at *controlling*
   outward behaviour which springs from prejudice: 'Education on
   Aboriginal culture is not necessarily the answer' he said (p.3);
5. That everyone must realise that the regulation of public officers by such
   institutions as Ombudsmen, legal aid services, tribunals and so on, is here
   to stay and is increasing substantially. He argued that senior police have
   got to get the message across to 'hundreds of young policemen all over
   the country' to stop thinking along the lines that 'Aboriginal Legal Aid
   services ... just get in the way of a conviction'. Tatz maintained that the
   prevalence of this line of thought is due to basic ignorance of the
   adversary nature of our justice system (p.4). He expressed amazement
   at such ignorance which was apparently Australia-wide;
6. That training of police about Aboriginal culture must include the histories
   of particular, relevant regions where police happen to be located: i.e.
   situational histories of Yalata, Maralinga, Port Adelaide, etc.; and, that
   this should be part of all on-site briefings when new officers arrive,
   however brief is their intended stay.

In addition, he recommended several broader strategies to the senior police
present:

a) That Australia needs to follow the American example that aims to provide for the same proportion of black staff in the fire brigade, police department, and so on, as the relevant proportion of blacks in the immediate, surrounding population not merely a '1% scheme'. This is intended to 'defuse racial tension' (p.4). Whether it has achieved this end remains a moot point, but he suggested for South Australia: 'Initially, let's have a target of at least 3, 4, or 5 Aboriginal police in Ceduna?' ... 'I think this is terribly important' (p.5); and, that they be 'properly gazetted jobs' (p.20) in the force that enable portability to other States and types of employment or to subsequent 'fully-fledged' police officer status.[13]

b) High quality skills-training in conflict-resolution (p.20) were absolutely vital to the kinds of situations that often lead to Aboriginal arrests.

c) 'Smart policing' - which avoids involvement until absolutely necessary - allows communities to put in practice their own values and strategies for dealing with offenders, especially when property is involved rather than lives. 'Police have got to believe that with support, those communities *are* capable of dealing with things themselves ...'.

This was also linked to:

d) 'Community justice mechanisms' and issues of decriminalization of further crimes. Tatz advised the meeting to consider an Australian Law Reform Commission Report of some five years ago which was not acted upon.

e) Sport and Police Youth Clubs for Youth: Tatz proposed a two-pronged approach for Aboriginal youth: a) an examination of sporting facilities available to increase year-round opportunities (as this tends to defuse violence and trouble generally); and, b) the re-establishment of Police Youth Clubs (still common in New South Wales, but not longer so in South Australia).

Finally, Tatz emphasized the need for two fundamental changes. Firstly, for structural/administrative change in the relationship between the police department and Aboriginal people. On this, he implored senior officers to push for a special separate Aboriginal section in police headquarters: ' ... there must be acknowledgement that we are talking about a totally different cultural group', which itself is 'quite diverse'. Such a unit should not become specialized and exclude all else but Aboriginal issues, 'but until such time as you put the Aboriginal issues right out in front ... around the Commissioner, problems will remain ...' (p.9). And secondly, Tatz reminded everyone present that 'the responsibility for changing the kind of social mess that is occurring in some Aboriginal communities is the responsibility of Aboriginal communities ... the police are just one party in all of this'. This too, must gain greater recognition by Aboriginal groups, he proposed. The meeting was then open to discussion for some hours.

In summary, there were six highly significant features of this Tandanya meeting:

1. An open acknowledgement of past racist behaviour by some police (within the context of some appalling uses of policing in the previous 200 years) and *including* the most recent past. Expressions of Aboriginal perceptions at the meeting concerning such racism were neither countered nor subjected to qualification by police officers present. Rather, several officers referred directly to racist behaviour and attitudes amongst some members of the force along these lines: that it is as entrenched in at least some areas and age-groups in the police force, as are the criminal lives of some Aboriginal adults who have been breaking the law since they were very young.
2. Both 'sides' indicated their own past aggravation of the situation from time to time.
3. There was agreement that there have been very good relations apparent in particular regions of Adelaide between certain police officers, Aboriginal leaders and Aboriginal community members - but that such good rapport has often been shattered by the high mobility of police personnel transferred elsewhere.
4. Innovative schemes (some still experimental) were operating in an attempt to break down barriers. By creative involvement of police officers in Aboriginal kindergartens and in primary schools with significant Aboriginal student numbers, these schemes have been perceived by Aboriginal people as successful. Moreover, they have been warmly welcomed by care-givers.
5. Aboriginal leaders acknowledged that police necessarily perform difficult and 'dirty' tasks, and that their role is currently undergoing a major shift.[14] Policing burdens have increased due to a wider chain of events related to 'strain in the welfare state'. That is, as social problems have increased, social workers have diminished in both number and hours, and Commonwealth Aboriginal Affairs monies have dried up while the States have not 'picked up the tab'.[15] Consequently, community development workers (both Aboriginal and non-Aboriginal) have become

'scarce on the ground', increasing demands upon police precisely when they are attempting to embrace a more community-based, proactive approach (p.12). Police admitted this was a long-term change issue effecting everyone in the force. In response 'some officers do not want to be, are not paid to be, and feel ill-equipped to be, "social workers" '.

6. The Aboriginal Education Foundation Inc. offered its services to assist the police force in any way it could, including assisting police research as it considered long-term strategies toward improving Aboriginal/police relations in South Australia.

Tentative comparisons between Aboriginal and non-Aboriginal sole parents in state housing

The results of stage two of the AEF/FUSA study, released since the Tandanya conference, tend to endorse the findings in *Taking Control*: that is, that Aboriginal people seem to be in receipt of negative 'special attention' from police in Adelaide.

Police/Aboriginal interaction, and sole parenthood

Sole parents are one of the most disadvantaged groups in Australia. Using the same Aboriginal-initiated, and collaboratively produced methods and research approach, 52 female Aboriginal sole parents were compared with 45 female non-Aboriginal sole parents also in state housing, and with similar incomes, welfare reliance, education, and health profiles.[16]

Due to the sample size and composition characteristics we must exercise caution in any such comparisons. Nevertheless, with regard to some aspects of police interaction within the community, results suggest, to a statistically significant level, that sole parents may not be treated by police in a uniform manner. That is, non-Aboriginal sole parents appear to be less likely to receive the kind of negative 'special attention' from police, that Aboriginal sole parents apparently receive.

For example, police 'harassment' of participants outside of their homes, was reported by nearly ten times as many Aboriginal sole parents as non-Aboriginal ones (40% compared 4% respectively).[17] Another trend was indicated: that is, that alleged physical violence by police toward participants or members of their households was approximately 2.5 times greater in Aboriginal households (27% compared to 11%). It is interesting, then, to note that one in ten non-Aboriginal sole parents alleged police violence in this manner.

Violence, lack of acceptance, and self-harm

As has been mentioned, one focus of the study and the issue which proved
to be a catalyst for research in the Adelaide Aboriginal community, was self-
harm.   In stage one of the AEF/FUSA study, variables which were
statistically significant,[18] differentiated Aboriginal suicide attempters from
Aboriginal non-attempters.   Of these, four out of twenty related either
directly to police/judicial issues, to lack of acceptance in society generally,
or to physical violence experienced (regardless of its source).   Aboriginal
informants reported that the following events brought major distress in their
lives:

Law enforcement intervention:
    i)   High numbers of police visits to their homes;

Personal perceptions - in relation to the law:
    ii)   The impact of even minor violations of the law upon self esteem.

Abuse experience:
    iii) Experiences of abuse, particularly in early life (usually by a
relative) and subsequent fear of violence.

Personal perceptions - generally:
    iv) Perceptions of 'non-acceptance' by the rest of society.

(Due to the sample size, regression analyses to explore the possible
interelationship of these and other variables was not possible.)

Aboriginal and non-Aboriginal suicide attempters.   In stage two, when
comparing Aboriginal and non-Aboriginal suicide attempters, (and bearing
in mind that both groups had very similar imprisonment profiles - just over
one-in-four), police intervention again was much more likely amongst the
Aboriginal female sole parents.   For example, 38% of Aboriginal attempters
reported incidents of 'harassment', as against nil non-Aboriginal attempters.[19]
Aboriginal attempters were twice as likely to allege physical abuse by police
of a household member than non-Aboriginal attempters, 31% compared with
15% respectively.   However, it must be noted these numbers are small and

should only be considered as indicative of a trend.

To summarize the results of this AEF/FUSA study, the reported experience of police by these urban Aboriginal households in state housing would appear not to be echoed amongst similar non-Aboriginal households.

Discussion

With regard to stage two data, we should be mindful that allegations were made by randomly-selected households, the heads of which were female care-givers who resided in an area that spanned the sprawling suburbs of Adelaide. Participants were not asked more particularly about police issues than about a wide range of other matters such as financial ones, sexual abuse, housing, education, and self-harm. It is also salient to realize that 40% of Aboriginal people regarded 'usual' police behaviour as 'courteous and responsive' - although the same figure for the non-Aboriginal people was 65%. Therefore, by no means all police officers are perceived to behave in a racist or otherwise unsatisfactory fashion, and these data revealed that some Aboriginal people still regard most police quite favourably, even after alleging an incident of considerable violence by police.

Caution is called for in interpreting all these results. This is most certainly the case when considering questions as to why people seem to engage in self-destructive action. Causality cannot be inferred from association - and we must be clear we are dealing with small numbers especially in stage two of this study (that is, 52 Aboriginal and 45 non-Aboriginal sole parents: 13 and 19 suicide attempters respectively). However, the trends seem clear, and it is noteworthy that many allegations made to interviewers were described in some detail in response to open questions (both in stages one and two). Furthermore, as the tenor of allegations made in both stages would appear to be supported by several less random inquiries revealing the reported experiences of minority groups generally[20] or Aboriginal people in particular[21] there would seem to be little doubt that concern over police attitudes and behaviour is considerably greater amongst Aboriginal people than amongst most non-Aboriginal people.

Furthermore, since the publication of *Taking Control*, the validity of this study seems to have been particularly enhanced when, in the Tandanya meeting, 'calling a spade a spade' took place. That is, senior police acknowledged that racism remains a serious problem for some in the police force and in response, they put forward their ideas and personal experiences aimed at overcoming it. Such concern therefore, appears well-founded, and it can be surmised that if a careful, systematic cross-cultural study of this issue was mounted amongst a larger sample of urban households, much more relevant information would be likely to emerge. The apparent relationship between police behaviour and self-harm evident in the results is a quite separate, and indeed problematic, matter. This is a particularly disturbing result and one which tends to lend urgency to this debate and to suggest its potential to fuel positive outcomes for the Aboriginal community.

It is important to conclude this discussion by highlighting a consideration of gender. We should not forget that the allegations made in stage two were exclusively female in origin. It is well established in the literature, particularly by the Royal Commission into Aboriginal Deaths in Custody, that Aboriginal males are subjected to a very high level of police interaction and incarceration. Many of the women referred to incidents which allegedly took place involving their own partners, ex-partners, or children, which would include an element of male perceptions known to them, but it is reasonable to conclude that had this study been able to incorporate a greater Aboriginal male perspective, results may well have further differentiated Aboriginal and non-Aboriginal reports.

Mental health study highlights police issues

In addition to the AEF/FUSA study another study led by a Health Commission psychiatrist, which focused upon mental health in the Adelaide Aboriginal community, is of particular interest. It was carried out in the same period in Adelaide by the Aboriginal Health Organization (AHO) and the Mental Health and Evaluation Centre (MHEC) of the South Australian Health Commission (Clayer et al 1991). It too posited an association between police action and Aboriginal self-harm. Despite its much larger sample (n=530), its purely quantitative approach, and its different methodology, this study tends to corroborate the AEF/FUSA study results with regard to police/Aboriginal interaction (see Chapter 9: Problems with Police). There was no collaboration between research teams beyond very early discussions which clarified the quite different study objectives and approaches.

In relation to suicide attempt, Clayer et al (1991: 45) concluded on a disturbingly similar note as the AEF/FUSA study, namely, 'there is a significant correlation between attempted suicide and police problems (p=.0017) and between the consumption of alcohol and police problems'.

Conclusion

It would seem reasonable to interpret the apparent accord between the results of these independent, household population studies which went about their respective research tasks in quite different ways[22] as further strengthening the case that there remains a serious problem in Aboriginal police relations which is yet to be either acknowledged in official police views or addressed by the kind of comprehensive approach that Professor Tatz has recommended. This problem continues to be responsible for considerable distress in the Aboriginal community.

Given the recent Los Angeles experience of riots arising from the verdict in the Rodney King (police bashing video) case, it is of long term social and economic good sense that a strategy for structural change in the relationship between police and the Aboriginal community be established in Australia. One lesson to be drawn from that ugly event in the United States of America, by no means the first of its kind, must be that *perceptions* are of utmost social significance, and that the question of what may be considered 'fact' is potentially explosive in any society. It would appear to be time we learnt to read the signs well in advance, if we are to be truly proactive rather than reactive. Quite apart from the results of systematic research, one of those signs could be seen in the comment of the South Australian Police Complaints Authority (PCA 1992:4) that relationships with Aboriginal communities 'continue to be an area of substantial concern', and that despite several initiatives already taken by police and government, it is 'likely that there will continue to be complaints'. Another, is the apparent refusal of the Police Commissioner to support the recommendations of the Authority that criminal charges of assault be laid against three police officers. This has meant a considerable dilution of its effect, and a further undermining of confidence in complaints mechanisms which, in South Australia, continue to lack sufficient resources.[23]

Finally, it is vital to acknowledge the goodwill that has been extended to police by many Aboriginal leaders, and vice-versa, so far as several high-ranking police officers are concerned. As a participant, this author has to agree with Colin Tatz. It *was* a remarkable spirit of openness on both sides which prevailed at that Tandanya meeting - and no one has questioned Professor Tatz's assertion that it was truly 'unique and historic'. That momentum must not be allowed to wane like so many earlier initiatives in

Aboriginal/police relations. It would appear that in South Australia there is a genuine desire for further collaboration. Should wider Aboriginal community consultation endorse it, and the South Australian government and police show sufficient political will and resources for its support, it might be possible to move towards the comprehensive plan for restructuring and reform proposed by Tatz.

Such a plan however, seems to remain outside the scope of recent proposals advanced by a national forum of police Commissioners in Canberra (reported in the *Advertiser* 11 May, 1992: 'Police Aim to End Clash of Cultures'). It also goes beyond official government responses to the recommendations of the Royal Commission into Aboriginal Deaths in Custody, as those responses merely addressed issues of police behaviour and language toward Aboriginal people[24] - positive, important, and most welcome though such measures have been.[25]

References

Aboriginal Deaths in Custody: Response by Governments to the Royal Commission (1992) Vol. 1, Canberra: Australian Government Publishing Service.

Aboriginal Education Foundation of South Australia Inc. (1990) *Police/Aboriginal Relations Seminar*, unedited transcript of seminar held on the 2 and 3 July 1990 at Tandanya Aboriginal Cultural Institute, Adelaide (addressed by Professor Colin Tatz): 1-31.

Bevan O. (1991) 'Changing the Face of Policing' in J. Vernon and S. McKillop (eds) *The Police and the Community*, Conference Proceedings No. 5, held at Brisbane October 23-25, 1990, Canberra: Australian Institute of Criminology.

Clayer J.R. and Divakaran-Brown C. (1991) *Mental Health and Behavioural Problems in the Urban Aboriginal Population,* Report of a Study Conducted by The Aboriginal Health Organization and The Mental Health Research and Evaluation Centre of the South Australian Health Commission, November.

Goldsmith A.J. (1991) 'Complaints against the Police: A "Community Policing" Perspective' in J. Vernon and S. McKillop (eds) *The Police and the Community*, Conference Proceedings No. 5, held at Brisbane October 23-25, 1990, Canberra: Australian Institute of Criminology.

Human Rights and Equal Opportunity Commission (1991) *The Report of the National Inquiry into Racist Violence in Australia*, Canberra: Australian Government Publishing Service.

Johnston E. (1991) *Royal Commission into Aboriginal Deaths in Custody National Report* Vol. 4, Canberra: Australian Government Publishing Service.

Little M. and Trezise P. (1991) 'Policing in South Australia as it Affects Aboriginal People', *Aboriginal Law Bulletin*, 2: 49, April: 18-19.

McConnochie K., Hollinsworth D., and Pettman J. (1988) *Race and Racism in Australia*, Wentworth Falls: Social Science Press.

Police Complaints Authority (1992) *Fifth and Sixth Annual Reports* covering the period 1 July 1989 to 30 June 1991, Adelaide.

Radford A.J., Harris R.D., Brice G.A., Van der Byl M., Monten H., Matters D., Neeson M., Bryan L. and Hassan R. (1990) *Taking Control, A Joint Study of Aboriginal Social Health in Adelaide with Particular Reference to Stress and Destructive Behaviours, Stage One: Aboriginal 'Heads of Household' Study 1987-1989*. Monograph No. 7, Department of Primary Health Care, Adelaide: The Flinders University of South Australia.

Tatz, Colin (1990) 'Aboriginal Violence: A Return to Pessimism', *Aboriginal Journal of Social Issues* 24: 4, 245-260.

Vernon J. and McKillop S. (eds) 1991 *The Police and the Community,* Conference Proceedings No. 5, Canberra: Australian Institute of Criminology.

Appendix 1

Relevant questions used in the AEF/FUSA study semi-structured questionnaire.

Legal trouble and imprisonment
Have [you/your partner or ex-partner/your child(ren)] ever been in any trouble with the law? ... imprisoned?
(If yes, ... when ... what for? ... age(s) ... total time in custody ...)
Note: 'Trouble with the law': 'trouble' was assessed by the participant.

Police: household visits
In the last two years, have the Police come *to* your door without you having called them there? (If yes, how many times?)

Police: household entry
Have Police ever *entered* your house without invitation or a warrant, and without proceeding to arrest someone? (If yes, how many times in the last two years ? ... brief outline of what allegedly happened).

Police: attitudes and behaviour
Do you *usually* find the Police? (tick one)
- Courteous and respectful
- Indifferent but fair

- Rude and intrusive
- Abusive and violent

Police: physical abuse

Has anyone from this household claimed Police have physically abused them? (If yes, how many times in last 2 years? ... who claims this? ... brief outline of circumstances and any follow-up?).

Police: 'harassment'

Has anyone from this household claimed to have been the subject of very unreasonable attention by Police outside of the home? (If yes, how many times in last 2 years? ... who? ... give example).

Notes

1.   Graham Brice (B.A.) Hons. is Senior Research Officer with the Aboriginal Health Council of South Australia which is the main advisory body to the State government on Aboriginal health matters.   His background is in Sociology (currently completing his candidature for an MA by research thesis) with extensive experience in collaborative, cross-cultural research with a community and social health orientation.   Particular interests include indigenous health and colonialism, research methods, philosophy of social science, contemporary issues of racial reconciliation, violence and the law. He has been working closely with Aboriginal people for many years including research carried out in response to Royal Commission into Aboriginal Deaths in Custody recommendations, and is the co-author of several reports and papers: most recently, *Neporendi: Social Health and Social Action*, based on research with an urban Aboriginal community.

2.   See *Royal Commission into Aboriginal Deaths in Custody* (RCIADIC) *National Report* (1991) Vol. 4, 29.5.2: 124; see also McConnochie K., Hollinsworth D., and Pettman J. (1988) *Race and Racism in Australia*, Wentworth Falls: Social Science Press.

3.   *The Report of the National Inquiry into Racist Violence in Australia*, op. cit.(69-137; 209-213) not only highlights the breadth and depth of the problem but also the reluctance to lodge such formal complaints. Over six years of informal 'participant observation' while a member of the Management Committee of the Aboriginal Education Foundation of South Australia Inc., having initially been employed to assist them with social research on a contract basis, revealed to the author how strong was the concern over police issues.

4. This comment was apparently made in response to the claims of the *Report of the National Inquiry into Racist Violence in Australia*, op. cit.; see 'The Advertiser', 20 April 1991, 'Police Slam Claims of Race Violence'.
5. However, this would seem to have taken place only at limited levels of the police force, as discussed below.
6. This may raise suggestions of bias - a matter addressed below. See *Appendix* 1 for an outline of relevant questions used in the research.
7. The study partners were The Aboriginal Education Foundation Inc. (AEF) and The Flinders University of SA (FUSA) Department of Primary Health Care and Discipline of Sociology. This author was research officer for the project, and a co-author of *Taking Control*. Having been seeded by the AEF the project was funded through the Department of Aboriginal Affairs, the South Australian Health Commission, and the National Health and Medical Research Council. The Chief Investigator was Professor Anthony Radford, Primary Health Care, FUSA.
8. Some examples were: i) 'My son-in-law was followed by police a couple of times. He has very dark features and drives a Commodore. Police suspected it to be stolen because it was a nice car'; (ii) 'My son was riding a new bike - police stopped him in the street to ask him if it was stolen'; (iii) 'When I first got a car - police checked ownership (assumed it to be stolen) ... they also suspected it had been used in robbery, and did a licence check ... when I opened the glove-box to get my licence, police pulled a gun on me and told me if put my hand in the glove-box "he would blow my black head off" ... I lodged an official complaint'; (iv) 'During Grand Prix a mob of us walking down Hindley St. Police harassed us, kicked my *de facto* in the knee and told us to "get out of Hindley St"'. Other reports of physical violence by police while at the police station or 'lock-up' included: 'I was put in cell at Elizabeth in winter time - I asked for a blanket and police said "no". There was a pile of blankets nearby so I took one ... I ended up with a broken tooth and they took the blanket away'. For further details see *Taking Control* (Radford *et al* 1990: 61-65).
9. See e.g., Huizer, G. and Mannheim, B. (eds) (1979) *The Politics of Anthropology: From Colonialism and Sexism toward a View from Below*, Paris: Mouton.
10. This association was statistically significant at $p < .01$: the result was $p = .003$ after Yates Correction.
11. Professor Tatz described it as 'unique and historic' on public radio the next day - and said that in his estimation it could not have taken place elsewhere in Australia.
12. Colin Tatz has over 30 years experience in Aboriginal affairs and research including a nation-wide study of Aboriginal violence and sport conducted with significant police backing and involvement (Tatz 1990).
13. On this, the meeting learnt from police spokespersons that recommendations

had already been put to the Commissioner by senior police (based on a training scheme already established); in addition, we were told that 'an Aboriginal person' will also be employed 'in a liaison capacity when we get office space' (p.15). A police officer commented: *'we are just waiting to hear and to begin interviewing people chosen by the Aboriginal community ...'*

14. This has been highlighted by an Australian Institute of Criminology conference proceedings publication *The Police and the Community* (Vernon and McKillop 1991).

15. The Aboriginal and Torres Strait Islander Commission is currently trying to overcome this problem.

16. The tentative results of this project were first reported by the AEF and Flinders University at the 'Indigenous Health' conference conducted by the Public Health Association, October 1991 at Alice Springs and have since been submitted to public health journals for consideration for publication, with A.J. Radford as principal author.

17. The result (after Yates Continuity Correction due to small sample size) was $p = .00011$.

18. That is, significant at $p = <.05$.

19. The Fishers Exact Test result was $p = .006$.

20. See for example, *The Report of the National Inquiry into Racist Violence in Australia*, op. cit.

21. See for example, the Royal Commission into Aboriginal Deaths in Custody Report of the Inquiry into the Death of Mark Quayle; the *Police Complaints Authority Fifth and Sixth Annual Reports* covering the period 1 July 1989 to 30 June 1991, Adelaide, which included at Appendix B, a detailed assessment of Aboriginal cases (though a quantitative, race-related summary was still lacking).

22. For example, the average interview discussion time in the AEF/FUSA time was 2.5 hours with some spread over two days, which was much longer than was common in the AHO/MHEC study (Clayer and Divakaran-Brown 1991) which used mainly standardized questionnaires.

23. See the Police Complaints Authority (1992) Report for 1989-91 op. cit., and *The Advertiser* 30 April 1992 'Police Complaints Soar'. Some commentators have indicated that complaints made by Aboriginal people to this Police Complaints Authority, a statutory authority with considerable power in South Australia, have not been particularly excessive. However, in the absence of race-related summary data we have only the Authority's own comments. Furthermore, with rare exceptions, (one of which was reported in *Radford et al 1990* as an incident which resulted in the suspension by a judge of a police officer for two weeks), it is understandable if few official complaints are made by already allegedly 'harassed' individuals, or, that few result in 'justice being *seen* to be done' to the satisfaction of the Aboriginal community. The Director of the Aboriginal Legal Rights Movement in South Australia, Ms

Sandra Saunders, reportedly claimed that 'Aborigines had no faith in the police complaints system and feared they would be victimized if they made complaints' (*The Advertiser* 20 April 1991) - a point echoed by the RCIADIC Report (see 29.5.6-7, Johnston 1991: 125) which stated 'the existing mechanisms for dealing with complaints against police rarely give confidence to Aboriginal people that their complaints will be fairly evaluated'. Many investigations (irrespective of race) do not result in what is perceived as strong corrective actions (see also Little and Trezise 1991). As has been mentioned, the sheer workload of the Authority is not matched by its available staff even after recent expansion in South Australia, a problem noted repeatedly in the press. Goldsmith (1991) calls for an independent complaints forum by broadening the discussion of complaints mechanisms to stress the political nature of all policing. However, the South Australian experience, where such independence is more apparent, highlights the need to increase reporting requirements, as the current lack of detail about complaints lodged add to the distrust felt in the Aboriginal community.

24. *Aboriginal Deaths in Custody: Response by Governments to the Royal Commission* (1992: 203). These were in response to Recommendations 60 and 61 of the Royal Commission into Aboriginal Deaths in Custody.

25. **Acknowledgements** This essay is based on research, action in the wake of research results, and a discussion paper prepared for the Aboriginal Work Group of the Aboriginal and Torres Strait Islander Congress of the Uniting Church of Australia (South Australian Synod). Thanks are due to: Rev Bernie Clarke and Kingsley A'Hang of the latter group; and to Dr Anthony Radford, Professor of Primary Health Care, Centre for Health Advancement, Flinders University who was Chief Investigator of the original project; and Muriel Van Der Byl, Liz Johnston, Effie Best, and Helen Monten of the Aboriginal Education Foundation of SA Inc (AEF), the joint-study partner. The AEF Executive Management Committee (of which the author has been a member since 1987) approved this essay and its publication. I am grateful to all these people for their helpful and constructive comments on drafts. For the original research, approval was received from the Aboriginal Health Research Ethics Committee of South Australia (see Radford *et al* 1990 for details). Finally, this essay would not have eventuated if Ms Marj Tripp, an Aboriginal elder in Adelaide with much experience in Aboriginal police relations, had not convened a special seminar with the AEF and police. At that seminar, Professor Colin Tatz assisted the Aboriginal community in Adelaide to consider the implications of the research; extracts from his taped address are reproduced with kind permission from him.

X Retrieving the 'Decent Society': Law and order politics in New Zealand 1984–1993

Paul Havemann and Joan Havemann[1]

Introduction

In 1984 the fourth Labour government began a radical monetarist experiment, in 1990 National continued this under the slogan of achieving a 'Decent Society'. Our focus in this essay is on the evolution of the competing discourses which vie with each other in the process of reshaping the New Zealand state to retrieve a 'decent society' based on free market principles, a small state and a crime control apparatus integrated into the 'community'. In particular, we are concerned with explicit and implicit discourses in the law, order, and justice platforms of the major parties in their election campaigns 1984, 1987 and 1993, government policies and official discourse, and media coverage.

In recent times real increases have occurred in recorded violent crime in New Zealand - including a sevenfold increase between 1960 and 1985, and an increase of 80% from 1980 to 1989 (Newbold 1992: 85) - but the crime problem is fuelled to panic-inducing proportions by extensive, daily, hard news reporting on the activities of police, courts, offenders and victims. Crime is then analysed and 'explained' in soft news features presenting a more complex but nonetheless fear and retribution-justifying form.

In the process, the crime wave becomes associated with 'race' and moral decay and the demise of good parenting in political and media discourses. Links to unemployment or loss of self esteem, lands, or self determination, or connections between the crime wave, a violence-ridden gendered culture, discourses on the need for habilation not rehabilitation, and the negative impact of worklessness, are disarticulated or coopted.

The current crime wave in our view, is a feature of an anomic *gesellschaft* society structured by a decade under two economic rationalist governments. The 1993 election platforms of both major parties demonstrate commitment to achieve crime control through greater technological efficiency in the formal apparatus but more particularly by promoting *gemeinschaft* through 'community' prevention, safer 'communities', 'community' policing, and reintegrating the family into the archipelago of control (Cohen 1985: 118-127).

Superficially, then, Labour's platform is similar to National's, but whereas privatization of the crime control apparatus is envisaged by National's, temporarily held up, *Penal Institutions (Amendment) Bill (New Zealand Herald*, 22 September 1993), private prisons are explicitly rejected by Labour. The detail of Labour's platform also reveals explicit commitments to enforce the rights of the accused, and to address domestic violence and exercise greater gun control.

Reshaping the state 1984-1994

We take the political economy of the state as our starting point for understanding crime but reject visions of the state (or 'the system') as a static, reified, monolithic entity, in favour of a more complex concept of the state as dynamic 'processes of structuration' (Giddens 1976: xiii; Cerny 1990: ix-xii; Skocpol 1985: 4-25; Franzway, Court and Connell 1989: 42, 52-53). This view envisages constant interplay, conflict, and contradictions not only between the state on the one hand, and social forces on the other, but even within, between, and among separate, relatively autonomous parts or agencies of the state. Thus mutual influence and change are possible (Havemann and Turner 1994).

The New Zealand state's attempts to manage the fiscal crisis and related ideological crises have exemplified an interplay between social democratic and corporatist, and New Right and market liberatarian, approaches by both major parties. The parties and governments bearing these ideologies and strategies have consistently denied the contradictions inherent in their programmes. Repressive, traditional law and order policies and platforms have been juxtaposed with explicit acknowledgements of the links between crime and unemployment and anomie, yet the links between unemployment, anomie, and Labour and National's social and economic policies are consistently unacknowledged.

Between 1950 and the 1970s, New Zealand/Aotearoa was characterized by its own dependent agricultural fordism (O'Brien and Wilkes 1993) or social democratic fordism (Mathews 1989). Colin James dubs this period 'the prosperity consensus' (James 1992: 6), while Jesson refers to the 'Labour tradition' (Jesson 1992). It represented widespread commitment to a vision of New Zealand as a land of opportunity in which voluntary conformity was both expected and rewarded: thanks to education, employment and state support, everyone - or at least, everyone assimilated into the predominant culture of that 90% of the population of Anglo-Celtic descent - had a 'fair go'.

The Anglo-Celtic majority, confident in its racial and cultural superiority, accepted cultural, military, political-legal and economic dependency on Britain. The prevailing values of the society were esteem for individualism tempered by understanding of the need for material security (provided by the welfare state, collective bargaining and a highly regulated economy), coupled with a sense of belonging to the dominant geopolitical bloc. New Zealand wanted to join NATO. SEATO and, later, ANZUS were consolation prizes.

Equality and the right to self-improvement and social mobility regardless of class were features of male labourism which permeated the assumptions about work and welfare, largely leaving the cult of domesticity intact. The corporatist state was seen by the employed beneficiaries of this social order as a 'friend' rather than as an authoritarian 'nanny'. Unemployment was extremely low. Governments played a 'never-ending role' as arbitrators, protectors, regulators and mediators between interest groups (James 1992: 13-18). As in Britain and western Europe, the welfare state functioned to reconcile the constituent elements of capitalist accumulation with the demands of legitimation (O'Connor 1973; Offe 1972: 479-488).

The 'prosperity consensus' is no more, and the 'Labour tradition' has disintegrated; the 'decent society' has disappeared for all but the top third of income earners and their dependants. The social order of most industrialized nations, including Aotearoa/New Zealand, is increasingly characterized by a post-fordist diversity, differentiation and fragmentation amounting to ideological and fiscal crises for the welfare state.

Antagonisms flowing from diversity, differentiation and fragmentation have been part of Aotearoa's 'Old Times' and are being carried forward into the 'new'. The 'New Times' (Hall and Jacques 1991) are such that ideological uncertainty and political de-alignment (Vowles and Aimer 1993) are acute, yet claims for settlements of old and new antagonisms are so pressing that the existing juridical-political and coercive institutions of the state must accommodate differences and change.

The big question, as ever, is how will these institutions react to these pressures? A great deal has been written about 'transformation of New Zealand 1984-92' (James 1992), 'the privatization of power in Aotearoa/New Zealand' (Kelsey 1993), New Zealand's bureaucratic revolution (Boston et al 1991), New Zealand's constitution in crisis (Palmer 1992), and New Zealand in crisis (Novitz and Willmott 1992), the transition from dependent agricultural fordism to Labour monetarism (O'Brien and Wilkes 1993).

The redesign of New Zealand's welfare state, state trading enterprises (Duncan and Bollard 1992), and civil service has rapidly followed a well-worn path. Residual welfarism (Shannon 1991; Boston and Dalziel 1992), in the form of a contracted public core and expanded privatized or voluntary penumbra, has been the project of both the fourth Labour government 1984-1990 and the National government 1990-1993. The consequent growth of worklessness engendered by the abandonment of neo-Keynesianism has meant no savings in social security spending.

New right or neo-liberal ideology dominates economic policy: economic policy is consistently privileged over social policy, which is eclectic, marginal, or non-existent (Koopman-Boyden 1990). The usual Treasury and Business Roundtable arguments that the state is too large, the deficit and public debt too high, social security too poorly-targeted, the margin between benefits and wages too narrow, and so on, have won the day (Boston and Dalziel 1992: 8).

The usual user-pays and targeting approaches to education, health care, housing, social security, and superannuation, and environmental policy have occurred, coupled with 'liberalization' of the labour market (Harvey 1992), 'deregulation' of the finance and manufacturing sectors, and privatization and corporatization (Duncan and Bolland 1992; Dalziel and Boston 1992; Kelsey 1993).

Under the Labour government, it must also be said, some less usual aspects of reshaping the state were attempted which contradict Labour's image as dogmatic market rationalists and reveal clear traces of the party's social democratic and labourist pedigree (James 1992).

Indeed, the combination of legislative interventions and official discourse in the form of commission and review processes and reports underlines the processes of structuration which were going on. These social-democratically inspired interventions, reviews and reports attempted to create new platforms of process for citizenship in the juridical-political complex which appear to be irreconcilable with the kind of comprehensive and deliberate shift to a repressive society seen elsewhere (Havemann 1987).

One of Labour's most promising, but least effective, efforts was one to promote citizenship - albeit in a limited legal form - through a bill of rights found in the *New Zealand Bill of Rights Act* 1990 (Arseneau 1990).

Attempts to try to 'settle' the antagonisms grounded in ethnic inequalities, such as the *Treaty of Waitangi (Amendment) Act* 1985, enabled the Waitangi Tribunal to promulgate principles which would curb the corporatization process (Kelsey 1990). An attempt was made to devolve power to Maori under the *Rununga Iwi Act* 1990 to promote biculturalism (O'Reilly and Wood 1991). These interventions and the courts' responses have been described by Palmer as the 'Maori Constitutional Revolution' (Palmer 1992).

Structured gender inequalities in employment were tackled by rigorous reviews of equal employment practices (Tremaine 1991) and analysis of the potential for a non-discriminatory regulatory framework for women in the workforce, which led to the *Employment Equity Act* 1990 (Wilson 1992). This Act was instantly repealed by National and replaced by the *Employment Contracts Act* 1991 which dismantled the entire collective bargaining, award and arbitration scheme in place since 1894. Harbridge claims that women and the low-paid and unorganized have suffered dramatically as a result (Harbridge 1993), whereas the government claims that the gap between men's and women's earnings has narrowed (*Waikato Times*, 25 September 1993).

The Report of the Royal Commission on Social Policy (1988), though ignored by government at the time, set out a radical participatory social democratic agenda for citizenship based on the principles of voice and choice. The Report of the Ministerial Committee of Inquiry into Violence (1987) chaired by Sir Clinton Roper went to the heart of New Zealand's gendered culture of violence at a structural rather than victim-blaming level.

As dramatically, the Report of the Ministerial Committee of Inquiry into Prison Systems (1989) was decisively abolitionist. Though 'habilitation', a concept advanced within this Roper Report, echoes through 1993 Labour, National and Alliance manifestos, the Roper reports have had little formal expression in government policy but serve as rhetorical resources for counter-hegemonic action against the economic libertarian and moral authoritarian tendencies in the dominant political formations.

Labour's perceived softness on crime - perhaps attributable to such championing of social democratic initiatives - may have cost the party the 1990 election:

Although Labour had freed the economy, on matters of crime and penal policy its public talk seemed to tie the party firmly to its social democratic base (Pratt 1988: 257).

The contradiction between social democratic, New Right/economic libertarian and moral authoritarian ideologies remains acute and has been exacerbated by three years of National Party government. Electoral politics - somewhat surprisingly - may be the site in which this struggle takes place over the next few years. The Labour-initiated Report of the Royal Commission (1986) on the Electoral System proposed the abandonment of the first-past-the-post, majoritarian system (FPP) and recommended mixed member proportional representation (MMP) along the German model. The 1993 general election ballot included a binding referendum question for or against this. Though electoral reform was thought to be a sleeping issue in the mid-1980s, a non-binding referendum in 1992 saw FPP resoundingly defeated and the popularity of the third party 'Alliance' rise dramatically, reflecting a profound alienation from the major parties and, presumably, their platforms. The 1993 referendum supported MMP which is to be the basis of the 1996 general election. The election result almost produced a 'hung' parliament with the Alliance holding the balance. This National Government however sustained its tiny majority but a new style of consensus politics is already under way.

Reconstituted representative institutions based on MMP were, in the view of most New Zealanders then, the only means through which New Zealand could address the turmoil produced by ideological contradictions and their programmatic outcomes. The question remains, will MMP subvert the evolution of a market society buttressed by a repressive state apparatus? In particular, how will a new order grounded in the present confront the problems of crime, of worklessness, of alienation and of anomie?

Law and order for a 'decent society' 1984-1994?

Overall, the 1984-1994 evidence points towards the evolution in New Zealand of a state increasingly turning to coercion rather than legitimation to manage the crisis. Consent is increasingly purchased by promises of more public spending on law and order. Is the price of the 'decent society' a repressive state form verging on what Gramscian Marxist theorists have described as an 'exceptional state' (Hall et al 1978: 23; Ratner and McMullan 1983)?

Such a state form depends upon constructing 'active popular consent' to the management of fiscal and ideological crises in such a way that, while democratic, representative institutions appear to be left intact, the welfare state is dismantled and policies of 'coercion and containment' are legitimated, provided that they are targetted at marginal groups. At the same time, marginalization increases as more and more groups become a burden. Spoonley rejects the relevance of the 'exceptional state' concept to the New Zealand context because the New Right agenda is not neo-fascist here and does not entail 'exceptional' treatment such as programmatic genocide of racial minorities (Spoonley 1987: 264).

The diagnosis of the causes of New Zealand's fiscal crisis and the remedies proposed by elites (Jesson 1987, Holland and Boston 1990) within the major political parties, the bureaucracy, and big business from 1984 onwards appear to have constructed a 'common sense' which has legitimated support for law and order policies, for privatizing the so-called command economy, including state-owned assets, and for streamlining 'the inefficient welfare state'. This new post-fordist 'common sense' (Rogernomics) has displaced the dominant 'Labour tradition' (Jesson 1992) and appears to have brought successive governments to office since 1984 (James 1992; Vowles and Aimer 1993; Gold and Webster 1990; McLoughlin 1992; O'Brien and Wilkes 1993; Havemann 1994), though seldom, we would argue, with the *informed* consent of the electorate (Mulgan 1990, 1992), and despite the disastrous social impact New Right policies are known to have had elsewhere (Taylor 1991).

In New Zealand, the infrastructure of representative institutions has allowed for a peculiarly unbridled form of power to be exercized by the executive, whether Labour or National (Palmer 1987). We have actively cautioned (Havemann 1992) against the dangers of 'simply transporting analyses which make sense of political developments in Britain or the U.S. to the programme of liberal [economic] reform here' (Kelsey 1993: 296). Notions like the 'exceptional state', 'authoritarian populism', 'friendly fascism', or 'the law and order society' may be too extreme, though they may describe discernible repressive tendencies in the re-shaping of the New Zealand state.

As we illustrated above, unlike the Reagan-Bush U.S.A., the Thatcher-Major U.K. and Mulroney-Campbell Canada, 'the great moving right show' has been accompanied in New Zealand by some equally dramatic, almost 1960s-like, social democratic reforms and rhetorical gestures.

It is therefore hardly surprising that New Zealanders are de-aligned. Ambiguity and complexity have blurred the parameters of a law and order agenda over the decade, especially under Labour. But the concrete reality of immiseration caused by New Right economic policy implementation, despite attempts at the realization of social democratic policies, has been accompanied by increased crime and the legitimation of law and order policies of coercion and containment.

Apart from Kelsey (1993), Pratt (1987), and Treacher (Pratt and Treacher 1988), little detailed attention thus far has focused on the extent to which the New Zealand state's crisis management strategies have included the evolution of a law and order agenda inexorably driving towards the shaping of an increasingly repressive state. Over the last two decades, political economists of crime in Britain (Hall et al 1978; Taylor 1981), the U.S. (Michalowski 1981; Platt 1981) and Canada (Taylor 1980; Ratner and McMullan 1983) have identified patterns of association between the rise of the Right and law and order. Cohen summarized their indices of the drift to a repressive state as:

· increasing rates of imprisonment;

· increasing severity of punishment (renewed emphasis on deterrence and incapacitation and longer determinate sentencing);

· a widening net of criminalization;

· an expansion of the repressive parts of the apparatus to deal with political and industrial unrest;

· a cut back of liberal 1960s gains in areas such as abortion and women's rights, with a corresponding ascendence of right-wing moral crusaders;

· greater publicity given to street crimes; and

· a transformation of the discrete moral panics of the 1960s into a deliberate climate of hostility to marginal groups and racial minorities, who become scapegoats for the crisis (Cohen 1985: 108).

Trends

Below, we attempt somewhat eclectically to match trends in New Zealand over the 1984-1994 period against these indices. A contradictory combination of progammes and policies emerges under Labour, whose election platforms and policies in office consistently try to reconcile contradictions between social democratic, economic libertarian and moral authoritarian tendencies within the hegemonic ideology (Kelsey 1993: 296). National's conservative agenda, however, is largely unambiguous. Their project has been to de-regulate the labour market and impose austerity measures to cut the costs of the welfare 'safety' net.

Increasing rates of imprisonment? The imprisonment rate per 100,000 has increased significantly in recent years, from 86 in the decade from 1978 to 1988, to 107 in February 1990. The comparable February 1990 figure for Australia was 75 per 100,000. The Canadian figure for 1986 was 109 and the U.S. figure for 1987 was 358 (Norris and MacPherson 1990: 42-43).

The average daily prison muster increased from 2,518 sentenced inmates in 1985 to 3,205 in 1989 (Norris and MacPherson 1990: 41) and to 3,821 on 14 November 1991 (Braybrooke and Southey 1992: 25). The total prison population, including remand prisoners, on that date was 4,232.

Increasing severity of punishment (renewed emphasis on deterrence and incapacitation and longer determinate sentencing)? In 1982 only 18% of those convicted of other than road traffic offences were sent to prison. By 1991 that figure had risen to 39% (Minister's foreword to Spier, Norris and Southey 1992: 3).

The average length of sentence for rape increased from 49.3 months in 1984 to 65.8 months in 1991 (an increase of 30%): for aggravated robbery, the increase was from 28.8 months to 36.3 months in the same period. Typically, sentence lengths have increased for all other violent offences during this period. The maximum sentence for sexual violation was increased from 14 to 20 years, effective September 1993, under the *Crimes Amendment Act* (No 3) 1993. In addition, courts now have power to impose preventive detention on first offenders convicted of sexual violation.

In spite of widespread use of diversion because of the *Children, Young Persons and Their Families Act* 1989, custodial sentences for young offenders who are *not* diverted have climbed from 3.4% of sentences in 1986 to 7.1% in 1991, though the actual numbers of young persons sentenced to custodial sentences dropped from 321 to 73 during that period. Supervision under the Department of Social Welfare has similarly climbed from 22.5% to 40.1% over the same period (dropping from 2,132 to 415 in actual numbers). And, perhaps reflecting the dire straits of young people, monetary penalties have plummeted from 31.7% of sentences in 1986 to 9.2% in 1991 (from 2,998 to 95 in actual numbers).

A widening net of criminalization? The catalogue of activities prohibited under the criminal law has neither expanded nor contracted significantly under Labour or National, though existing offences have undergone refinement to underscore their culpability. There have also been suggestions that the parents of young offenders should be culpable under law for the wrongdoing of their children.

If we associate net-widening with diversion from the formal juvenile (or adult) criminal justice system, then the impact of the *Children, Young Persons and Their Families Act* may be net-widening. Diversion has widespread support though it lacks any means of either reviewing practices to identify disparate outcomes reflecting race or gender bias or fettering the discretion of those who impose it (Kelsey 1993: 220). Because of diversion, the number of children coming before the courts dropped sharply from 7,236 in 1989 to 1,887 in 1990.

An expansion of the repressive parts of the apparatus to deal with political and industrial unrest? Repressive legislation of this kind characterized the Muldoon years. Labour and the current National Government are seen to be relatively benign, though Maori continue to be the focus of surveillance (Kelsey 1993: 317) and are grossly over-represented as 'clients' of the criminal justice system (Newbold 1992: 137-138; Spoonley 1993).

Data matching to curb welfare fraud, the exchange of information between Revenue, Social Welfare, the Accident Compensation Corporation (ACC) and the police facilitated by new technology, and the gradual evolution of a 'smart' ID card for keying clients into services and for costing their use of, and eligibility for, them are promoting a drift towards a 'surveillance society', especially for the poor (Kelsey 1993: 317).

Neither access to official information nor protection of privacy, nor indeed official accountability, has been reciprocally strengthened. The current election campaign has exposed the fact that some police are 'secondarily employed' (making six-figure incomes) from computerizing data and selling services (such as keyholder directories) based on information previously gathered and used in the normal course of their employment.

A docile labour force has been created under the *Employment Contracts Act 1991* without the need to deploy the state's repressive apparatus directly (Harbridge 1993). In a recent review of the Act, the New Zealand Employers' Federation has suggested the statutory removal of any requirement of procedural fairness as a separate issue in determining whether a dismissal is unjustifiable (New Zealand Employers' Federation 1991: 20). Meanwhile unemployment, which stood at 160,000 three years ago (when Mr Bolger was wont to call the then Prime Minister 'Mr Unemployment'), now stands at about 210,000, or 9.8% of the population.

Police have attacked the *Bill of Rights* and the *Children, Young Persons and Their Families Act* for curbing police powers by their due process provisions while, by and large, the courts have defended the legislation.

A cut back of liberal 1960s gains in areas such as abortion and women's rights, with a corresponding ascendence of right-wing moral crusaders? New Zealand enjoyed a citizens' rights based albeit 'reluctant' welfare state in the 1960s and through to 1984. That period brought many gains including the path-breaking accident compensation legislation of the 1970s (Shannon 1991).

Labour began a process of attrition in 1984 (Kelsey 1990; Holland and Boston 1990; Boston et al 1991) which has accelerated dramatically under National. National's attacks on income maintenance, accident compensation, labour market strategy, health care, housing, and tertiary education, and the 'downsizing' of the public sector have been well-documented (Boston and Dalziel 1992; Novitz and Willmott 1992; Kelsey 1993).

The attempt to address gender-based wage inequities in the labour force was suffocated at birth when Labour's *Employment Equity Act* was repealed almost as soon as it was passed in 1990 (Wilson 1992).

One area of note with respect to the law and order debate in recent times is the suppression of the Victims' Task Force report by Busch, Robertson and Lapsley (1992), which exposed the lamentable inadequacy of the criminal justice system to protect women victims of domestic violence. Another area of note is a $20 million cutback to legal aid.

Women, Maori, Pacific Islanders and the poor have been consistently immiserised, while the top income earners have benefitted from a 33% income tax rate and more of the tax take comes from regressive goods and services taxes levied on everyone.

The Cohen indices do not highlight privatization and voluntarization of public services, yet 'the retreat of the state is associated with a reassertion of the family - that is, with the role of women as the providers of services' (Bunkle 1992: 74) and with an enhanced role for charity such as foodbanks. As we shall be addressing, the family and the community have been coopted into the 'archipelago of social control' by both Labour and National. National's tone is victim-blaming while Labour appeals to the social democratic idiom of participation. Public opinion polls show widespread public support for the idea of police/community cooperation.

Greater publicity given to street crimes? In our view, hard news reporting and police commentary have traditionally focused on street crime, but it could be argued that increasing media publicity and police attention are now being given to domestic violence, including child abuse, and to *road* crimes, with the introduction of compulsory breath testing and speed cameras.

A transformation of the discrete moral panics of the 1960s into a deliberate climate of hostility to marginal groups and racial minorities, who become scapegoats for the crisis? Kelsey (1993) identifies several categories of 'folk devils' targetted within New Zealand as 'the enemies within': Maori, 'overstayers', Asian immigrants, feminists, and lesbians and gay men. There is not space here to examine the validity of her analysis. We would argue, however, that the evidence is equivocal for the deliberate scapegoating of Maori in the media. Fox (1992) complains, with undoubted justification, about the coverage of Maori issues in the mainstream media. Prime Minister Jim Bolger tried in January and on Waitangi Day (6 February) 1992 to scapegoat Maori for the high rate of violent crime, and though both Hobson MP Ross Meurant and criminologist Greg Newbold joined in with criticism of the parenting skills of Maori and Pacific Islanders, a flurry of news articles ensued in which this scapegoating was rejected by Maori and Pakeha alike.

Gisborne police commander Superintendent Rana Waitai rejects the race/crime nexus and points to the role of unemployment in the crime equation: he is backed by the Anglican Bishop of Wellington (*Dominion*, 1 February 1992). In an article headlined 'Bishop takes PM to task' (*New Zealand Herald*, 31 January 1992), the then Anglican Bishop of Waikato, the Rt Rev Roger Herft, accuses Bolger of trying 'to draw people's attention away from economic policies that have created more unemployment and redundancies', and also accuses him of victim-bashing. On the same page, in an article headlined 'Job lack, crime link backed', Professor Ian Shirley of the social policy research unit at Massey University, without referring to race, draws on the evidence of over 700 overseas studies showing a link between high levels of unemployment and crime. He blames the government (and the previous Labour government) for creating 'incredible insecurity' with social and economic policies which have produced 'long-term unemployment, economic deprivation and social disorder'.

Pita Rikys of Auckland District Maori Council, in an article headlined 'Govt policy blamed for crime' (*New Zealand Herald*, 7 February 1992) criticizes Bolger's statements about Maori criminal behaviour as a 'public relations ploy' to draw attention away from new health charges: he, too, sees unemployment as a major cause of crime, and blames Government policies which include 'the pursuit of free market economic goals irrespective of social costs' for high levels of Maori unemployment and Maori imprisonment.

A *Dominion* editorial on 'Maoris and violence' (3 February 1992) calls on the Government to implement recommendations contained in the 1987 Roper Report on Violence, and to obtain Maori involvement and commitment by building the future on a new base - and points out that though the solutions will cost, the costs of not implementing them will be far greater.

Law and order as an electoral issue

The control of crime, especially violent offending, was identified by political parties as a key issue in the elections of 1949, 1969, 1972 (Newbold 1990: 148), 1987 (Newbold 1989: 293; Vowles and Aimer 1993) and 1990 (Vowles and Aimer 1993), and emerged as one of the 'non'-economic issues in 1993. The common theme of law and order planks has been 'coercion and containment': parties have ignored public fear of crime and public outrage at their peril.

In 1984 neither Labour under Lange nor National under Muldoon isolated law and order as an issue. Both were primarily concerned with economic policy to manage the dramatic crisis facing new Zealand at that time arising from Muldoon's 'Think Big' policies and the failure of the 'only command economy in the western world'. Labour had an alternative platform on economic management and distinctive policies on defence, environment, and women.

The New Zealand Party assembled by millionaire Sir Robert Jones had a 'Law and Order' plank promising immediately to 'declare war on crime'. The policy statement described crime as 'epidemic' and a reflection of a 'sick and stagnant society', declared that 'this nation has the second highest rate of prison inmates per capita', and promised 'hard labour', 'greatly increased police numbers', 'compensation by offenders for all crimes', and the 'decriminalization of victim-less crimes', including smoking marijuana.

Its economic libertarianism was matched by a strong moral liberalism which enabled it to appeal to many disenchanted supporters of the major parties. Spectacularly, the New Zealand Party captured 12.3% of the vote in its first bid for power. No analysis exists of the specific impact its Law and Order plank had on voters' choices.

In 1984, when Labour took over as government, the penal system was 'troubled and restless' (Newbold 1989: 293). As the then Minister of Justice, Geoffrey Palmer, attempted to lower the prison 'muster', which stood at an all time high. The *Criminal Justice Act* 1984 reduced prison terms for property crimes, automatically deducted periods in remand from sentences, and promoted parole. At first prison numbers dropped to a 16-year low, but parolees re-offended in large numbers and the numbers again reached an all time high. A spate of violent murders and gang-related activity put crime back on the political agenda.

The Roper Report on Violence (1987) found that over the preceding decade conviction rates were up 55% for rape, 200% for robbery and aggravated robbery, 115% for murder, and 234% for manslaughter! Also in 1987, the *New Zealand Herald* carried numerous hard-news crime stories and 25 major crime articles (Newbold 1992: 140), while public opinion polls revealed that the percentage of those polled who regarded law and order as the most serious issue increased from 5% to 13% during that year. Law and order was found to be level-pegging with education as 'very important', and fewest respondents judged it to be 'not important' in the election study of that year (Vowles and Aimer 1993: 166).

Though both Labour and National went into law and order mode for the 1987 election, Labour launched a $950,000 campaign to sell its 'get tough', 'law and order' programme but did not formally put law and order into its election manifesto. Its management of the economy, and environmental, human rights, international relations, and anti-nuclear policies were foregrounded.

Labour's law and order package had a tough side which was found mostly in the legislation amending the *Crimes Act* 1961 which expanded by five the types of activities specified as violent offences, and in the *Criminal Justice Act* 1985, which delivered harsher penalties, reduced parole options, and imposed a ten-year non-parole period for murder. Labour also attempted to refocus attention on to the victim and to promote the 'community' as the basic resource for crime prevention. As we shall see, these themes are now mandatory elements of any New Zealand law and order campaign.

The Police Association campaigned vigorously for increased resources and against the Labour government, which responded by promising up to 100 more police. The Leader of the Opposition, National's Jim Bolger, promised a tough crime control programme. Several child murders and gang rapes during the run-up to the election were seized on by the Opposition to amplify their law and order promises: they responded to several marches demanding the restoration of capital punishment by promising a free vote in parliament and a national referendum on hanging. Pratt suggests that this particular tactic was perceived by the media as opportunistic and incoherent. So was an attempt to show Labour as soft on rape, which brought a rebuttal demonstrating that penalties under Labour were in fact harsher than they had been under National (Pratt 1988: 261).

Aside from these tactics, the National Party's *'Freedom, Law and Justice'* platform highlighted that 'the cornerstone of our democracy is personal and community law and order', and that 'no New Zealander should be afraid to walk the streets at night ... or be afraid in their own home'. Key elements of this campaign to combat the fear of urban crime were victims and police. National promised to 'give the police the manpower and resources', to meet any reasonable request for equipment and legal powers', to 'deal with the gang problem', and to protect and compensate 'the forgotten victim'.

Despite the global stock market crash (or perhaps because of it) Labour won the 1987 election with 48% of the valid vote against National's 44%. The only minor party to achieve more than 5% of the vote was the red/green Values Party with 5.6%.

Notably, the impact of the New Right 'Rogernomics' agenda did not appear to affect adversely the popularity of the fourth Labour government at this stage. Rogernomics still represented a dynamic alternative to the 'stagflation' of the Muldoon era and may indeed have been a contributing factor to Labour's electoral appeal (Vowles and Aimer 1993: 82), especially since National acknowledged that its economic policies were the same as Rogernomics (*Dominion* 26/09/87).

Summarizing the 1987 election campaign, Pratt (1988: 265) concludes: 'The complexities and possibilities of penal policy were reduced at times to a matter of who would lock offenders up the longest'.

In 1987-1990, however, the Labour government saw the social impact of Rogernomics coming home to roost. The crime 'wave' continued, 'few tangible benefits could be seen by voters from Labour's initiatives, and the purpose of the initiatives was far from clear' (Vowles and Aimer 1993, 1984). The New Zealand values survey of 1989 found a national perception of increasing criminality and almost universal affirmation of the need for 'stiffer jail sentences' [75 + %] and 'increased police powers' [80 + %]:

There is little difference in viewpoint among social groups: women and regular church goers are a little more conservative on these items than men or infrequent church-goers. European and Maori seem to think alike. There is minor variation by age. Labourites are a shade less keen than National supporters on these approaches in dealing with crime, but three out of four Labour identifiers favour them (Gold and Webster 1989: 27).

We concur with Pratt's prescient assessment that, though they lost the

1987 election battle, National won the war to establish the parameters of crime talk and set down the terms on which Labour was forced to compete to be tough on the law and order front during 1987-1990 (Pratt 1988: 265). To their credit, Labour did so half-heartedly.   Though the Labour government made some attempts to address the public's demands for crime control, its most conspicuous initiatives again pushed in the opposite direction, towards rights, due process, and rehabilitation.

Palmer launched the Ministerial Inquiry into prison systems whose report (Roper 1989) had a substantially abolitionist message. He also initiated a major overhaul of the *Crimes Act* 1961, intending to modernize the substantive criminal law. This bill was opposed by the judiciary and the legal profession and perceived to be very much a lawyers' law project. It came to nothing.

Reform of the law relating to neglected children and, notably, young offenders completed a lengthy period of gestation culminating in the *Children, Young Persons and Their Families Act* 1989. This Act created an apparently soft regime based on diversion, family group conferences, and restrictions on the use of police powers.

The *New Zealand Bill of Rights Bill* debate raged and the 1990 Act passed - drastically watered down - the 1985 proposal. Yet it, too, appeared to enhance individual rights against officialdom. None of these initiatives did anything, it seems, to allay the public's fear of crime and to restore confidence in the government's commitment to wage war on crime.

The National Party continued to exploit the crime wave. Shadow police minister John Banks promised in 1989 to increase police numbers by 900. Hard and soft news presented details of rising crime, unemployment and social dislocation. The Opposition took the opportunity to present the Government as both responsible for rising crime and unwilling to take a tough approach to combat it. National's slogan was the return to a 'decent society'.

Could it be that the 'crime problem' provided a lightning-rod for the insecurity and confusion engendered by the rapid and radical changes wrought by Labour in the period 1984-1989, and legitimated a strong law and order agenda for the 1990 election?

The populist and opportunistic National manifesto attempted to appeal to a broad spectrum of voters who were not normally National supporters. '*Restoring Law and Order*' focused on fear of crime, street crime and white collar crime. It declared that 'all offenders will be treated equally before the courts, whether the crimes are committed in fortified gang headquarters, or in glitzy high rise office towers'. It promised to 'vary from the present government ... by admitting that the problems exist', to provide 'rehabilitation of young offenders' and to 'get very tough on those who refuse the chance', and to provide 'a great deal of assistance for at risk groups' while those who avoided assistance would be 'appropriately dealt with'. It also promised more police again and stiffer prison sentences - despite overwhelming expert evidence that such strategies are ineffectual such as Roper (1989) and the New Zealand Police (1989).

One of the ways to restore 'the decent society' promised in National's law and order platform was to 'tackle the underlying causes'. Thus National promised to launch a major offence on unemployment, the cause of so much crime and antisocial behaviour'. National's platform appealed to voters across the political spectrum. It was astute and did the job. The 1990 election survey data led Vowles and Aimer to comment:

> In 1990, Labour's loss of political popularity combined with the public's perception of social disorder and rising crime lifted National to a pinnacle of electoral approval on the law and order issue (1993: 167).

Electors questioned about the need for more government spending on police and law enforcement show 64% of Labour, 84% of National, 62% of Green, and 69% of New Labour Party supporters wanting more spending (Vowles and Aimer 1993: 168). Labour supporters ranked law and order fourth below unemployment, education and health as an extremely important issue. National supporters put it number one.

When asked whether their party's political platform was closest to the supporter's own position on the issue, only 28% of Labour supporters, compared with 84% of National supporters, indicated this was so respecting their party's law and order platform. (Labour achieved a 50% association from its supporters on only three issues, whereas National achieved 50% association on eight!) Those who switched from Labour, and who therefore contributed to a landslide victory for National of 47% of the vote (compared to Labour's 35%), expressed 'least residual feeling of support for Labour' on law and order. Further: 'Empathy with Labour on the law and order issue had collapsed, even among its stable voters, more of whom felt closer to National' (Vowles and Aimer 1993: 74).

The same was true for the unemployment issue. Interestingly, by late 1991 - early 1992, the National government's Prime Minister had repudiated the causal link between crime and unemployment so pointedly articulated in the election-winning 1990 manifesto, thereby throwing a potentially interesting curve into the 1993 campaign, though one which did not materialize explicitly. Justice Department data collected for the first time in 1990 found 44% of inmates were unemployed at the time of arrest (*Dominion Sunday Times* 9 February 1992). Justice officials presented the statistics as showing a correlational, rather than causative, relationship between crime and unemployment.

Law and order agendas: National and Labour

The National Government continued its predecessor's Rogernomic policies and even some of its more progressive environmental, anti-nuclear and Maori policy initiatives. The parameters of the law and order agenda set for Labour in 1987, which also contributed to National's 1990 victory, continued in 1993 to form the basis for what National sees as a winning combination: 'Crime prevention', 'Law and Order', Victim 'Support' and community. The National Party's September 1993 *'Justice and Law and Order Policy'* asserted that 'the only way to solve the problem of crime is for communities to join with the police in taking responsibility for crime prevention'. The slogan it carried was *'Building Secure Communities'*.

Labour's August 1993 *'Plan for Law, Order and Justice'* is entitled *'Making Our Neighbourhoods Safe Again '*. It seemed that Labour had learned from 1987 and 1990. It was taking seriously the crime and crime control agenda which National controlled, and matched National item for item, though the 1993 platforms differed somewhat in substance, tone and emphasis.

National highlighted Crime Prevention; Labour opens with *'Helping Communities to Become Safer'*. National's Law and Order category embraced issues addressed by Labour under Police Issues, Creating a More Just and Tolerant Society (e.g. anti-porn legislation) and Justice issues (e.g. sentencing). National had a section on Victim Support; Labour has a section headed Victims/Survivors of Crime.

A summary of the points of convergence and divergence in the platforms illustrates that both parties shared objectives to allay the fear of crime, to be seen to be addressing the crime problem, and yet to sustain fidelity to their historical value bases. These objectives are always fraught with more contradictions for Labour than for National, especially since National has been enabled to set the parameters of the law and order debate while Labour must operate within the parameters of an unpopular economic and social policy framework of its own making:

Crime prevention, community and the family

·   Both major parties coupled crime prevention with support for the system (piloted by Labour) of Safer Community Councils.

·   Labour incorporated Maori community control of some justice programmes and respect for Maori values, while National's community focus stressed programmes for good parenting, identifying children and families at risk and child abuse prevention.

Crime control and law enforcement

·   Both promised support for community policing and more police (Labour explicitly criticizing National's centralization approach).

·   Both promised more crime detection high technology.

·   Both promised support for the Serious Fraud Office (Labour expressing concern that the SFO is currently under-resourced, and considering re-incorporating the Office as a branch of the police to ensure its backing 'by the institutional strength that a law enforcement agency needs', National promising 'strong continued support for the Serious Fraud Office and the Securities Commission as separate bodies').

·   Labour promised to review the operation of the police/traffic merger, while National regards the completed integration of the two services as a positive given.

·   National promised enhanced police powers to question juveniles.

·   Labour promised to set up a Public Prosecutor's service to free-up police from this role.

·   Labour promised to modernize the *Crimes Act*, promote diversion, and improve the efficiency of the courts.

·   Both acknowledged the need to combat pornography.

·   Both tackled enhanced gun control.

- Both promised forfeiture of the proceeds and tools of crime.

Due process and (prisoners') rights

- National boasted a $20 million dollar saving on the legal aid bill through its amendments to the *Legal Services Act*, while Labour promised to investigate creation of a public defenders office, to increase funding to community law centres, to promote eligibility for legal aid to groups including refugee status claimants, and to sustain commitment to the *New Zealand Bill of Rights Act* 1990.

Containment, punishment and (re)habilitation

- Both favoured experimentation with the home confinement of some non-violent offenders.

- Both supported 'habilitation' centres. Labour, however, articulated a concern for the size of the prison population and the nature of the prison experience based on the Roper Report (1989), while National stressed inmate education and work and especially tough deterrent measures - a maximum penalty for sexual violation (penile or otherwise) of up to 20 years, no parole for violent offenders, tighter bail conditions, tighter recall provisions for parolees, and restricted inmate privileges.

- National proposed to privatize two correctional facilities, while Labour explictly affirmed its position that providing prisons will continue to be a state responsibility.

The victim

- National's approach to the victim was streamlined down to increased funding, directing courts to consider reparation by offenders to victims in all cases, and requesting the Parole Board to take account of victims' views when considering parole.

- Labour's detailed policy included promises to: implement recommendations of the Victims' Task Force Report; explore better reparation provisions; establish a victims' charter of rights; investigate the need for victims' access to advocacy and advice before, during and after the trial; coordinate and resource support and advocacy groups; require services for victims to be responsive to victims' needs, culturally appropriate and geographically spread; and ensure victim-oriented training for all levels of personnel in the legal system. Labour highlights domestic violence and promises to explore changing the *Domestic Protection Act*, to monitor police performance under the Act, and to promote police training on the subject.

The platform of the third contestant, the 'Alliance' - an association of red/green/populist and Maori minor parties, entitled *'Fair Justice'*, highlighted 'Access to Justice and Law', revamped legal aid, law centres, public defenders, a public prosecutor service, and appropriate Maori legal structures. Under 'Prisons and Habilitation Centres' the Roper reports on violence (1987) and prisons (1989) informed their position. (All three major contestants in the 1993 election have adopted Roper's habilitation centre idea.) Labour and the Alliance had a more holistic approach to solutions to the crime problem than National; perhaps Labour and the Alliance know the words *and* the music.

The Alliance saw anti-violence training modules at all levels of the education system. The Alliance's 'Victims of Crime' programme involved reparation, compensation, and representation for victims, as well as the opportunity for them to participate in making the perpetrator confront the consequences of his or her actions.

Labour and National have presented their approaches to the management of the crime problem within the parameters of: Crime Prevention, Community and the Family; Crime Control and Law Enforcement, Due Process and (Prisoners') Rights; Containment, Punishment and (re)Habilitation and the Victim. Labour and the Alliance both included explicit references to the links between crime and unemployment. National's flip-flop on this linkage from 1990 to 1992 deserves another article.

A formative conclusion: 'bringing the *community* back in'?

The *Justice and Law and Order* (National) and *Law and Order and Justice* (Labour) 1993 platforms relied heavily on promises involving 'community' prevention, safer 'communities', 'community' policing, and supporting the 'at risk' family or reintegrating the family into the school and the state with 'Parents as First Teachers'.

We close by examining the process we have described by reference to Cohen's work on the 'quest for community' (1985: 118-127) and

'controltalk' (Cohen 1985: 273-281), since Cohen's analysis adds dimensions
to our understanding of the ideological management of the crisis. What are
the meanings of community/neighbourhood and family in 'controltalk'? If
they are 'euphemisms', then what subtle but negative connotations are
disguised which should be unmasked? Or should we merely accept their
emphasis as evidence of belated attempts to restore the supposed
gemeinschaft of previous times to replace the alienation and anomie of the
gesellschaft which the New Right's economic rationalism has produced?

In the victim-blaming idiom of the National platform, is 'family' a vehicle
for the reintegration of the family into the 'carceral archipelago', and does
it open the family to expert invasion, albeit in a residual welfare state?
'Neighbourhood and community' are potent symbolic terms which are easily
coopted as adjuncts to conservative and social democratic projects.
Community is seen in 1993 'controltalk' as the resource to assist police with
crime prevention and control.

The rich iconography of the village or the Maori *pa* may lie behind the
current impulse. Yet little or no real attempt to reinforce Maori legal
structures is stressed in the manifestos. Maori lore, instead of Pakeha law,
has in the past two years been invoked by now-adult, former victims of child
sexual abuse to do marae justice resulting in the shaming of several kaumatua
(elders) responsible by stripping them of their status. When this process of
marae justice was featured in the media recently it attracted ambivalent
responses.

For conservatives, the 'community' may be a bastion against modern and
postmodern values such as individualism and autonomy which have enabled
women and men to break repressive bonds of tradition, class or patriarchy.
Cohen suggests that 'most attempts to recreate community in fact constitute
evidence of the end of community': he asks whether it is likely that the same
interests and forces which destroyed the traditional community -
'bureaucracy, professionalization, centralization, [and] rationalization' - can
now be used to reverse the process (1985: 122-3).

In New Zealand, leaflets shaped like police helmets were being distributed
door-to-door encouraging residents to make contact with their neighbours and
collect their phone numbers so that people can look out for one-another. But
even if police and a few neighbourly residents make 'a community', it is
hard to see what difference they could make to a crime wave which results
from still unaddressed structural causes.

Cohen tells us that 'community and neighbourhood' entered the glossary
of 'controltalk' as a response to the destructuring ideology of the 1960s and
1970s. Community and neighbourhood achieved positive connotations when

contrasted with 'the state' and 'the institution'. A convergence of perpectives is reflected in this outcome:

1. a pragmatic recognition that the formal system was not working (echoed in Roper 1989);

2. a humanitarian and civil libertarian view that formal institutions denied rights and were brutalizing and degrading (very muted in the present);

3. a social scientific finding that 'institutionalization' induced labelling by the system and negative self-imagery, dependency, and secondary forms of deviation on the part of the client; and

4. a conservative, rationalist cost/benefit analysis that institutions were costly and unproductive.

New Zealand politicians' quest for *gemeinschaft* will have to be analyzed to discover what intellectual supports underpin it. The destructuring ideology of the 1960s and 1970s juxtaposed the state-funded institution with the state-funded community-based programme and came out for the community through informalism, alternatives, de-institutionalization and all those 'good things'. The residual post-fordist welfare state of the 1990s juxtaposes state/market, market/family (hapu), market/charity or nothing. The old community with all its ancient antagonisms remains but is juxtaposed with the new market society and enhanced state repression. Citizenship has been emptied of meanings achieved under even imperfect social democracy.

We now face an altogether different platform of process upon which settlements are to be attempted. The market society and its unacknowledged repressive apparatus is supposedly a platform of process upon which currently hegemonic political formations aim to deliver the 'decent society'. The major political parties pay lip-service to the ideas of income redistribution, income security, and the creation of meaningful employment, but appear unable or unwilling to pursue radical policies for achieving them. Unless different social movements are radically re-aligned and empowered, socially just outcomes for all which might mitigate crime and violence seem unlikely. The 1996 general election fought on the basis of MMP offers New Zealanders a chance to check the transition to post-fordism and assert a communitarian ecologically sound social order based on an authentic partnership of Maori and Pakeha peoples.

References

Arsenau, T. (1990) 'A Bill of Rights', in M. Holland and J. Boston (eds) *The Fourth Labour Government: Politics and Policy in New Zealand*, Auckland: Oxford University Press.

Boston, J. (1991) 'The Theoretical Underpinnings of Public Sector Restructuring in New Zealand', in J. Boston et al (eds) *Reshaping the State: New Zealand's Bureaucratic Revolution*, Auckland: Oxford University Press.

Boston, J. *et al* (eds) (1991) *Reshaping the State: New Zealand's Bureaucratic Revolution* Auckland: Oxford University Press.

Boston, J. and Dalziel, P. (1992) *The Decent Society? Essays in response to National's Economic and Social Policies*, Auckland: Oxford University Press.

Braybrook, B. and Southey, P. (1992) *Census of Prison Inmates 1991*, Wellington: Department of Justice.

Bunkle, P. (1992) 'The Economy: Restructuring and Growth', in D. Novitz and B. Willmott (eds) *New Zealand in Crisis*, Wellington: GP Publications.

Busch, R., Robertson, N. and Lapsley, H. (1992) *Domestic Violence and the Justice System: A Study of Breaches of Protection Orders* [suppressed: the expurgated version is available as Victims Task Force Report (1992)].

Cerny, C. (1990) *The Changing Architecture of Politics: Structure, Agency and the Future of the State*, London: Sage Publications.

Cohen, S. (1985) *Visions of Social Control: Crime, Punishment and Classification*, Cambridge: Polity Press.

Dominion Sunday Times, Wellington: Independent News Ltd.

Duncan, I. and Bollard, A. (1992) *Corporatization and Privatization: Lessons from New Zealand*, Auckland: Oxford University Press.

Fox, D. (1992) 'The Maori Perspective of the News', in M. Comrie and J. McGregor (eds) *Whose News?* Palmerston North: Dunmore Press.

Franzway, S., Court, S., and Connell, R. (1989) *Staking a Claim: Feminism, Bureaucracy and the State*, Sydney: Allen and Unwin.

Giddens, A. (1976) *New Rules of Sociological Method*, London: Hutchinson.

Gold, H. and Webster, A. (1990) *New Zealand Values Today*, Palmerston North: Alpha Publications.

Hall, S. et al (1978) *Policing the Crisis: Mugging, the State and Law and Order*, London: Macmillan.

Hall, S. and Jacques, M. (1991) *New Times: the Changing Face of Politics in the 1990s*, London: Lawrence and Wishart.

Harbridge, R. (ed.) (1993) *Employment Contracts: New Zealand Experiences*, Wellington: Victoria University Press.

Harvey, O. (1992) 'The Unions and the Government: the Rise and Fall of the Compact', in J. Deeks and N. Perry (eds) *Controlling Interests: Business, the State and Society in New Zealand*, Auckland: Auckland University Press.

Havemann, P. (1987) 'Marketing the New Establishment Ideology in Canada',

Crime and Social Justice, 26, 11-37.

Havemann, P. (1992) 'Canadian Realist Criminology in the 1990s: some Reflections on the Quest for Social Justice', in J. Lowman and B. MacLean (eds) *Realist Criminology: Crime Control and Policing in the 1990s*, Toronto: Toronto University Press.

Havemann, P. (1994) 'Regulating the Crisis from Fordism to Post-fordism in Aotearoa/New Zealand 1984-1994. Some Contraditions in the Interregnum, Morbid and Otherwise', forthcoming in *Humanity and Society*.

Havemann, P. and Turner, K. (1994) 'The Waitangi Tribunal: Theorising its Place in the Re-Design of the New Zealand State', unpublished paper (forthcoming).

Holland, M. and Boston, J. (1990) *The Fourth Labour Government: Politics and Policy in New Zealand*, Auckland: Oxford University Press.

Hughes, J. (1993) 'Personal Grievances', in R. Harbridge (ed.) *Employment Contracts: New Zealand Experiences*, Wellington: Victoria University Press.

James, C. (1992) *New Territory: the Transformation of New Zealand 1984-92*, Wellington: Bridget Williams Books.

Jesson, B. (1987) *Behind the Mirror Glass*, Auckland: Penguin Books.

Jesson, B. (1992) 'The disintegration of a Labour Tradition: New Zealand Politics in the 1980s', *New Left Review*, 192, March/April.

Kelsey, J. (1990) *A Question of Honour? Labour and the Treaty 1984-1989*, Wellington: Allen and Unwin.

Kelsey, J. (1993) *Rolling back the State: Privatisation of Power in Aotearoa/New Zealand*, Wellington: Bridget Williams Books.

Koopman-Boyden, P. (1990) 'Social Policy: has there been one?', in M. Holland and J. Boston (eds) *The Fourth Labour Government: Politics and Policy in New Zealand*, Auckland: Oxford University Press.

Mathews, J. (1989) *Age of Democracy: the Politics of Post-fordism*, Melbourne: Oxford University Press.

McLoughlin, D. (1992) *The Undeveloping Nation*, Auckland: Penguin Books.

Michalowski, R. (1981) 'The Politics of the Right', *Crime and Social Justice*, 15: 29-35.

Mulgan, R. (1990) 'The changing electoral mandate', in M. Holland and J. Boston (eds) *The Fourth Labour Government: Politics and Policy in New Zealand*, Auckland: Oxford University Press.

Mulgan, R. (1992) 'The Elective Dictatorship in New Zealand' in H. Gold (ed.) *New Zealand Politics in Perspective*, Auckland: Longman Paul.

Newbold, G. (1989) *Punishment and Politics: the Maximum Security Prison in New Zealand*, Auckland: Oxford University Press.

Newbold, G. (1990) 'Violence in New Zealand', in P. Green (ed.) *Studies in New Zealand Social Problems*, Palmerston North: Dunmore Press.

Newbold, G. (1992) *Crime and Deviance*, Auckland: Oxford University Press.

New Zealand Employers' Federation (1991) *Submissions on the Employment Contracts Bill*.

New Zealand Herald, Auckland: Wilson and Horton.

New Zealand Police (1989) *Resource Management Review*. Strategos Consulting Limited.

Norris, M. and MacPherson, S. (1990) *Offending in New Zealand: Trends and International Comparisons*, Wellington: Department of Justice.

Novitz, D. and Willmott, B. (eds) *New Zealand in Crisis*, Wellington: GP Publications.

O'Brien, M. and Wilkes, C. (1993) 'The Tragedy of the Market', Palmerston North: Dunmore Press.

O'Connor, J. (1972) *The Fiscal Crisis of the State*, New York: St Martin's Press.

Offe, C. (1972) 'Advanced Capitalism and the Welfare State', *Politics and Society*, (Summer) 479-488.

O'Reilly, T. and Wood, D. (1991) 'Biculturalism and the Public Sector', in J. Boston et al (eds) *Reshaping the State: New Zealand's Bureaucratic Revolution*, Auckland: Oxford University Press.

Palmer, G. (2nd edition 1987), *Unbridled Power - an Interpretation of New Zealand's Constitution and Government*, Auckland: Oxford University Press.

Palmer, G. (1992) *New Zealand's Constitution in Crisis*, Dunedin: John McIndoe.

Platt, A. (1981) 'Managing the Crisis: Austerity and the Penal System', *Contemporary Marxism*, 4: 29-39.

Pratt, J. (1987) 'Taking Crime Seriously: Social Work Strategies for Law and Order Climates', *New Zealand Sociology*.

Pratt, J. (1988) 'Law and Order Politics in New Zealand 1986: A Comparison with the United Kingdom 1974-9', *International Journal of the Sociology of Law*, 16: 103-26.

Pratt, J. and Treacher, P. (1988) 'Law and Order and the 1987 New Zealand Election', *Australian and New Zealand Journal of Criminology* (December) 21: 253-268.

Ratner, R. and McMullan, J. (1983) 'Social Control and the Rise of the "Exceptional State" in Britain, the United States and Canada', *Crime and Social Justice*, 19: 31-43.

Roper, C. (1987) *Report of the Ministerial Committee of Inquiry into Violence*, Wellington: Government Printer.

Roper, C. (1989) *Te Ara Hou: The New Way. Report of the Ministerial Committee of Inquiry into the Prisons System*, Wellington: Government Printer.

Royal Commission on the Electoral System (1986) *Report of the Royal Commission on the Electoral System 'Towards a Better Democracy'*, Wellington: Government Printer.

Royal Commission on Social Policy (1988) Vols. I-IV, Wellington: Government Printer.

Shannon, P. (1991) *Social Policy*, Auckland: Oxford University Press.

Skocpol, T. (1985) 'Bringing the State Back In: Strategies of Analysis in Current Research', in P. Evans et al (eds) *Bringing the State Back In*, Cambridge

University Press.

Spier, P. , Norris, M. and Southey, P. (1992) *Conviction and Sentencing of Offenders in New Zealand: 1982 to 1991*, Wellington: Department of Justice.

Spoonley, P. (1987) *The Politics of Nostalgia: Racism and the Extreme Right in New Zealand*, Palmerston North: Dunmore Press.

Spoonley, P. (1993) *Racism and Ethnicity*, Auckland: Oxford University Press.

Taylor, I. (1980) 'The Law and Order Issue in the British General Election and the Canadian Federal Election of 1979: Crime, Populism and the State', *Canadian Journal of Sociology*, 5: 285-311.

(ed.) (1991) *The Social Effects of Free Market Policies*, London/New York: Harvester/Wheatsheaf.

Tremaine, M. (1991) 'Equal Employment Opportunity in State Sector Reform', in J. Boston et al (eds) *Reshaping the State: New Zealand's Bureaucratic Revolution*, Auckland: Oxford University Press.

Victims Task Force (1992) *Protection from Family Violence*, Wellington: Department of Justice [See Busch, R., et al above].

Vowles, J. and Aimer, P. (1993) *Voters' Vengeance: the 1990 Election in New Zealand and the Fate of the Fourth Labour Government*, Auckland: Auckland University Press.

Wilson, M. (1992) *'Employment Equity Act* 1990: A Case Study in Women's Political Influence, 1984-90', in J. Deeks and N. Perry (eds) *Controlling Interests: Business, the State and Society in New Zealand*, Auckland: Auckland University Press.

Notes

1. Paul Havemann is a foundation Professor of Law at the University of Waikato, New Zealand. Before going to Waikato in 1990 he was at La Trobe University in Melbourne. He served as head of the School of Human Justice at the University of Regina, Saskatchewan 1980-87. His major areas of interest include the rights of indigenous First Nations peoples, juvenile justice law and policy, social policy and crime control and human rights. He holds LLB (Hons), LLM degrees from the University of London.

    Joan Havemann is currently tutoring in business communication and public relations at the University of Waikato. Her research interests are in public policy and discourse analysis. She contributed freelance articles to magazines and commentaries to CBC radio while living in Canada where she was an organiser and spokesperson for peace and anti-nuclear groups. She holds an honours degree from the London School of Economics.

XI Towards a cross-cultural theory of Aboriginal criminality

Russell Smandych, Robyn Lincoln and Paul Wilson[1]

Introduction

Despite extensive research, no attempt has yet been made systematically to compare the experience of aboriginal people in the criminal justice systems of Canada and Australia with the aim of developing a more generalized cross-cultural theory.   In search of a more adequate theoretical framework for explaining the apparently similar patterns of criminal justice outcomes found among aboriginal peoples, this essay explores a number of different approaches.[2]   The concern with developing a cross-cultural theory of aboriginal criminality[3] is motivated by the notable similarities that can be observed in the way in which indigenous peoples have been caught up in the criminal justice systems of different countries that have undergone the process of European colonization.

Criminologists in a number of different countries have examined the experience of aboriginal people and their patterns of involvement in the criminal justice system, and the academic study of aborigines and the law is an 'established enterprise' (Waller 1984).   However, much of the research centres on small localized studies of offending behaviour, sentencing disparities and police or public attitudes.   At the national level there is considerable evidence from police and prison figures to provide a general picture, but there is little that synthesises all these data in a way that moves us from 'description to explanation' (Parker 1987).   In addition, very little systematic comparative research has been carried out for the purpose of attempting to develop a more adequate cross-cultural understanding of these patterns.

Canada and Australia both have substantial aboriginal populations and both have similar British colonial histories. Their legal and criminal justice institutions are alike, based on the common law tradition. They are both federal states in which the responsibility for enacting and enforcing criminal laws are shared by state/provincial and federal governments. Because of these common features, these two nations provide a suitable context for undertaking systematic comparative research on aboriginal criminality.

Contemporary developments in Canada and Australia involving aboriginal people and the criminal justice system add further justification for selecting these two nations. In recent years, the federal government of Canada and several provincial governments have funded commissions of inquiry to investigate and make recommendations aimed at improving the treatment of aboriginal people in the criminal justice system, and developing criminal justice policies more sensitive to the traditional legal customs and culture of Canada's aboriginal peoples (Law Reform Commission of Canada 1991; Alberta 1991; Manitoba 1991; Nova Scotia 1988).

Likewise in Australia, the treatment of Australian Aboriginal and Torres Strait Islander people in the criminal justice system at both the state and federal level has been long investigated. The Law Reform Commission of Australia (1986) examined the possible use of customary law methods as a measure of reducing over-representation of aboriginal people in arrest and imprisonment statistics. More recently, public concern about the number of deaths of aborigines held in police and prison custody culminated in the *National Report* of the Royal Commission into Aboriginal Deaths in Custody (1991). While this Royal Commission, established in 1987, has been criticized sharply by aboriginal leaders and criminologists (Broadhurst and Maller 1990; Wilson and Lincoln 1991), its brief and findings are comparable to recent government inquiries that have occurred in Canada (McNamara 1992a).

In the academic arena, both Canadian and Australian criminologists have given a great deal of attention to research aimed at developing more adequate explanations of the causes of aboriginal over-representation, and at developing more adequate criminal justice and social policies affecting aboriginal peoples.[4] Despite the clear parallels, no systematic collaborative and comparative research has been carried out on these issues. Rather, the research and theorizing around aboriginal criminality in Canada and Australia have remained quite insular. In the following sections, we provide an overview of the current state of research and theorizing about aboriginal involvement in the criminal justice system in Canada and Australia with the aim toward laying the groundwork for the development of a more adequate theory, or set of theories, that can help to explain similar cross-national patterns of recorded criminal behaviour by indigenous peoples.

Politicization of Aboriginal crime and justice issues

The topics of aboriginal crime and justice are now receiving unprecedented interest in Canada and Australia, even prior to the UN-declared Year of Indigenous Peoples. There are many factors that have contributed in bringing academic, public and government attention to bear on issues surrounding aboriginal crime and justice in both countries. One significant factor is the strengthening political voice of aboriginal people and their leaders. In recent years, descendants of the original indigenous peoples have become increasingly politically active and demanding in their call for action aimed at undoing the harm caused by government policies of assimilation, cultural genocide and political cooption, and also at the harm caused by a long history of institutionalized and widespread racism (Daniels 1986; York 1990; Read 1988; Langton 1983).

Canada, for example, is at a crossroads in its political history and the history of its treatment of aboriginal people (Boldt 1993; Wotherspoon and Satzewich 1993). This has been forced on Canada's federal and provincial governments by a series of events participated in by aboriginal people, the most symbolically significant of which include: the six-week armed blockade and confrontation between Mohawk warriors and the Quebec police and Canadian military at Oka, Quebec, in the summer of 1990; the death of the Meech Lake Constitutional Accord orchestrated by Canadian aboriginal leaders; the Donald Marshall Inquiry in Nova Scotia (Nova Scotia 1988); and the recently completed three-year Aboriginal Justice Inquiry in the province of Manitoba (Manitoba 1991).

The Aboriginal Justice Inquiry of Manitoba was established in 1988 to investigate the manner in which aboriginal people were being dealt with in the criminal justice system and to make recommendations for improving the system. The two Commissioners of the Aboriginal Justice Inquiry, one of whom is the only aboriginal judge in Manitoba, called for a massive overhaul of the province's criminal justice system and a fundamental change from the way in which aboriginal people have been perceived and treated by 'white society' in the past. In a recently published book, *Surviving as Indians: The Challenge of Self-Government,* Menno Boldt (1993) sums up the current state of critical opinion on the fairness of Canadian courts in dealing with Canada's indigenous peoples, noting:

Official statistics, which show Indians to be grossly overrepresented among those arrested, convicted, and imprisoned, lend support to Indian grievances that racism in the Canadian justice system is pervasive and runs deep. Indians have experienced it and proclaimed it for years, but, except for the recent provincial inquiries, the justice system has denied the validity of such grievances (Boldt 1993: 13).

The recent events that have brought the issue of aboriginal crime and justice to the forefront in Canada have been watched closely by many Canadian criminologists, who have long recognised the problem of over-representation of aboriginal people in the Canadian criminal justice system (Bienvenue and Latif 1974; Hagan 1974, 1975a, 1975b, 1977). However, it is only more recently, in the wake of the increasing political power of aboriginal peoples and the growing concern of Canadian governments to address aboriginal matters, that criminological research on issues surrounding aboriginal crime and justice has begun to receive more extensive attention.

In Australia, there has been a similar process of politicization. As a result of widespread public concern about Aborigines dying in police and prison cells, the Royal Commission into Aboriginal Deaths in Custody (RCIADIC) was established on 17 June 1987. The Commission was given the brief to inquire into the reasons for this national tragedy at a time when Australia was approaching its Bicentennial celebrations. The Commission, which has been described as a 'lawyers' picnic' (NAILSS 1989), cost at least $A30 million. It recommended no criminal charges against custodial officers involved in the cases, despite evidence that some lied under oath, fabricated evidence, unlawfully arrested and detained aboriginal people, and in other cases, assaulted them (Lincoln and Wilson 1993). There were many protests and actions undertaken by aboriginal communities in an attempt to see justice done.

One of the major findings to emerge from the research conducted by the Commission was that the proportion of aborigines in both police and prison custody was similar to the proportion of aboriginal deaths in each form of custody (Grabosky et al 1988). This was interpreted as meaning that there were no differences between the black and white rates of custodial deaths. Those who had opposed the establishment of the Commission therefore asserted that the issue of aboriginal deaths in custody was not a problem of special significance.

However, the Commission's research found that across the country there were 75 aboriginal deaths per 100,000 of the adult aboriginal population and a 3.3 non-aboriginal deaths per 100,000 of the adult non-aboriginal population. In other words, aboriginal adults died in custody at a rate 23 times that of non-aboriginal people (Biles, McDonald and Fleming 1990) and if non-aborigines had been imprisoned at the same rate there would have been 8,500 deaths in the study period studied (Tickner 1992). The differences in custodial deaths were attributed to over-representation of aborigines in police cells and prisons - a finding that was not unknown previously in the Australian criminological literature. Any attempt to explain the social or cultural causes of over-representation became bogged down in a lack of resources and a legally-dominated inquiry.

The Commission did bring the position of aboriginal people to world attention. An Amnesty International team visited Australia in 1993 and characterized the Australian criminal justice system as making aboriginal people vulnerable to 'highly disproportionate levels of incarceration and to cruel, inhuman or degrading treatment' (Amnesty International 1993: 5). The political response has been the allocation of over $A70 million to employment strategies, police services, cross-cultural training schemes, changes in custodial procedures, improvements in legal services and the establishment of 'watchdogs' to oversee the implementation of the 338 accepted recommendations (Tickner 1992).[5] In addition, a reconciliation (treaty) council has been established to devise strategies for national redress of the historical disadvantage of aboriginal peoples flowing from the 'terra nullius' concept and more recently, a High Court decision in what is known as the 'Mabo' case has placed aboriginal land rights issues back on the public and political agenda.

Within this context of politicization of aboriginal issues, we offer a critical overview of the research on aboriginal criminal justice that has been completed to date. This overview is undertaken, first, for the purpose of describing what is known about experiences of indigenous people and crime, and secondly, for the purpose of showing how criminologists have attempted to explain the problem of the over-representation of indigenous people in the criminal justice system.

Research on Aboriginal criminal justice issues

Many attempts have been made to document the extent to which indigenous peoples, as compared to non-indigenous peoples, are processed through the criminal justice system. Determining the precise extent to which aboriginal people are represented in the criminal justice system is hindered by the fact that official statistics generally include only status or registered Indians in

Canada while few data exist on the involvement of non-status Indians, Métis and Inuit (Griffiths and Verdun-Jones 1989; Yerbury and Griffiths 1991). In Australia, aboriginality is not always identified in official data and indeed under-counting in both custodial and non-custodial settings is probable (Biles and McDonald 1992).

Despite this and numerous other data collection problems, over the past 20 years researchers have compiled a wide range of data on the socio-economic and demographic characteristics of indigenous peoples and the nature of their involvement in the criminal justice system. Research has looked at the manner in which indigenous peoples are processed and at the extent to which they are over-represented in custodial settings. Research to date has been mostly descriptive and anecdotal and the generalizations that can be made based on available data should be used with considerable caution. Provided below is a summary of the findings of recent research that has looked at patterns of criminal behaviour for indigenous peoples recorded in official statistics (derived from Amnesty International 1993; Australian Institute of Criminology 1988; Broadhurst 1987; Cunneen and Robb 1987; Eggleston 1976; Hazlehurst and Dunn 1988; Hazlehurst 1987; Griffiths and Verdun-Jones 1989; Manitoba 1991; Walker 1987; Yerbury and Griffiths 1991).

· indigenous peoples tend to commit less serious crimes and are imprisoned generally for offences against good order including vehicle related charges, petty theft, resisting arrest and drunk and disorderly charges;

· in Canada, aboriginal peoples comprise 7% and up to 70% of federal and provincial corrections institutions respectively, and in Australia the proportion is around 17% nationwide;

· aboriginal peoples are arrested at a greater rate than others in the population (up to 29 times) and overall there is less likelihood that non-custodial dispositions will be invoked;

· there is a considerably higher rate of recidivism among aboriginal groups which is estimated at up to 80% in some regions;

· indigenous women are over-represented in police and prison statistics which can be up to 70% of admissions in some states/provinces and this disproportion appears to be increasing;

- the age of incarceration of aboriginal youth appears to be declining and they too are over-represented in the juvenile justice system;

- in comparison with their non-indigenous counterparts, indigenous offenders are first identified by the criminal justice system at an earlier age, and in many jurisdictions, indigenous youth evidence rates of arrest between three and 90 times that of their non-indigenous counterparts;

- alcohol use is present in a high percentage (up to 90% in some jurisdictions) of crimes committed by indigenous peoples;

- a high proportion of aboriginal violent crimes are intra- and inter-personal and are usually directed against family or community members; and

- there has been a trend toward more serious violence, namely rape and domestic assault, within communities and groups in recent years.

There are, of course, wide variations in the patterns of indigenous crime between and within Canada and Australia. The pattern varies according to the urban, rural or remote geographic location, socio-economic variables, cultural factors and local historical and political influences. However, at every step of the criminal justice processing, aboriginal peoples are disadvantaged and from arrest to disposition their relative position deteriorates even further.[6]

Explanations of Aboriginal over-representation

In addition to documenting the extent of over-representation of indigenous peoples in the Canadian and Australian criminal justice systems, various attempts have been made to explain it. There is a cluster of explanations that focus on some form of direct or indirect racism and discrimination within the system that results in such over-representation. When analyzed more closely, the findings centre on racist bias, visibility, cultural factors, legal and extra-legal considerations and over-policing. Such explanations are often provided at the micro-level to explain differences found in specific data, but they fail to provide general explanatory value. In the following review we provide a summary of the findings of research in this area.

Racist bias. One of the most common explanations for over-representation is that there is systematic bias in the criminal justice system discriminating against aboriginal peoples. Racism in operation does appear to have cogency given many of the glaring examples that are found at the individual level (see Cowlishaw 1987). Parker suggests that 'the discriminatory attitudes and actions of many members of the police force are important contributory factors to the existence of disproportionate numbers of Aboriginal prisoners' (Parker in Graham 1989: 67). However, some studies have found no basis for racism in practice (Wundersitz, Bailey-Harris and Gale 1990).

The studies of John Hagan (1974, 1975a, 1975b, 1977) on the criminal justice processing and sentencing of native offenders in Alberta have provided a wealth of material in this area. In 1974 Hagan published a study of the sentences received by Indian and Métis inmates incarcerated in five Alberta correctional institutions. Although Hagan found that native offenders were represented at least four times as often among newly-incarcerated offenders than among the general population, he concluded that this had less to do with racial discrimination than with the fact that native offenders were much more often convicted and sentenced to serve short prisons sentences for minor offences.

Visibility. In an early study which examined the statistics for persons 18 years of age and older who were arrested by the Winnipeg Police Department, Bienvenue and Latif (1974) found that although native Indians comprised only 3% of the total population of Winnipeg, they accounted for 27.5% of all male arrests and 69.5% of all female arrests. In light of the fact that a major category of native over-representation in arrest statistics was for liquor offences, Bienvenue and Latif (1974) concluded that, relative to their non-indigenous counterparts, Indians were arrested for offences of a more minor nature and that a major contributor to this high arrest rate was the visibility of native Indians in the urban environment.

This visibility factor has also been found in Australia. Rees (1982) suggests that the combination of alcohol use, poor execution of crimes and police need to achieve high clear-up rates mean that aboriginal people may be apprehended more easily and be 'loaded-up' with additional charges. This unintended racism could be excused simply as laziness on the part of police but there does seem to be a systematic tendency for such targeting to occur, confounded by the visibility of aboriginal offenders.

Cultural factors. Another area of indirect racism includes an incongruence between aboriginal cultural practices and the predominantly Anglo-Celtic criminal justice system. There are linguistic differences which may result in confusion in arrest and interview situations (Foley 1984). As Rees (1982:

38-39) points out, 'Aborigines are particularly vulnerable to police interrogation techniques; secondly, police treat Aborigines differently and thirdly, Aborigines experience greater difficulty than other members of the community in exercising the right to refuse to answer questions'. However, these cultural differences should not be seen merely as misunderstanding at the level of interpersonal communication. They are embedded in social and cultural inequalities and in many jurisdictions, police training colleges have now instituted courses for their officers in cross-cultural awareness.

Legal factors. Racism can come in the form of separate legislation for aboriginal peoples. McCorquodale (1987) provides a summary of all Acts passed in all Australian jurisdictions that concern indigenous people, or the ones that mention them as a specific group. A cursory glance at his digest shows how far-reaching the stretch of the law has been into the lives of aboriginal people. Some of these laws may appear favourable (like the various *Fisheries Acts* that enable persons of Australian Aboriginal descent to fish in ways precluded to others). Other pieces of legislation are personally intrusive (like the various *Dog Acts* restricting the numbers of pets that could be owned). While much of this legislation can be, but no longer is, invoked, there *are* rarely-used pieces of legislation, such as 'riotous assembly' and 'consuming liquor in a public park', that are often used exclusively against aboriginal people.

Extra-legal factors. From his study of the treatment of native offenders by probation officers and the content of their pre-sentence reports, Hagan (1975b, 1977) concluded that although probation officers' recommendations for sentence were a source of unfavourable treatment for Indian and Métis offenders, particularly in rural areas, there was no clear evidence that rural probation officers recommended more severe sentences for native offenders in their pre-sentence reports because of racial discrimination. Hagan explained the recommendations for more harsh sentences by the fact that the probation officers more often emphasized extra-legal factors in formulating their evaluations of offenders, and in particular, their assessment of the offender's 'demeanour' (or show of remorse and cooperation) and likelihood of success on probation.

A number of more recent studies aimed at addressing the question of native over-representation in the Canadian criminal justice system (Boldt, Hursh, Johnson and Taylor 1983; LaPrairie 1990; Taylor 1982; Wynne and Hartnagel 1975) have also addressed this issue. For example, in their study of pre-sentence reports and the incarceration of natives in the Yukon, Boldt

et al (1983) attempt to determine whether Hagan's (1975b, 1977) findings on
the content and influence of pre-sentence reports written by rural probation
officers in Alberta are consistent with data that exist for the Yukon. While
Boldt et al (1983) found, contrary to Hagan, that 'extra-legal' factors did not
play as important a role in the sentences handed out to convicted offenders
in the Yukon, they do not offer a clear alternative explanation for the
apparent vast over-representation of aboriginal offenders in the Yukon.

In Australia, Gale and her colleagues (1990) highlight the confounding
effect of extra-legal factors as individuals pass through from arrest to
disposition. They argue that while there appears to be no systemic
discrimination, there are value judgements made by police and other justice
personnel on the basis of social class, location of home, and perceived ability
to respond to directions. Aboriginal youth are more likely to be arrested
rather than reported because police believe that they will not attend a panel
or court. This label of arrest is then carried through the system, where a
caution is less likely for Aborigines because they were arrested in the first
instance — and this initial contact is perceived as reflecting a more serious
offence or an intractable offender. The decision-making process then
continues to discriminate in an unintended way. Thus, the police play an
important role throughout the whole system as their initial action 'exerts a
crucial influence on subsequent outcomes' (Wundersitz et al 1990: 14).

Overpolicing. Another significant aspect of racist discrimination comes from
research which examines the role that police play in the criminal justice
system and in local communities. Edmunds (1990: 6) points out that 'police
practices that involve the unnecessary surveillance of all aspects of
Aboriginal daily life, such as constant patrolling of living areas' needs to be
reviewed. Her research raises the spectre of indirect racism through a
combination of police surveillance practices and high police numbers that
conflict with Aboriginal cultural practices and a high, visibile indigenous
population in regional centres (see also Edmunds 1987).

The ratio of police to aboriginal persons has been documented extensively
in some areas of Australia. The Human Rights and Equal Opportunity
Commission report found that communities with high aboriginal populations
also had high police numbers. In 1990 the ratio for Wilcannia was 1:73 and
for Walgett it was 1:96 (both small rural townships with high aboriginal
populations); whereas for the whole state of New South Wales the ratio was
1:459 (Amnesty International 1993). Amnesty International, when
completing its report on Australia, witnessed several first-hand examples of
overpolicing. They noted that this contributed to a 'sense of provocation

within the context of the tensions that often characterize Aboriginal-police relations' (Amnesty International 1993: 23).

Other explanations

The most significant and sustained efforts to develop a more adequate theoretically-grounded knowledge of the causes of indigenous over-representation in the Canadian criminal justice system, are those of Carol LaPrairie (1984a, 1984b, 1987, 1990, 1991, 1992). LaPrairie points out that the recent 'politicization of criminal justice issues within the agendas of land claims, self-government, and constitutional matters' has created a 'prevailing discourse' within which (both non-aboriginal and aboriginal) political interest groups have found it convenient to ignore many of the outstanding questions that still exist about the relationship between sentencing and over-representation. In her attempt to bring more adequate theory and research into the aboriginal justice debate, LaPrairie provides an important and highly critical re-examination of the 'meaning' and causes of aboriginal inmate over-representation, including:

· that 'reliance on the standard of aboriginal population ratios, i.e. inmate versus general populations, has obscured other ways of understanding over-representation. For example, if one changes the standard to aboriginal and non-aboriginal age distributions in the general population, the "over-representation" picture might look quite different'; and

· that 'if one follows the theoretical approach of the critical criminologists and uses class (based on socio-economic level) as the standard and predictor of who goes to jail, aboriginal people may well be statistically under-represented' (LaPrairie 1990: 429-30).

LaPrairie also attempts to clarify the current state of theorizing about the causes of over-representation. In doing so, she points out that there are three basic 'competing but not mutually exclusive explanations for the disproportionate representation of aboriginal people in correctional institutions', namely: differential treatment by the criminal justice system; differential commission of crime; and differential offence patterns. Most importantly, LaPrairie makes a case for the argument that focusing attention exclusively on the alleged discriminatory processing of aboriginal people in the criminal justice system - while perhaps serving a number of political agendas - does little to advance our overall level of theoretically-based knowledge of the causes of over-representation. In essence, she argues 'the need for the criminal justice system to redirect the issue (of aboriginal over-representation) to where it belongs - in the social, political and economic spheres'. LaPrairie (1990: 430-31) suggests that we must also look to these spheres, or fundamental aspects of 'social structure and economic disparity', in order for us to better understand the causes of crime among indigenous people and aboriginal criminal offence patterns.

LaPrairie's views are for the most part quite consistent with the conclusions that have been arrived at by other critical criminologists in Canada and Australia (Havemann, Crouse, Foster and Matonovich 1984; Havemann 1989; Brogden 1990; Wilson 1982; Cowlishaw 1987; Edmunds 1990). One of the common features underlying this recent critical work is the extent to which the authors' analyses of the problems of crime and justice experienced by aboriginal people are based on more in-depth critical and historical research. As we will see more clearly in the discussion taken up later in this essay, the work of these investigators is also linked together by the common thread that all of it is undertaken starting, either implicitly or explicitly, from a Marxian World-System perspective (Neuman and Berger 1988). Although more conventional-liberal and state-employed criminologists routinely acknowledge and incorporate the arguments advanced by more critical historically-informed criminologists (cf Hartnagel 1987; Griffiths and Verdun-Jones 1989; Griffiths, Yerbury and Weaver 1989; Yerbury and Griffiths 1991), they rarely follow through very far on these arguments, either in terms of developing more adequate theoretically-informed research, or more appropriate (theoretically defensible) criminal justice policy.

All of this work points to the need for more systematic comparative research aimed at developing a better cross-national understanding of the problems that indigenous peoples face in the criminal justice systems imposed on them as a result of the process of European colonization. With few exceptions, research carried out on aboriginal crime and justice in Canada and Australia has lacked a comparative dimension. More generally, owing at least in part to the underdeveloped state of the sub-field of comparative criminology in universities, criminologists have made sparse use of the cross-cultural theories of crime that are now being developed and tested by comparative criminologists. It is this comparative dimension that may provide more adequate avenues in which to develop an integrated theory.

Developing a cross-cultural theory of Aboriginal criminality

In the remainder of this essay, we offer a discussion of the considerations that need to be taken in order to develop and test a cross-national theory of aboriginal criminality. We begin with a review of the current state of cross-cultural theories of crime and some of the recent research undertaken by comparative criminologists aimed at testing these theories. We then turn to developing a theoretical framework for approaching the cross-national study of aboriginal criminality that attempts to integrate and build on the recent work of comparative criminologists and aboriginal crime researchers in North America and Australia (LaPrairie 1992; Marenin 1992).[7]

Cross-cultural theories of crime

Within the field of comparative criminology there is ongoing debate and disagreement surrounding the need for, and possibility of, developing widely generalizable cross-cultural theories of crime. On the one hand, authors such as Beirne (1983a, 1983b), Groves and Newman (1989) and Beirne and Messerschmidt (1991), have pointed out the many conceptual, definitional and measurement problems associated with attempting to study crime cross-culturally. On the other hand, in recent years an increasing number of comparative criminologists have undertaken research which has been aimed at developing more generalizable cross-cultural theories of crime based on the systematic collection and analysis of cross-national crime data (Bennett 1991a, 1991b; Bennett and Basiotis 1991; Bennett and Lynch 1990; Heiland, Shelley and Katoh 1992; Rosenfeld and Messner 1991). The following review of different theoretical approaches to the empirical literature provides several suggestions about the steps that must be followed in any effort undertaken to develop a cross-cultural theory of aboriginal criminality.

Neuman and Berger (1988) assess the strengths and weaknesses of three competing cross-cultural theories of crime: the dominant Durkheimian-Modernization perspective; the Marxian World-System perspective; and the emerging Ecological-Opportunity perspective. The key causal concepts and theoretical propositions associated with each of these perspectives are summarized by Neuman and Berger (1988: 282-89) as follows:

Durkheimian-Modernization (DM) Perspective

· In the DM perspective crime is caused by a disruption or breakdown of a prior, stable normative order. The transition to 'modern' society creates a temporary disequilibrium when modern values and norms come into contact with and disrupt older cultural patterns, weakening informal social controls and traditional normative restraints on criminal impulses.

· Urbanization and rural-urban migration have a significant impact on normative patterns of criminal behaviour. In urban areas, 'modern' values are strongest and traditional norms, socializing agents and social control mechanisms are less effective. Consequently, anomie, social disorganization, cultural heterogeneity, criminal sub-cultures and juvenile delinquency are more likely to develop.

Marxian World-System (MWS) Perspective

· The MWS perspective explains the past three centuries of socio-economic change in terms of historical events that spread the capitalist mode of production and social relations unevenly across the globe. The world system is the unit of analysis, and the interrelations or inequalities among social formations are used to analyse structures and processes within and between nations. In addition, social change is shaped by a semi-autonomous international system of states and internal political factors.

· Economic inequality and social classes are key elements of the MWS explanation of crime. More specifically, this explanation argues that the expansion of the capitalist mode of production creates new inequalities and gives rise to new social classes. Capitalist social relations replace pre-capitalist patterns of economic self-sufficiency and communal methods of dispute resolution. Legal mechanisms redefine property rights to facilitate capitalist expansion and help create, maintain and control a new rural and urban proletariat.

· According to the MWS perspective, urban crime is generated by the uneven expansion and contraction of the capitalist production process within and between nations, not by anomie, social disorganization or urbanism per se.

The Ecological-Opportunity (EO) Perspective

· The EO perspective on cross-national crime synthesises an ecological approach to social change and an opportunity theory of criminal behaviour. The EO approach connects macro-level changes in economic and social structure to a micro-level explanation of crime through the concept of opportunities. Crime increases when evolutionary processes create a societal surplus which expands the quantity of material goods available to be stolen.

· The EO perspective explains collective political behaviour by the same processes that generate crime. Both take place in a structural context of competing interests and the rational calculation of costs and benefits.

In the five years that have passed since Neuman and Berger (1988) provided their review of the current state of theoretical perspectives in comparative criminology, theorists have continued to develop and test variants of these three approaches, while at the same time introducing other relevant theoretical perspectives. For example, most recently, Heiland and Shelley (1992) have offered a restatement and defence of the Durkheimian-Modernization perspective, while at the same arguing the need for incorporating a theoretical perspective that takes into account the potential connection linking civilization (or the 'civilizing process'), modernization and crime. In their defence of the DM perspective, Heiland and Shelley remark that:

> The modernization concept has great explanatory powers because it permits a multi-dimensional model. To analyze the process of modernization, it is possible to combine empirically verifiable data along with historical and ethnographic description (Heiland and Shelley 1992: 6).

Furthermore, Heiland and Shelley argue that:

> Examining crime and crime control from the modernization perspective does not focus on societal transformation as a consistent (one-way evolutionary) process. Rather, it focuses on the confusion, the relapses, and the regional differences in modernization. It suggests that modernization proceeds at different rates and in some areas or subcultures, it may be only a very partial process. Many societies do not completely modernize but retain elements of traditional and pre-modern societies. In former colonies, the traditions of the pre-colonial past merge with those of the colonial power. The norms that emerge may reflect the

adaptation of those of the colonial power rather than the modernization of the legal system (ibid).

The social process attached to colonialism noted by Heiland and Shelley (1992) above is expanded upon in considerably more detail by Wright (1992: 150) in his discussion of 'syncretism', or 'the growing together of new beliefs and old ... [as] a way of encoding the values of a conquered culture within a dominant culture'. In his study, *Stolen Continents: The 'New World' Through Indian Eyes*, Wright (1992) examines the impact of European contact and conquest on the indigenous peoples of North and South America, and the centuries of accommodation and resistance that have followed.

This connection is drawn out at this point in our discussion to show that adopting a Durkheimian-Modernization perspective does not lead inevitably to accepting a consensus-based functionalist view of the causes of aboriginal crime. As Heiland and Shelley indirectly point out, the modernization perspective allows for an examination of how processes associated with modernization can affect the behaviour of individuals (and perhaps the amount and type of crime committed) within different subcultural groups. Heiland and Shelley also argue that the concepts of modernization and civilization can be combined in a complementary manner to develop a more adequate theoretical perspective for explaining changing patterns of crime and social control. According to the synthesis they propose:

The paradigm of civilization claims that two substantial processes have occurred. First, civilizing has altered interpersonal relations and individual standards of conduct. It has altered the attitude towards the use of violence against others (which helps to explain the DM finding of the shift from violent crime to property crime). The theory of civilization as well as the concept of modernization, both expect a structural change in the forms and patterns of crime, as well as an increase in the level of crime (Heiland and Shelley 1992: 7).

In recent years, the other theoretical approaches outlined by Neuman and Berger (1988) have been similarly defended and expanded upon by comparative criminologists concerned with developing more adequate cross-cultural theories of criminal behaviour and social control. In his call for a 'critical comparative criminology', Gordon West (1990: 99) argues the need for a guiding theoretical framework 'based on a world system and/or dependency model', coupled with an active concern for the protection of human rights. West criticizes the dominant modernization perspective associated with 'traditional comparative criminology' for its naive assumptions about linear-evolutionary social progress. To take its place, he elaborates a 'global critical justice problematic' that builds on the ideas of MWS or dependency theorists, critical feminists and human rights advocates. West (1990) concludes by calling on comparative criminologists to become involved in research and political activities that contribute to greater (global) social and economic equality. Specifically, he notes that:

In part through cultural imperialism and lack of local resources, in many third world countries such as Nicaragua, there is not, as yet, an indigenous criminology (a specific theory, or even much written from a criminological perspective), but there certainly are crime and justice experiences which need explication and explanation, and raise comparative questions. These criminological practices demand a critical comparative criminology capable of revealing the theory implicit in such practices and their necessary preconditions, one which is historically and cross-culturally grounded (West 1990: 108).

It is possible to derive specific theoretical propositions from the MWS perspective for testing with quantitative empirical data. For instance, Neuman and Berger (1988: 287) note that while the DM perspective 'predicts an homogenization of international crime rates for nations at similar levels of development, and explains anomalies (e.g. Japan, Switzerland) *post hoc* in cultural, historical, and geographic terms', the MWS perspective 'argues that the effect of industrialization on crime depends on how modes of production articulate with one another'. Although a great deal of potentially interesting work could be undertaken aimed at the quantitative empirical testing of propositions derived from the MWS perspective, for the most part critical comparative criminologists have moved in the direction (advocated by West 1990), of undertaking comparative-historical research aimed at documenting the manner in which the global expansion of capitalism affects changing definitions of crime and dominant mechanisms of social control. As noted earlier, a number of researchers in Canada (cf. Brogden 1990; Havemann 1988; Manitoba 1991) have also adopted elements of this perspective.

Within the last five years there has been a substantial amount of research aimed at testing propositions derived from the EO perspective and integrating it with other theoretical perspectives in an attempt to explain cross-national crime patterns for different types of crime. In a recent article, Bennett

(1991a) looks at cross-national time-series data that allow him to evaluate competing DM and EO models 'by analyzing the effects of level of development and rate of (economic) growth on crime rates'. Using theft and homicide rates for 38 developed and developing countries, Bennett analyzes the extent to which they are correlated with level of development, rate of economic growth, form of economic growth, urbanization, proportion of juveniles and degree of economic inequality. Bennett's data analysis points to a number of 'unexpected curvilinear relationships' linking these dependent and independent variables; which tends to contradict (or refute) propositions derived from the DM perspective and 'offer qualified support' for a newly-specified 'opportunity model'.

Several similar attempts at testing hypotheses derived from specific (and often integrated) modernization, opportunity and routine activities models, have been undertaken by quantitatively-oriented comparative criminologists in recent years (Bennett 1991b; Bennett and Basiotis 1991; Rosenfeld and Messner 1991). Contrary to the critique advanced by radical criminologists (West 1990) that this type of quantitative research tends to be overly-simplistic and naive, a strong argument could be made that the collection and analysis of cross-national crime data is indispensable if we are ever going to be able to more adequately explain the existence of different types and rates of crime in different historical and social settings. As Neuman and Berger conclude:

> Comparative criminology is currently plagued by a hiatus between theory and research. The different levels of theoretical explanation need to be explored with data that simultaneously employ variables at the structural/contextual and individual levels ... Such data is not likely to become available for many countries. Regardless, quantitative studies must be complemented by in-depth historical research in order to examine the specific processes occurring within nations. Quantitative cross-national studies with aggregate data remain appropriate to evaluate the alternative perspectives, but it is important to be explicit about the 'metatheoretical' assumptions underlying such research (Neuman and Berger 1988: 301).

A cross-cultural theory of Aboriginal criminality

Although elements of several different cross-cultural theories of crime are implicit in Canadian and Australian research on aboriginal crime, no attempt has yet been made by researchers to develop a more explicit integrative comparative theoretical framework for helping to explain the criminalization of indigenous peoples. However, this does not mean that criminologists have not recognized the need for moving in this direction. In his review of 'Contemporary Crime and the American Indian', May (1982) noted the need for 'comparative studies' that would better help to explain the underlying causes of the high rate of aboriginal crime in different jurisdictions. Despite the useful suggestions for future research offered by May (1982), little appears to have been done in the last decade to advance cross-cultural research and theorizing directed at explaining similar cross-national patterns of recorded criminal behaviour by indigenous peoples.

Two notable exceptions to this are the recent discussions offered by LaPrairie (1992) and Marenin (1992) on what they feel should be the direction taken by theorizing and research on aboriginal criminal justice issues. LaPrairie (1992) introduces a discussion of John Braithwaite's (1989) reintegrative theory of shaming as a way of connecting the different types of research and research findings that now exist on aboriginal crime. LaPrairie notes that:

> Braithwaite addresses the most central issues in the etiology of crime by focusing on the effectiveness of shaming. He suggests that who commits crime depends largely on the degree to which individuals are 'connected' to the institutions of family, school, work, and community because their interdependence with these institutions dictates the power of shaming ... Inherent in societies with high levels of crime is the belief that the control over some members, through informal structures and traditional institutions has been weakened dramatically. Braithwaite contends that reintegrative shaming will work best in societies where interdependency, communitarianism, and cultural homogeneity exist (LaPrairie 1992: 285).

LaPrairie indirectly connects Braithwaite's theory with cross-cultural theories of crime in her remark that his theory 'is useful when examining the high rates of aboriginal crime both on and off-reserve and the corresponding weakening of traditional aboriginal institutions through processes of colonization and modernization, and more recently, through mass communication'. LaPrairie argues that many of the research findings that have been reported show 'disproportionate levels of crime and violence, both on and off-reserve', and suggest that these are the result of 'a serious rupture of traditional control mechanisms in contemporary aboriginal communities'. LaPrairie implies in her discussion that both the processes of colonization

(MWS theory) and modernization (DM theory) have contributed to creating the social and economic conditions faced by indigenous peoples, and that these conditions have in turn led to serious ruptures in (and sometimes even the total disintegration of) more traditional ('communitarian') aboriginal methods of dispute settlement and social control.

In his recently completed study aimed at 'Explaining Patterns of Crime in the Native Villages of Alaska', Otwin Marenin (1992: 339) develops a 'situation-specific perspective' that focuses on 'the interactive dynamics of dominant and dominated cultures' as one element needed in order to explain specific patterns of aboriginal crime. Specifically, in outlining his view on the type of theoretical perspective that is needed to better explain high rates of aboriginal crime, Marenin notes that:

> Explanations deduced from general approaches are insufficiently specific to account for divergent patterns of criminality among and within native American communities. Explanations of criminality which use dependency or cultural dislocation or alcohol use as crucial explanatory concepts need to be 'linked down' theoretically to specific situations in native American communities and to observed patterns of criminal behaviour. Explanations need to account for the process by which native groups were and continue to be incorporated into the larger environment and need to show how criminogenic conditions and individual criminality arise from the dynamics of interaction between dominant and dominated groups (Marenin 1992: 340).

Marenin's approach is consistent with, and displays elements of, several different more general cross-cultural theories of crime. His reference to the need to study the dynamics of interaction between dominant and dominated groups is consistent with MWS theory, while his emphasis on the need to examine the specific situations that exist in different aboriginal communities is in keeping with the method followed by adherents of the EO perspective, who are concerned with learning about the different opportunity structures for crime that exist in different communities and different countries, and with how the 'routine activities' engaged in by people either increase or decrease their chances of becoming involved in crime, either as an offender or a victim.

When looked at as related contributions, the recent work of comparative criminologists and aboriginal crime researchers in North America and Australia can be seen to provide the basic ingredients required in order to develop a more adequate theoretical framework for approaching the cross-cultural study of aboriginal criminality. In our opinion, at the most basic level, what these diverse bodies of work indicate is that while we may never be able to build a 'general theory of aboriginal crime', we may well be able to carry out different types of research that contribute to an explanation of the (individual, community, regional, national and even global) causes of the over-representation of indigenous peoples in the criminal justice systems of many different countries around the world.

One of the indispensable first steps in this effort resides in the need to undertake more comparative historical work, taking into account the insights offered by MWS theory (McMichael 1990). In particular, we need to learn more about how, historically and in different countries, European colonizers have applied their laws to indigenous peoples, and how in turn indigenous peoples have struggled to resist having these laws imposed (Berger 1991; Bienvenue 1983; Bourgeault et al 1992; Dyck et al 1985; Fisher 1980; Hazlehurst 1993; Smandych and Linden, in press; Wright 1992). At the same time, however, more quantitative and qualitative/ethnographic research is needed in order to learn more about the 'specific situations' faced by indigenous peoples today in the different countries in which they appear to be more often criminalized than non-indigenous peoples who are now members of the currently more dominant cultural group.

This essay has canvassed the extant literature on aboriginal over-representation and the theories or middle-range explanations that have been advanced to explain the different arrest and imprisonment rates. What we shall be attempting in the future as the second stage of our research is to examine aboriginal offending patterns, some of which lie outside the official picture of over-representation. In this second stage we will draw on ethnographic, historical and anthropological, as well as criminological, data to examine social, local, political, cultural and historical differences in criminal behaviour among aboriginal groups, examine the meaning of such criminality and analyse the explanations posited for the differences in criminal activity.[8]

References

Alberta Government (1991) *Justice on Trial, Report of the Task Force on the Criminal Justice System and Its Impact on Indian and Métis People, Vol. 1: Main Report,* Edmonton: Attorney General of Alberta.

Amnesty International (1993) *Australia: A Criminal Justice System Weighted Against Aboriginal People*, Sydney: Amnesty International.

Atkinson, J. (ed.) (1990) *Beyond Violence: Finding the Dream*, Aboriginal and

Islander Sub-Programme, National Domestic Violence Education Programme, Canberra: Office of the Status of Women.

Australian Institute of Criminology (1988) *Crime Digest*, Canberra: Australian Institute of Criminology.

Beirne, P. (1983a) 'Cultural Relativism and Comparative Criminology', *Contemporary Crises* 7: 371-91.

Beirne, P. (1983b) 'Generalization and its Discontents: The Comparative Study of Crime', in I. Barak-Glantz and E. Johnson (eds) *Comparative Criminology*, Beverly Hills: Sage, 19-38.

Beirne, P. and Messerschmidt, J. (1991) *Criminology*, New York: Harcourt Brace Jovanovich.

Bell, D. and Napurrula Nelson, T. (1989) 'Speaking About Rape is Everyone's Business, *Women's Studies International Forum* 12: 4, 403-15.

Bennett, R. (1991a) 'Development and Crime: A Cross-National, Time-Series Analysis of Competing Models', *The Sociological Quarterly* 32: 343-63.

Bennett, R. (1991b) 'Routine Activities: A Cross-National Assessment of a Criminological Perspective', *Social Forces* 70: 147-63.

Bennett, R. and Basiotis, P.P. (1991) 'Structural Correlates of Juvenile Property Crime: A Cross-National, Time-Series Analysis', *Journal of Research in Crime and Delinquency* 28: 262-87.

Bennett, R. and Lynch, J.P. (1990) 'Does a Difference Make a Difference? Comparing Cross-National Crime Indicators', *Criminology* 28: 153-82.

Berger, T. (1991) *A Long and Terrible Shadow: White Values, Native Rights in the Americas, 1492-1992*, Vancouver: Douglas and McIntyre.

Bienvenue, R. (1983) 'Comparative Colonial Systems: The Case of Canadian Indians and Australian Aborigines', *Australian-Canadian Studies: An Interdisciplinary Social Science Review* 1: 30-43.

Bienvenue, R. and Latif, A.H. (1974) 'Arrests, Disposition and Recidivism: A Comparison of Indians and Whites', *Canadian Journal of Criminology* 16: 105-16.

Biles, D. and McDonald, D. (eds) (1992) *Deaths in Custody Australia 1980-1989*, Canberra: Australian Institute of Criminology.

Biles, D., McDonald, D. and Fleming, J. (1990) 'Aboriginal and Non-Aboriginal Deaths in Custody', *Australian and New Zealand Journal of Criminology* 23: 1, 15-23.

Boldt, E., Hursh, L., Johnson, S. and Taylor, W. (1983) 'Presentence Reports and the Incarceration of Natives', *Canadian Journal of Criminology* 25: 269-76.

Boldt, M. (1993) *Surviving as Indians: The Challenge of Self-Government*, Toronto: University of Toronto Press.

Bourgeault, R., Broad, D., Brown, L. and Foster, L. (eds) (1992) *1492-1992: Five Centuries of Imperialism and Resistance*, Halifax: Fernwood Publishing.

Braithwaite, J. (1979) *Inequality, Crime and Public Policy*, London: Routledge and Kegan Paul.

Braithwaite, J. (1989) *Crime, Shame and Reintegration*, Cambridge: Cambridge University Press.

Braithwaite, J. (1992) 'Los Angeles and the Pathologies of Criminal Justice', *Criminology Australia* April/May: 2-5.

Broadhurst, R.G. (1987) 'Imprisonment of the Aborigines in Western Australia, 1957-1985', in K.M. Hazlehurst (ed.) *Ivory Scales: Black Australia and the Law*, Sydney: University of New South Wales Press, 153-89.

Broadhurst, R.G. and Maller, R.A. (1990) 'White Man's Magic Makes Black Deaths in Custody Disappear', *Australian Journal of Social Issues* 25: 279-89.

Brogden, M. (1990) 'Law and Criminal Labels: The Case of the French Métis in Western Canada', *Journal of Human Justice* 1: 13-32.

Cowlishaw, G. (1987) 'Policing the Races', unpublished paper, Sydney: Mitchell College of Advanced Education.

Cunneen, C. and Robb, T. (1987) *Criminal Justice in North-West New South Wales*, Sydney: NSW Bureau of Crime Statistics and Research.

Daniels, D. (1986) 'The Coming Crises in the Aboriginal Rights Movement: From Colonialism to Neo-Colonialism to Renaissance', *Native Studies Review* 2: 97-116.

Dyck, N. (ed.) (1985) *Indigenous Peoples and the Nation-State: Fourth World Politics in Canada, Australia and Norway*, St. John's: Memorial University, Institute of Social and Economic Research.

Edmunds, M. (1987) *'They Get Heaps': A Study of Attitudes in Roebourne Western Australia*, Canberra: Aboriginal Studies Press.

Edmunds, M. (1990) 'Doing Business: Socialisation, Social Relations and Social Control in Aboriginal Society', discussion paper, Canberra: Royal Commission into Aboriginal Deaths in Custody.

Eggleston, E. (1976) *Fear, Favour or Affection: Aborigines and the Criminal Law in Victoria, South Australia and Western Australia*, Canberra: Australian National University Press.

Fisher, R. (1980) 'The Impact of European Settlement on the Indigenous Peoples of Australia, New Zealand, and British Columbia: Some Comparative Dimensions', *Canadian Ethnic Studies* 12: 1-14.

Foley, M.(1984) 'Aborigines and the Police', in P. Hanks and B. Keon-Cohen (eds) *Aborigines and the Law*, Sydney: George Allen and Unwin, 160-90.

Gale, F., Bailey-Harris, R. and Wundersitz, J. (1990) *Aboriginal Youth and the Criminal Justice System*, Melbourne: Cambridge University Press.

Grabosky, P., Scandia, A., Hazlehurst, K. and Wilson, P. (1988) 'Aboriginal Deaths in Custody', *Trends and Issues in Crime and Criminal Justice*, No. 12. Canberra: Australian Institute of Criminology.

Graham, D. (1989) *Dying Inside*, Sydney: Allen and Unwin.

Griffiths, C. and Verdun-Jones, S.N. (1989) 'Native Indians and the Criminal Justice System', in C. Griffiths and S. N. Verdun-Jones (eds) *Canadian Criminal Justice*, Toronto: Butterworths, 545-88.

Griffiths, C., Yerbury, C. and Weaver, L. (1989) 'Victimization of Canada's Natives: The Consequences of Socio-Cultural Deprivation', in E. Fattah (ed.) *The Plight of Victims in Modern Society*, New York: St. Martin's Press, 118-38.

Groves, W.B. and Newman, G. (1989) 'Against General Theory in Comparative Criminology', *International Journal of Comparative and Applied Criminal Justice* 13: 23-29.

Hagan, J. (1974) 'Criminal Justice and Native People: A Study of Incarceration in a Canadian Province', *Canadian Review of Sociology and Anthropology Special Issue* 220-36.

Hagan, J. (1975a) 'Parameters of Criminal Prosecution: An Application of Path Analysis to a Problem of Criminal Justice', *Journal of Criminal Law and Criminology* 65: 536-44.

Hagan, J. (1975b) 'The Social and Legal Construction of Criminal Justice: A Study of the Pre-Sentencing Process', *Social Problems* 22: 620-37.

Hagan, J. (1977) 'Criminal Justice in Rural and Northern Communities: A Study of the Bureaucratization of Justice', *Social Forces* 55: 597-612.

Hanks, P. and Keon-Cohen, B. (eds) (1984) *Aborigines and the Law: Essays in Memory of Elizabeth Eggleston*, Sydney: George Allen and Unwin.

Hartnagel, R. (1987) 'Correlates of Human Behavior', in R. Lindon (ed.) *Criminology: A Canadian Perspective*, Toronto: Butterworths.

Havemann, P. (1989) 'Law, State, and Canada's Indigenous People: Pacification by Coercion and Consent', in T. Caputo et al (eds) *Law and Society: A Critical Perspective*, Toronto: Harcourt Brace Jovanovich, 54-72.

Havemann, P. (1988) 'The Indigenization of Social Control in Canada', in B. Morse and G. Woodman (eds) *Indigenous Law and the State*, Dordrecht, Netherlands: Foris Publications, 71-100.

Havemann, P., Crouse, K., Foster, L. and Matonovich, R. (1984) *Law and Order for Canada's Indigenous People: A Review of Recent Research Literature Relating to the Operation of the Criminal Justice System and Canada's Indigenous People*, Ottawa: Solicitor General of Canada.

Hazlehurst, K.M. (1993) *Political Expression and Ethnicity: Statecraft and Mobilization in the Maori World*, Westport, CT: Praeger.

Hazlehurst, K.M. (ed.) (1987) *Ivory Scales: Black Australia and the Law*, Kensington: New South Wales University Press.

Hazlehurst, K. and Dunn, A.T. (1988) 'Aboriginal Criminal Justice', *Trends and Issues in Crime and Criminal Justice*, No. 13. Canberra: Australian Institute of Criminology.

Heiland, H.-G. and Shelley, L.I. (1992) 'Civilization, Modernization and the Development of Crime and Control', in H. Heiland, L. Shelley and H. Katoh (eds) *Crime and Control in Comparative Perspectives*, Berlin: Walter de Gruyter, 1-19.

Heiland, H.-G., Shelley, L.I. and Katoh, H. (1992) *Crime and Control in Comparative Perspectives*, Berlin: Walter de Gruyter.

Independent Commission on International Humanitarian Issues (1987) *Indigenous Peoples: A Global Quest for Justice*, London: Zed Books.

Langton, M. (1983) *After the Tent Embassy*, Woollahra, New South Wales: Valadon.

LaPrairie, C. (1984a) 'Selected Criminal Justice and Socio-Demographic Data on Native Women', *Canadian Journal of Criminology* 26: 161-69.

LaPrairie, C. (1984b) 'Native Juveniles in Court: Some Preliminary Observations', in T. Fleming and L. Visano (eds) *Deviant Designations: Crime, Law and Deviance in Canada*, Toronto: Butterworths, 337-50.

LaPrairie, C. (1987) 'Native Women and Crime: A Theoretical Model', *Canadian Journal of Native Studies* 7: 121-37.

LaPrairie, C. (1990) 'The Role of Sentencing in the Over-representation of Aboriginal People in Correctional Institutions', *Canadian Journal of Criminology* 32: 429-40.

LaPrairie, C. (1991) *Justice for the Cree: Communities, Crime and Order*, The Grand Council of the Crees, Quebec: Cree Regional Authority.

LaPrairie, C. (1992) 'Aboriginal Crime and Justice: Explaining the Present, Exploring the Future', *Canadian Journal of Criminology* 34: 281-98.

LaPrairie, C. and Griffiths, C.T. (1982) 'Native Indian Delinquency and the Juvenile Court: A Review of Recent Findings', *Canadian Legal Aid Bulletin* 5: 39-46.

Law Reform Commission of Australia (1986) *The Recognition of Aboriginal Customary Laws*, Report No. 31, Law Reform Commission of Australia, Canberra: Australian Government Printing Services.

Law Reform Commission of Canada (1991) *Report on Aboriginal Peoples and Criminal Justice: Equality, Respect and the Search for Justice*, Ottawa: Law Reform Commission of Canada.

Lincoln, R. and Wilson, P. (1993) 'Aboriginal Offending: Patterns and Causes', in D. Chappell and P.R. Wilson (eds) *The Australian Criminal Justice System*, 4th edition, Sydney: Butterworths, 61-86.

Manitoba Government (1991) *Report of the Aboriginal Justice Inquiry of Manitoba, Volume 1: The Justice System and Aboriginal People, Volume 2: The Deaths of Helen Betty Osborne and John Joseph Harper*, Government of Manitoba: Queen's Printer.

Marenin, O. (1992) 'Explaining Patterns of Crime in the Native Villages of Alaska', *Canadian Journal of Criminology* 34: 339-68.

May, P.A. (1982) 'Contemporary Crime and the American Indian: A Survey and Analysis of the Literature', *Plains Anthropologist* 27: 225-38.

McCorquodale, J. (1987) *Aborigines and the Law: A Digest*, Canberra: Aboriginal Studies Press.

McMichael, P. (1990) 'Incorporating Comparison within a World-Historical Perspective: An Alternative Comparative Method', *American Sociological Review* 55: 385-97.

McNamara, L. (1992a) 'Autonomy-Based Solutions and Criminal Justice Reform: A Comparison of the Recommendations of the Australian Royal Commission into Aboriginal Deaths in Custody and the Aboriginal Justice Inquiry of Manitoba', *Aboriginal Law Bulletin* 2: 54, February, 4-7.

McNamara, L. (1992b) 'The Aboriginal Justice Inquiry of Manitoba: A Fresh Approach to the "Problem" of Overrepresentation in the Criminal Justice System', *Manitoba Law Journal* 21: 49-79.

McNamara, L. (1992c) 'Aboriginal Peoples, the Administration of Justice and the Autonomy Agenda: An Assessment of the Status of Criminal Justice Reform in Canada with Reference to the Prairie Region', LLM thesis, University of Manitoba.

National Aboriginal and Islander Legal Services Secretariat (1989) 'An Interesting and Informative Chat Is Not What I Had in Mind', *Aboriginal Law Bulletin* 36: 12-14.

Neuman, W.L. and Berger, R.J. (1988) 'Competing Perspectives on Cross-National Crime: An Evaluation of Theory and Evidence', *Sociological Quarterly* 29: 281-313.

Nova Scotia Government (1988) *Royal Commission of Inquiry into the Donald Marshall Jr. Prosecution,* Sydney and Halifax: Queen's Printer.

Parker, D. (1987) 'The Administration of Justice and its Penal Consequences, in K.M. Hazlehurst (ed.) *Ivory Scales: Black Australia and the Law,* Sydney: University of New South Wales Press, 136-52.

Read, P. (1988) *A Hundred Years War,* Canberra: Australian National University Press.

Rees, N. (1982) 'Police Interrogation of Aborigines, in J. Basten, M. Richardson, C. Ronalds and G. Zdenkowski (eds) *The Criminal Injustice System,* Sydney: Australian Legal Workers Group and Legal Service Bulletin, 36-61.

Royal Commission into Aboriginal Deaths in Custody (1991) *Royal Commission into Aboriginal Deaths in Custody: National Report,* Canberra: Australian Government Publishing Service.

Sackett, L. (1990) 'Aboriginal Violence: Responding to the Tatz View', *Australian Journal of Social Issues* 26: 68-70.

Sackett, L. (1993) 'The Panopticon Re-Visited: The Royal Commission into Aboriginal Deaths in Custody', *Australian Journal of Social Issues* 28: 3, 229-44.

Schneider, H.J. (1992) 'Life in a Societal No-Man's Land: Aboriginal Crime in Central Australia', *International Journal of Offender Therapy and Comparative Criminology* 36: 5-19.

Smandych, R. and Linden, R. (1994) 'Co-existing Forms of Aboriginal and Private Justice: An Historical Study of the Canadian West', *Justice and Reform* 1, forthcoming.

Tatz, C. (1990) 'Aboriginal Violence: A Return to Pessimism', *Australian Journal of Social Issues* 25: 245-60.

Taylor, K.W. (1982) 'Multiple Association Analysis of Race and Plea Negotiation:

The Wynne and Hartnagel Data', *Canadian Journal of Sociology* 7: 391-401.

Tickner, R. (1992) 'Government Response to the Final Report of the Royal Commission into Aboriginal Deaths in Custody', *Aboriginal and Islander Health Worker Journal* 16-19.

Walker, J. (1987) 'Prison Cells with Revolving Doors: A Judicial or Societal Problem?' in K.M. Hazlehurst (ed.) *Ivory Scales: Black Australia and the Law*, Sydney: University of New South Wales Press, 106-17.

Waller, L. (1984) 'Elizabeth Eggleston, Aborigines, and the Law', in P. Hanks and B. Keon-Cohen (eds) *Aborigines and the Law: Essays in Memory of Elizabeth Eggleston*, Sydney: George Allen and Unwin, 304-9.

West, G. (1989) 'Towards a Global Criminal Justice Problematic', *Journal of Human Justice* 1: 99-112.

Wilson, P.R. (1982) *Black Death White Hands,* Sydney: George Allen and Unwin.

Wilson, P. and Lincoln, R. (1991) 'Black Death and White Commissions: The Politics of investigating Aboriginal deaths in and outside custody', paper presented at the annual meetings of the American Society of Criminology, San Francisco, November.

Wotherspoon, T. and Satzewich, V. (1993) *First Nations: Race, Class, and Gender Relations*, Scarborough, Ontario: Nelson Canada.

Wright, R. (1992) *Stolen Continents: The 'New World' Through Indian Eyes*, Toronto: Penguin.

Wundersitz, J., Bailey-Harris, R. and Gale, F. (1990) 'Aboriginal Youth and Juvenile Justice in South Australia', *Aboriginal Law Bulletin* 2: 44, 12-14.

Wynne, D. and Hartnagel, T.F. (1975) 'Race and Plea Negotiation: An Analysis of Some Canadian Data', *Canadian Journal of Sociology* 1: 147-55.

Yerbury, C. and Griffiths, C. (1991) 'Minorities, Crime, and the Law', in M. Jackson and C. Griffiths (eds) *Canadian Criminology: Perspectives on Crime and Criminality*, Toronto: Harcourt Brace Jovanovich, 315-46.

York, G. (1990) *The Dispossessed: Native Life and Death in Canada*, Toronto: Little, Brown.

Notes

1. Russell Smandych is Associate Professor in the Department of Sociology, University of Manitoba, Winnipeg, Canada; Robyn Lincoln is doctoral candidate in the School of Social Science, Queensland University of Technology, Brisbane, Australia; and Paul Wilson is Dean of Humanities and Social Science, Bond University, Gold Coast, Australia.

2. In line with the definition found in the report of the Independent Commission on International Humanitarian Issues, *Indigenous Peoples: A Global Quest for Justice* (1987: 6), we define 'indigenous' or 'aboriginal' peoples as people who are 'the descendants of the original inhabitants of a territory taken over

through conquest or settlement by aliens'. In the Canadian context 'aboriginal people' include status and non-status Indians, Métis and Inuit. In Australia, the term 'aboriginal people' includes Aboriginal people as well as Islanders from the Torres Strait, Tiwi and Melville Islands.

3.   Only official or recorded data are used in this comparative study. More recent evidence emerging from both Canada and Australia suggest that there is an extensive hidden level of black-on-black violence (rape, domestic assault, self-mutilation) occuring in aboriginal communities (Wilson 1982; Bell and Napurrurla Nelson 1989; Atkinson 1990; Tatz 1990; Broadhurst 1987; Hartnagel 1987).

4.   In aboriginal research generally the findings usually point to the relative poor status of aboriginal peoples compared with their non-aboriginal counterparts on a range of indicators. However, it should be stressed that this is not an 'aboriginal problem' but one of professional accountability and of non-aboriginal criminal justice structures and processes. As Braithwaite (1992: 2) points out, the 'Western criminal justice system is an abject failure' and is a 'major institutional cause of the tearing, bleeding rift between black and white communities'.

5.   These 'watchdogs' include the annual *State of the Nation Report* on Aboriginal Social Justice from the Human Rights and Equal Opportunity Commission and the monitoring programme for deaths in custody housed within the Australian Institute of Criminology.

6.   Walker (1987) and others have provided evidence that aboriginal peoples may receive 'lighter' sentences than their non-aboriginal counterparts. However, caution is needed in interpreting these findings as evidence to the contrary is also available.

7.   It is important to note that this essay centres on aboriginal involvement in the criminal justice system, i.e. the official picture. The other area yet to be explored in this cross-cultural context is that of aboriginal criminal behaviour and the cultural, socio-historical and political explanations for such patterns of criminality as shown in the research evidence. Braithwaite (1979) reminds us that crime is not homogeneous and should be disaggregated before commencing any generalized analysis.

8.   This essay is based on a paper presented at the 11th International Congress of Criminology, Budapest, Hungary, 22-27 August 1993.

Index

Aboriginal communities ii, iv, ix, 2, 6, 7, 10, 12, 13, 14, 15, 17-19, 58, 73, 74, 81, 86, 88, 87, 197, 198, 201, 203, 204, 206, 208, 209, 210, 245, 248, 263, 264

Aboriginal Education Foundation of South Australia/Flinders University of South Australia project (AEF/FUSA) 198, 199, 201, 202, 205-210

Aboriginal justice 1-8, 10, 12-19, 29, 35, 37, 181, 247, 255

Aborigines 74, 80, 209, 245, 246, 248, 249, 252-255

abuse 32, 34, 39, 42, 81, 178, 197, 199, 200, 206, 207, 212, 238

accountability vii, 119, 121, 145, 152, 170, 226, 246

addiction 83, 110

Alberta 2, 5, 30, 37, 40, 42, 246, 252, 254, 265

alcohol and alcohol abuse iv, v, xii, 29, 40, 41, 81, 83, 86, 99, 100, 101, 110, 178, 179, 184, 208, 251, 252, 264

alienation 56, 57, 222, 238

alliance 221, 222, 237

Amnesty International 249, 250, 254, 255

anomie x, 143, 218, 222, 238, 258

Aotearoa 147, 218-220 (see also New Zealand)

arrest viii, 1, 28, 37, 39, 40, 52, 76, 78, 102, 106, 109, 119, 124, 127, 144, 148, 154, 199, 234, 246, 250-252, 254

arson 56, 165

Assembly of First Nations 8, 12, 35, 190

assimilation 7, 22, 85, 182, 184, 247

Association of Iroquois and Allied Indians 187

Australia i, iv, vi, vii, viii, x, xii, xiii, 1, 4, 5, 18, 51, 55-57, 59, 61-65, 68, 71-73, 75-78, 80-85, 89, 144, 197, 198, 200-203, 205, 207, 209, 210, 225, 245-252, 254, 256, 257, 264

autonomy ii, 1, 24, 5, 6, 8-10, 12-16, 18-20, 58, 152, 175, 176, 178, 182, 187, 188, 191, 218, 238, 258

Band Council 175, 176, 184, 187

beat policing vii, 144, 145, 152, 153-155, 159

biculturalism ix, 221

Bill of Rights (New Zealand) ix, 220, 221, 226, 232, 236, 239

Britain (see Great Britain)

British Columbia vi, 10, 28, 31, 39, 41, 42, 119, 121, 123-125, 127-129, 136, 138

burglary 56, 166

Canada i, ii, iii, vi, x, xii, 1, 2, 4-16, 19, 27, 30, 31, 35, 36, 43, 99, 100, 119-122, 124, 126, 127, 137, 143, 175, 176, 178, 179, 180, 181, 184, 217, 223, 224, 245-248, 250, 251, 256, 261

Charlottetown Accord 9, 12, 19, 190
chiefs 7, 8, 20, 17, 31, 38, 39, 41, 128,
   135, 152, 153, 175, 184, 186, 187,
   197, 199, 210
child abuse 56, 228, 235
children iv, viii, 6, 18, 52, 53, 55, 56,
   58, 59, 61, 67, 74, 76, 81, 84, 85,
   100, 109, 110, 119, 147, 158, 162,
   165, 168, 199, 208, 225, 226,
   228, 230, 232, 235, 238
citizenship ix, 220, 221, 239
class iii, iv, xi, 10, 51, 55-58, 61-65,
   67, 68, 71-73, 76, 79, 89, 104,
   105, 162, 219, 238, 254, 255
colonialism iv, v, 71, 86, 197, 200,
   245, 256, 260
community aid panels 151, 153
community justice ix, 89, 203
community policing vi, x, 123,
   143-146, 151, 152, 180, 181, 189,
   210, 235
community service v, 52, 54, 66, 101,
   103, 111, 114, 148
compensation 53, 56, 156, 163, 226,
   227, 229, 237
conflict iv, viii, 17, 18, 33, 34, 81,
   203, 218, 254
conquest 245, 260
constitutional reform 9-13
control mechanisms ii, 19, 86, 258,
   263
conviction i, v, xii, 6, 10, 17, 31, 37,
   42, 43, 82, 83, 97, 99, 100, 106,
   114, 126, 132, 202, 230
correctional centres and institutions 30,
   62, 252, 255
courts v, vi, 2, 6, 7, 11, 13-16, 17, 30-
   36, 39, 40, 42, 44, 51-53, 59, 61,
   67, 75, 82, 83, 88, 95, 97, 98,
   99-104, 109-112, 114, 126, 144,
   146-150, 154, 155, 158-160, 166,
   168, 170, 183, 186, 217, 218, 221,
   225-227, 232, 235, 236, 247, 249,
   254
crime i, ii, v, vi, vii, viii, x, xi, xii, 3,
   17, 28, 29, 30, 32, 33, 34, 36, 38,
   39, 42, 43, 51-54, 56-68, 78, 81,
   86, 88, 95, 101, 119, 120,

121-127, 129, 136, 143-148, 153,
   155-159, 164, 168, 169-170, 175,
   177-181, 189, 191, 203, 217, 218,
   221-224, 225, 227-235, 237-240,
   247-249, 250-252, 255-265
crime control viii, 29, 62, 177, 178,
   180, 181, 189, 217, 218, 230, 232,
   234, 235, 237, 259
crime prevention vi, x, 3, 29, 39, 51,
   54, 61, 65, 66, 119, 121-125, 127,
   129, 147, 155, 230, 234, 235, 237,
   238
crime prevention through environmental
   design 128
criminal behaviour 53, 228, 247, 250,
   257, 258, 260, 263-265
criminal justice system i, ii, iii, iv, vi,
   xi, xii, 1-6, 13, 19, 27-31, 33-37,
   63, 65, 67, 71, 72, 75, 80, 86, 89,
   98, 100, 102, 122, 127, 134, 149,
   158, 159, 161, 180, 226, 227,
   245-257, 265
criminality i, iii, x, xii, 27-29, 62, 151,
   157, 231, 245, 246, 256, 257, 262,
   264
criminalization iv, 58, 74, 84, 85, 224,
   225, 262
criminology and criminologists xi, xii,
   27, 28, 71, 95, 100, 119, 128, 157,
   162, 168, 170, 204, 228, 246, 248,
   249, 250, 255-257, 259-262, 264
cross-cultural i, ix, x, xii, 3, 35, 182,
   197, 198, 208, 245, 249, 253, 256,
   257, 260, 262-264
crown 41, 42, 98, 101
cultural imperialism iii, 44, 261
culture ix, 3, 5, 11, 33, 34, 43, 72, 86,
   202, 217, 219, 221, 246, 260
custody 5, 31, 33, 60, 79, 82, 89, 101,
   103, 225, 248-250
customary law 17, 88, 246
deaths viii, 5, 22, 39-41, 71, 72, 74,
   76-80, 83, 85, 86, 197, 198, 201,
   207, 208, 210, 246, 247, 248, 249
deaths in custody viii, 5, 22, 71, 72,
   74, 76-78, 80, 83, 85, 86, 197,
   198, 207, 208, 210, 246, 248, 249
delinquency iii, 53, 57, 65, 66, 73, 258

detention iii, 38, 52, 59, 60, 75, 101, 114, 148, 149, 158, 225

discrimination ii, iii, v, xi, 1, 2, 27, 31-33, 43, 71, 73, 76, 87, 95, 180, 181, 202, 251-254

disorder 17, 51, 58, 59, 76-78, 81, 82, 228, 233

dispossession ii, 73, 86

dispute resolution ii, ix, 4, 15, 17-19, 131, 258

domestic violence iv, 56, 71, 81, 82, 87, 218, 227, 228, 237

drugs and drug abuse 57, 81, 95, 100-102, 104, 105, 110, 132, 133, 178, 179

drunkenness 76-78, 81, 82, 84

Durkheimian-Modernization (DM) 257, 259-263

Ecological-Opportunity (EO) 257, 258, 259, 261, 264

economic inequality 258, 262

economic policy 220, 223, 229

Edmonton 21, 41

education 10, 11, 28, 66, 146, 154, 170, 182, 198, 199, 202, 205, 207, 219, 220, 227, 230, 233, 236, 237

effective cautioning conference 156

effective cautioning scheme 145, 155, 156, 163

elders 10, 18, 35, 52, 89, 182, 238

employment v, ix, 55, 66, 68, 106-108, 133, 168, 203, 219, 221, 226, 227, 239, 249

empowerment i, 2, 65, 66, 161, 184

ethnicity i, xi, 31, 104

exploitation iv, 34, 72

family iv, vii, x, 16, 17, 37, 51, 53, 54, 60, 66, 76, 81, 86-89, 100, 104, 110, 131, 145, 147-156, 159-163, 165, 167-170, 193, 218, 227, 232, 234, 237, 238, 239, 251, 263

Family Group Conferences vii, 145, 147-149, 150, 151-154, 155, 156, 159-162, 163, 165, 168, 170, 232

fine default 76, 78, 83, 84

fines 10, 31, 52, 83, 101, 111, 112

First Nations 1, 8, 12, 13, 35, 175, 176, 182, 189, 190, 191, 217

first offenders v, 106, 161, 225

fraud 81, 102, 104, 105, 226, 235

gangs 58, 59

gaol (see incarceration)

gender iv, v, ix, 71, 72, 75-79, 82, 83, 89, 95, 97-103, 105, 107, 111, 112, 162, 175, 208, 221, 226, 227

gender relations 82, 91, 175

genocide 76, 223, 247

girls 37, 41, 74-76, 85

government i, ii, ix, x, xi, xii, 2, 3, 5-13, 16, 17, 19, 27, 34, 36, 37, 42, 44, 51-54, 56, 59-63, 66-67, 71, 73, 85, 89, 128, 138, 143, 144, 146, 148, 151, 153, 176, 177, 178, 181-183, 187-189, 197, 201, 209, 210, 217, 218, 219, 220-222, 223, 226, 228-234, 246-248, 255, 265

Great Britain v, vi, x, 98, 100, 143, 219, 223, 224

Hamilton 2, 5-7, 14, 15, 17, 27, 29, 32-34, 36, 37, 39, 41

harassment viii, 38, 41, 186, 198-200, 205, 206

health 10, 11, 56, 66, 79, 146, 179, 197-199, 201, 205, 208, 220, 227, 228, 233

High Court 104, 249

homicide 82, 86, 262

human rights 31, 38, 78, 87, 89, 197, 210, 217, 230, 249, 254, 260, 261

incarceration ii, viii, xi, 1, 2, 3, 10, 27, 30-33, 36, 40, 41, 59, 64, 67, 73, 77, 78, 80-85, 101, 104, 110, 114, 180, 201, 206, 208, 224, 225, 229, 246, 249, 250, 252, 253 (see also prison)

incident-driven policing vi, 121, 122, 124, 138

Indian Constable Programme 183, 184, 188, 189

Indians (see Native Canadians)

indigenous people ii, viii, xi, xii, 1, 3, 71, 72, 85, 95, 99, 149, 245, 247, 249-251, 253, 256, 260, 262, 263

inherent right 8, 9, 11, 12, 16

inmates 27, 225, 229, 234, 252

islander iv, 51, 52, 54, 60, 71, 72, 82,
    197, 204, 246
jail (see also incarceration)
James Bay 10, 15
Johnston 77, 78, 82, 200, 209
judges v, 2, 4, 30-33, 35, 36, 72, 82,
    88, 97, 98, 102, 110, 129, 148,
    150, 151, 164, 170, 209, 232, 247
jurisdiction 6, 9, 10, 12-16, 33, 35,
    185, 187, 188
justice administration 1, 2, 5, 12, 16,
    18, 19
justice agencies v, 73, 85, 87, 88, 144
justice reform ii, 1-3, 5-7, 12, 16, 19,
    54, 60, 151
juveniles i, iii, iv, vi, vii, ix, xii, 31,
    51-62, 63-68, 73-76, 78, 89, 123,
    130, 143, 145-151, 153-155,
    160-162, 163, 165, 169, 170, 178,
    203, 217, 225, 226, 235, 250, 251,
    254, 258, 262
juvenile crime 51, 52, 54, 56, 58, 59,
    62, 64, 65, 67, 145, 146, 148
juvenile justice iii, iv, vi, vii, 51-54,
    59-62, 65-67, 73, 89, 143, 145,
    146, 147, 149-151, 153, 162, 169,
    217, 251
Juvenile Justice Act iv, 51-54, 60, 61,
    67
Juvenile Justice Bill 51, 60
Labor Party (Australia) 151
labour iv, ix, x, 55, 72, 83, 197,
    217-234
Labour Party (New Zealand) 233
land 10, 11, 13-15, 21, 176, 217, 219,
    249, 255
language 11, 75, 78, 161
law iii, v, ix, x, 1, 3-8, 10, 11, 13,
    15-17, 27-32, 34-36, 43-44, 51, 56,
    60, 63, 65, 71, 76, 81, 85, 88, 97,
    122, 130, 131, 132, 133, 136, 143,
    150, 157, 158, 160, 163, 175, 178,
    183, 184-186, 197, 200, 203, 204,
    206, 217, 218, 222, 223-227,
    229-238, 245, 246, 253
law and order iii, ix, x, 13, 32, 43, 51,
    63, 65, 76, 85, 217, 218, 222, 223,
    224, 227, 229-234, 237

Law Reform iii, 4-8, 15, 16, 27, 28,
    32, 34-36, 60, 63, 65, 203, 246
Law Reform Commission of Canada
    4-8, 15, 16, 246
lawyers 4, 35, 42, 88, 150, 153, 232,
    248
leadership vi, 127, 135, 138
Manitoba 5-9, 14-18, 29, 37, 46, 47,
    180, 245-247, 250, 261
Manitoba Aboriginal Justice Inquiry 29
Maori i, v, ix, x, 101-104, 106, 108,
    110-112, 114, 147, 148, 162, 221,
    226, 227-229, 231, 234, 235,
    237-239
Maori Constitutional Revolution ix, 221
Maori Council (New Zealand) 228
marginalization iii, iv, 56, 67, 223
Marxian World-System (MWS)
    256-258, 261, 263-265
media 51, 58, 120, 123, 127, 129, 150,
    154, 156, 217, 227, 228, 230, 238
mediation 131, 132
Meech Lake Accord 10, 23
Métis 1, 2, 5, 8, 12, 27, 28, 30, 40,
    181, 245, 250, 252, 253
Métis National Council 12
Mi'kmaq 17
Micmac 37
military 181, 219, 247
minorities 32, 37, 38, 223, 224, 228
national iii, viii, x, xi, xii, 2, 5, 8, 9,
    12, 27, 28, 31, 77, 78, 80, 84, 85,
    87, 148, 153, 162, 175, 180,
    197-199, 201, 207, 217, 218,
    220-227, 229-238, 245-249,
    256-258, 261-263 National
    Government (New Zealand) 220,
    222, 226, 233, 234
Native Canadians 1, 5, 13, 14, 27,
    39, 180, 187, 245, 247-250, 252
    Cree 9, 10, 15, 37
    Cree-Naskapi 9, 10
    Inuit 1, 12, 27, 245, 250
Native Constables 182, 185, 188
Native Council of Canada 12
Native peoples ii, iii, 2, 4, 27-30, 37,
    32-43, 175-178, 182, 188, 190,
    191, 268

Native policing viii, 175-178, 181, 186, 87, 188, 189-191
neglect iv, 56, 62, 81
New Right 218, 220, 222, 223, 231, 238
New South Wales 58, 71, 74, 75, 79-81, 84, 85, 87, 89, 143, 144, 145, 149-154, 170, 198, 202, 203, 254
New Zealand i, ii, v, vi, vii, ix, x, xii, 95, 101, 103, 111, 114, 145, 147-151, 153, 162, 164, 165, 167, 168, 217-224, 226-233, 236, 238-239, 266
non-custodial 31, 33, 82, 103, 250
Northern Territory 77, 86, 88
Northwest Territories 45
Nova Scotia 5, 17, 37, 41, 134, 246, 247
offences iv, v, 10, 30, 33, 36, 40, 52, 57, 58, 62, 74, 76-83, 98-100, 102, 103, 104, 105, 125, 160, 166, 169, 179, 184, 185, 225, 230, 250, 252
offenders v, vii, xii, 3, 15, 30-33, 36, 41, 51, 52, 54, 58-60, 62-66, 82, 97, 98, 100, 101, 105, 106, 124, 145-150, 153-156, 158, 159, 160, 162-170, 203, 217, 225, 226, 229, 231-233, 236, 251-254
Ontario viii, 5, 38, 176, 182, 183, 185, 188, 189
Ontario Provincial Police (OPP) 183, 185-188
oppression iv, 29, 34, 72, 76
Ottawa 27, 138
over-representation ii, iv, xi, 1, 2, 28-31, 36, 65, 73, 77, 80-82, 95, 98, 99, 101, 102, 103, 109, 226, 246, 248, 249, 260, 251-255
ownership 4, 18, 132, 200
Pacific Islanders 102, 227, 228
Pakeha v, 101-103, 106, 108, 110-112, 114, 228, 238, 239
parole 27, 28, 33, 82, 83, 230, 236
paternalism xi, 7
penalties v, 33, 36, 51, 59, 62, 97, 101, 104, 157, 167, 225, 230, 236
physical abuse 39, 199, 200, 206

police iii, v, vi, viii, ix, x, xi, 2, 7, 14, 27, 29, 30, 33, 35-44, 57-59, 62, 74-79, 82, 83, 87-89, 102, 104, 106, 109, 119-138, 143, 144, 145-156, 159-161, 163, 164, 169, 175-183, 186-188, 190-191, 197-210, 217, 226-235, 237, 238, 245-250, 252-254
poverty iv, v, 32, 40, 55, 62, 63, 65, 83, 84, 99, 125, 131, 180, 226, 227, 246, 252
power ix, 10, 17, 31, 34, 59, 63, 65, 76, 79, 127, 147-149, 167, 183, 197, 200, 209, 220, 221, 223, 225, 229, 248, 259, 263
prison 27, 28, 30, 33, 36, 40, 41, 77, 80, 81, 83-85, 89, 95, 98-100, 102, 114, 180, 183, 185, 218, 221, 225, 229, 230, 231, 232, 233, 236, 245, 246, 248, 250, 255 (see also incarceration)
prisoners iii, 36, 80, 98, 225, 236, 237, 252
proactive 29, 89, 127, 134, 138, 180, 205, 209
probation 7, 31, 33, 52, 95, 98, 99, 101, 111, 114, 253, 254
problem-oriented policing vi, 119, 121-123, 125-132, 134-138
property 58, 65, 83, 102, 103, 132, 133, 144, 156, 163, 179, 185, 200, 203, 230, 258, 260
property crime 144, 260
prostitution 57
public drunkenness 76-78, 84
public order iv, vii, 36, 58, 72, 79, 145, 160, 183, 190
punishment vii, 27, 52, 60-64, 66, 67, 97, 99, 119, 151, 155, 157-159, 170, 224, 225, 230, 236, 237
Quebec 5, 9, 10, 15, 35, 38, 247
Queensland i, iii, iv, 51-53, 55, 56, 58-61, 64-68, 77, 81, 86, 87, 245
race i, iv, v, xi, 32, 38, 71-73, 75, 76, 78, 79, 87, 89, 95, 97, 98, 100, 101, 102, 103, 106, 108, 109, 111, 113-114, 181, 198, 207, 209, 217, 226, 228

racial discrimination v, 180, 252, 253
racism iii, iv, viii, ix, 11, 27, 31, 36,
    82, 197, 198, 202, 204, 207, 247,
    248, 251-254
recidivism vii, 146, 162, 163, 250
recognition i, 3, 7-12, 17, 37, 66, 88,
    190, 199, 204, 239
reconciliation 17, 145, 159, 197, 249
redress 38, 43, 249
reform i, ii, iii, vii, xi, 1-13, 15, 16,
    19, 27, 28, 32, 34-36, 51, 52, 54,
    60, 63-68, 80, 144-146, 150-152,
    170, 189, 191, 203, 210, 222, 223,
    232, 246
regenerating communities i, vi, xii,
    147, 169
Regina 45-47, 217
registered Indians 249
rehabilitation xii, 52, 62, 97, 217, 232,
    23
reintegration xii, 52, 153, 157-159,
    164, 166, 167, 169-170, 238
reintegrative shaming 153, 156, 159,
    161, 167, 263
reserves 14, 161, 33, 176, 183
resistance 81, 260
resources xiii, 4, 10, 11, 22, 56, 57,
    119-122, 125-127, 134-136, 149,
    163, 179, 182, 183, 187, 189, 191,
    209, 210, 221, 230, 231, 236, 238,
    249, 261
restitution 52, 53, 145, 159
retribution 62, 67, 156, 217
rights vii, ix, 7-9, 11-15, 20, 31, 35,
    38, 63, 67, 72, 78, 87, 89, 148,
    149, 157, 158, 170, 185, 192, 197,
    209, 217, 218, 220, 221, 224, 226,
    227, 230, 232, 236, 237, 239, 249,
    254, 258, 260, 261
Rogernomics 223, 231, 234
Roper, Sir Clinton and the Roper Report
    ix, 221, 229, 230, 236, 237
Royal Canadian Mounted Police
    (RCMP) 37, 39-42, 128, 130, 181,
    183-188
Royal Commission viii, ix, 5, 17, 37,
    41, 71, 72, 74, 76-78, 80, 83, 85,
    86, 119, 138, 197, 198, 207, 208,

    221, 222, 246, 248
SARA model 121, 123, 125, 132, 134
Saskatchewan 5, 40, 180, 217
school iii, ix, 37, 42, 55, 57, 71, 73,
    76, 119, 123, 125, 154-157, 162,
    163, 165, 170, 204, 180, 183, 217,
    237, 245, 263
self-determination 2, 3, 10, 18, 72, 217
self-government ii, 2, 3, 7-13, 16, 19,
    34, 177, 247, 255
self-harm 199, 206-208
sentences v, xi, 3, 30-33, 35, 36, 52
    54, 59-61, 64, 66, 67, 80, 82, 95,
    97-106, 109-112, 114, 224, 225,
    230, 231, 233, 234, 245, 251-254,
    255
settlement 13, 33, 40, 44, 79, 219,
    239, 245, 264
sexual abuse and assault iv, 37, 75, 81,
    82, 86-88, 207, 208
shame 153, 156-158, 164, 166, 167,
    169
shaming 153, 156, 159, 161, 167, 238,
    263
shoplifting 57, 58, 102, 104, 105, 114
social control ii, 3, 5, 19, 51, 61, 65,
    68, 86, 227, 258, 260, 261, 264
social policy ix, 51, 65, 66, 68, 217,
    220, 221, 228, 234
social structure 44, 199, 256, 259
socio-economic conditions 28, 29, 98,
    162, 180
sociology 45, 46, 68, 167, 175, 197,
    199, 245
South Australia 55, 80, 197, 198, 200,
    203, 205, 209
sovereignty viii, 14, 19, 34, 72, 178,
    190, 191
Status Indians 13, 245, 250
street crimes 29, 62, 224, 227
subsistence crime 57
suicide 56, 206-208
surveillance iii, 29, 36, 38, 56, 58, 63,
    75, 132, 226, 254
surveillance society 226
systemic discrimination ii, iii, 1, 27,
    32, 33, 43, 254
territory 13, 15, 16, 43, 44, 51, 56,

77, 85, 86, 88, 162, 245
theft 56, 58, 100, 102, 104, 105, 156, 166, 179, 180, 250, 261
Toronto i, 37, 179
Torres Strait Islander iv, 52, 71, 72, 82, 204, 245, 246
tradition 61, 178, 219, 223, 238, 246
traditional law v, x, 88, 218
treaty ix, 7, 221, 249
Treaty of Waitangi ix, 221
Tribal court 13, 14, 35
unemployment i, iii, iv, x, 33, 55, 57, 62, 63, 65, 84, 99, 106, 217-219, 226, 228, 232-234, 237
urban centres vi, 15, 38, 62, 84, 120, 122, 124, 127, 130, 197-199, 207, 208, 231, 251, 252, 258
vandalism 56, 57
verbal abuse 39, 42
victim iii, iv, v, vii, ix, 39, 56, 63, 64, 86, 89, 97, 124, 125, 131, 145-147, 149, 154-156, 159, 160, 162-164, 165-170, 217, 221, 227-231, 234, 236-238, 264
Victoria 95
visibility xi, 72, 76, 79, 251, 252
Wagga Wagga 145, 147, 152, 153, 156, 159, 160, 163, 164
Waitangi Tribunal 221
Walpole Island First Nation 175-177, 182-191
welfare 6, 10, 51, 56, 59, 61, 62, 64, 74, 76, 82, 83, 85, 106, 110, 146, 148, 149, 153-155, 161, 169-170, 185, 204, 205, 219, 220, 222, 223, 225-227, 238, 239
welfare state 204, 219, 220, 222, 223, 227, 238, 239
Western Australia 59, 73, 75, 77, 78, 80-84
Western Canada 120, 181
Winnipeg 8, 28, 37, 245, 252
women iv, v, viii, 8, 18, 27, 28, 40, 42, 55, 57, 71, 72, 73-89, 95, 98-103, 105, 106, 107, 109-112, 114, 133, 162, 180, 205-208, 221, 224, 227, 229, 231, 238, 250, 252, 265

working class iii, iv, 51, 55-58, 61-65, 67, 68, 79
working class youth iii, iv, 57, 58, 61, 62, 6
youth (see juveniles)
youth clubs ix, 203
Youth Justice Coalition 65, 75, 149, 150